Three Steel Teeth:
Wide Comb Shears and Woolshed Wars

Mark Filmer

Three Steel Teeth: Wide Comb Shears and Woolshed Wars

For Linda, Lauren and Nicole

Three Steel Teeth: Wide Comb Shears and Woolshed Wars
ISBN 978 1 76041 788 8
Copyright © text Mark Filmer 2019

First published 2019 by
GINNINDERRA PRESS
PO Box 3461 Port Adelaide 5015
www.ginninderrapress.com.au

Contents

	Foreword	7
	Preface	9
1	Canowindra Award Breach Escalates Dispute	13
2	Dubbo Meetings Set the Tone	20
3	Two Key Unionists	28
4	The Infiltration of Wide Combs	37
5	A Tale of Two Brothers	44
6	Preliminary Research Trials	50
7	Colonial History Provides Important Context	57
8	Two Key Strikes	64
9	The Pastoral Industry Award	72
10	The Arm Wrestle Over Trials	80
11	The Stalemate Continues	86
12	Mission Impossible	93
13	Why Oppose Wide Combs?	100
14	The Toughest Job of All	109
15	Enter the National Farmers' Federation	117
16	Shearers Prosecuted	125
17	The Sydney Showground Demonstrations	132
18	Evidence From the Showground Hearings	141
19	The Sunbeam Ban	149
20	Shed Inspections Begin	157
21	Commonwealth Hill and Snaigow Stations	163
22	The Long Wait	173
23	The Eromanga Ambush	182
24	Judgement Day	192

25	The Appeal Hearings	201
26	The Strike – Events Speed Up	209
27	The Strike – Riverina Rebellion	218
28	The Strike – Things Turn Nasty	231
29	The Strike – an End In Sight	244
30	More Trouble Arrives	258
31	'Son of Wide Combs'	266
32	More Woolshed Inspections	274
33	Sydney Hearings (October 1983)	279
34	Inspections Wrap Up	284
35	Meanwhile, the Bitterness Continued	294
36	The End Game	302
37	The Aftermath	315
	Afterword: Cut-out	324
	Glossary	326
	Timeline	328
	Acknowledgements	335
	Disclaimer	339
	Notes	341
	Index	357

Foreword

American car titan Henry Ford is reputed to have once said the Australian shearer was 'the most efficient machine on Earth'.[1] It's obvious to any observer that shearers are both highly skilled and hard-working labourers, who toil in what are sometimes literally back-breaking conditions that few people outside the industry could tolerate. Indeed, this book provides evidence that shearers are among the hardest-working members of the Australian workforce.

Putting aside the accuracy of Henry Ford's observation, it's clear that during the early 1980s most Australian shearers were not nearly as efficient as they might have been. Why? Because they were not permitted to use wide shearing combs, which were roughly 14 per cent more productive than narrow combs.

As this book chronicles, there were many facets to what became known as the wide comb dispute, but at its heart was the issue of technological change – in this case the introduction of the more efficient wide-tooth combs – and the ways in which any benefits from adopting an improved technology would be shared. There was also the issue of the perceived threat to Australian workers from immigrant labour – in this case New Zealand shearers. These issues played out in an era of confrontation between unions and the owners of capital, with a newly elected Labor government in power and seeking to reshape the nation's industrial framework.

Mark Filmer's meticulously researched and balanced account of this episode in Australian labour relations provides both a fascinating portrait of the economic landscape of the time, and a salutary set of insights for those tasked with guiding Australia's future prosperity. We now live in a world in which technology continues to replace labour across a range of sectors in the economy. It is also a world in which Australia grapples with an ongoing and potentially divisive debate about the appropriate level of immigration in the context of rapidly increasing global population mobility.

This book provides a welcome case study and range of lessons for those wise enough to realise the profundity of George Santayana's dictum that those who cannot remember the past are condemned to repeat it. Readers of this excellent account will be much better placed to avoid that mistake and I congratulate Mark on this readable and timely addition to our understanding of an important chapter in Australian history.

Professor Phil Dolan
La Trobe University

Preface

'Why would any person with a modicum of common sense want to corrupt a method of removing wool from sheep that has given such excellent results?' Ernie Ecob, the then New South Wales branch secretary of the Australian Workers' Union, posed this question to the union's pastoral industry members in a letter dated 3 December 1981. At the time, a small group of rebel shearers backed by the organisation that represented farmers in New South Wales, the Livestock and Grain Producers' Association, was pushing to have outlawed wide-tooth shearing combs approved for use throughout Australia. Their campaign was gaining momentum but the powerful AWU, which represented shearers, was vigorously opposing any change.

In the same letter to shearers, Ecob wrote,

> The ban on the use of wide combs was made by the Court [of Conciliation and Arbitration] in 1926. It has stood the test of time. It has served the employers' interest; the sheep are shorn clean and with a minimum of injuries. It is the basis of the formula on which the shearers' rate of payment per hundred sheep shorn is calculated. The use of standard combs has [an] enormous stabilising effect on the industry.

So why indeed would anyone want to 'corrupt' such a method? The answer, of course, was simple – they had an even better method!

Throughout the 1970s, millions of dollars of taxpayers' and wool growers' money was allocated to research projects to try to reduce the cost of wool harvesting and boost productivity in Australia's wool industry. The main focus was on robotic shearing and chemical defleecing techniques. There were significant advances but not to the point where these technologies could be commercialised. The single biggest productivity boost to take place in wool harvesting during the twentieth century was to occur in the early 1980s. It was the introduction of wide comb shears. This technology was not new – it had been around since the early 1900s but had been banned from use in Australia. Wide combs, which were manufactured in Australia, had three extra teeth and were about two centimetres wider than the standard narrow-gauge combs used by shearers to denude sheep. Wide gear was originally banned (following an application by wool growers) because it was believed it caused excessive damage to both the fleece and the sheep during shearing.

The catalyst for change took place during the 1970s, when Western Australia's wool growing industry experienced rapid growth. This created a shortage of shearers and resulted in many New Zealand shearers crossing the Tasman Sea to work in Western Australia. They brought with them their wide comb shears. Although illegal in Australia, they were able to be used with impunity in Western Australia because the shearing industry there was effectively unregulated. Many shearers from the eastern states also undertook contract shearing in the west and so were exposed to the wide-gauge equipment. Some shearers liked it so much they brought it back with them and used it illegally. However, the AWU strictly regulated the shearing industry in the eastern states and would not tolerate wide combs. Farmers' groups got involved because they could see benefits to wool growers, as well as shearers. The issue escalated to the point where the use of wide shearing combs became one of Australia's most bitter and protracted industrial disputes. It included a two-month national shearing strike that started in March 1983.

Ernie Ecob's letter to New South Wales shearers in December 1981 clearly showed the union's attitude toward change. As far as it was concerned, the system that had worked for the past 50 or so years could be relied upon for the next 50. It knew what was best for the industry, thank you very much. The trouble with that approach was it ignored the reality that wide combs were clearly superior to narrow combs. Every shearer who used them significantly increased his daily tally, and importantly, his pay. Wide combs were roughly 14 per cent more productive. It was obvious to everyone, except the AWU, that wide combs would be adopted in the industry because they allowed shearers to shear more sheep without any significant trade-off in terms of quality. The AWU's refusal to acknowledge this led to what must be one of the most spectacular own goals by a trade union in Australia's industrial relations history. Even powerful unions cannot stand in the way of technological change and progress. Many diehard AWU supporters look back on this dispute and still shake their heads in disbelief at the way the union handled it.

On 5 June 1984, immediately after the Arbitration Commission had handed down its final ruling in the wide comb dispute, a briefing note was prepared for the then federal Minister for Employment and Industrial Relations, Ralph Willis, to outline the commission's decision and reasons for its ruling. The briefing note included the following astute observation:

> For the AWU's part, its stubborn resistance to acknowledge the inevitable and failure to attempt to negotiate gains in exchange for an orderly introduction of wide combs was an abrogation of its responsibilities to its shearer members.

Spot on!

And the great, enduring irony for the AWU is that the farmers' groups involved in the campaign to legalise wide combs (the Livestock and Grain Producers' Association of New South Wales and the National Farmers' Federation) were not only expecting the union to seek some trade-offs in exchange for wide combs being legalised, they were more than willing to make some trade-offs. The union could have negotiated a range of improved conditions for its members. But it never asked! So, when the union lost the dispute, as it was always going to do, it completely imploded. In the words of Paul Houlihan, who was the industrial director for the National Farmers' Federation during the dispute.

They [the AWU] never went on big strikes willy-nilly – if they went on a big strike it was an important issue and it was do or die. When it was all over, and blokes started to use wide combs, they found that what the union had told them was simply bullshit. [The then federal secretary of the AWU] Frank Mitchell said to me that in the first six months after the blue they lost 60 per cent of their pastoral membership – as people used wide combs they realised they had been had, and they walked away from union membership in droves.

For me, Paul Woollaston, a rugged New Zealander who shore with wide gear throughout the dispute, summed it up better than anyone:

My argument was if they were no good they would die a natural death. Who is going to use them? It always amazed me that grown men could just blindly follow each other. That's what they did, without even thinking about something or trying something. If you are going to condemn something, at least you'd try it out, wouldn't you?

The wide comb dispute spanned roughly four years, divided many rural communities, engendered widespread violence and bitterness, and strained the traditionally close national friendship between Australia and New Zealand. Politically, it was the source of increased international tension between two great trans-Tasman allies, and it eventually sparked a Senate inquiry into the employment of 'visitors to Australia' (that is, New Zealanders) in Australia's shearing industry. The dispute also brought massive changes to the wool industry, ushered in a new era of industrial relations reforms and led to the total demise of the once mighty Australian Workers' Union in the nation's pastoral industry. Despite its significance, little has been written about the dispute. I hope this book provides an insight into these tumultuous years and helps readers understand why the wide comb dispute unfolded as it did.

Mark Filmer
Orange, New South Wales, March 2018

1

Canowindra Award Breach Escalates Dispute

On Monday 27 April 1981, the New South Wales branch of the Australian Workers' Union received a telephone tip-off. A caller informed the branch secretary, Ernie Ecob, that the banned wide comb shearing gear was being used to harvest the autumn wool clip at Canomodine Station near Canowindra in the state's central west.

At the time, wide comb shears could not be legally used in Australia, even though they were made here. The ban was mandated in the federal Pastoral Industry Award, dating back to 1926.[2] Also, the Australian Workers' Union (AWU), which represented shearers, had introduced a rule in 1910 effectively banning wide combs. However, there had been growing tension in the state's pastoral industry following reports that a small number of rebel shearers were using the outlawed gear. And the main farm lobby group in New South Wales, the Livestock and Grain Producers' Association (LGPA), had begun advocating for trials of wide combs to determine their suitability to shear the state's 46 million sheep. The AWU was vehemently opposed to wide combs and any proposed trials.

Immediately following the tip-off, Ecob made arrangements for a local union official to inspect the Canomodine shearing shed. His first choice for the job was the branch's vice president, Michael (Mick) Joseph O'Shea, who was based in Mudgee. However, O'Shea was laid up with a bad back. A few more phone calls revealed that Tom Anderson, an organiser based in Griffith, was at the time in Cowra, about half an hour's drive from Canomodine. Anderson was enlisted for the inspection, which was to take place the next day.

Canomodine Station was a 3,643-hectare property between Cargo and Canowindra and a 40-minute drive west of Orange. The property was gazetted during the state's early settlement. It was one of only a handful of large station holdings remaining in the district. Split by Canomodine Creek and adjoining the Belubula River, Canomodine featured a mix of alluvial creek flats ideal for cropping, and rolling hills and slopes. The property was owned by Prevost Trading Pty Ltd and managed by John Rothwell. It was prime wool growing country and in the early 1980s carried almost 20,000 merino sheep.

Rothwell had engaged Robert White to do the shearing at Canomodine Station that autumn. White ran a small contract shearing business with his wife Gayle from their property Robayle at Mandurama, south of Blayney. As well as the Canomodine contract, the Whites had also secured contracts to shear at two neighbouring properties, Rockdale and Millambri. This trio of relatively large contracts, secured in 1980, was a major boost for the couple's fledgling business.

White was an intriguing character. He was slightly built, weighing just over 50 kilograms, and was relatively short in stature; he could have been a jockey. He was a gun shearer and a hard-working, tenacious and determined man who refused to be intimidated. White was also developing some notoriety in the pastoral industry as someone who supported the use of wide combs. In doing so, he was putting himself directly in the line of fire of the then very powerful AWU – not something many shearers would volunteer to do!

White's team got word that Anderson would be inspecting Canomodine's 10-stand shed on 28 April. Until then, the handful of rebel shearers who were using or experimenting with wide gear would make every effort to conceal their use. If shearers were using wide gear, they would generally appoint a lookout to warn them if any strangers were approaching the shed. This would give them time to swap their combs and cutters to the standard narrow gauge and hide the wide gear before anyone could reach the shed.

However, when Anderson visited Canomodine Station on 28

April, White and his team made no effort to hide their banned wide gear. It was almost as if White wanted to provoke a confrontation and escalate the wide combs issue. Anderson observed each of the shearers along the stands on the board and noted that four were using the banned equipment. The four were White, New Zealand-born Paul Woollaston, Cliff Healey and Adrian Ridley. There was no confrontation or heated exchange and Anderson left within about five minutes. Upon arriving back in Cowra, he telephoned Ernie Ecob and confirmed that the previous day's tip-off had been accurate.

Unbeknown to any of the parties at the time, this seemingly benign incident at Canomodine Station that day was to have many far-reaching and unforeseen consequences. Almost immediately it escalated what at the time was only a relatively minor dispute. Looking back years later, the AWU said Canomodine was 'the torch that set the industry alight'.[3] The resulting upheaval and turmoil that occurred in the pastoral industry during the following years would give added momentum to important national economic and industrial relations reforms that were designed to make Australia a more competitive and reliable supplier in the emerging global marketplace. And Australia's iconic shearing industry was about to change. Indeed, a revolution was looming.

Black ban imposed

Repercussions of 'the Canomodine incident' started to play out almost immediately. Within days of Anderson's inspection, Ernie Ecob had worked behind the scenes with various union officials to organise a black ban of Canomodine Station. The effect of the ban was that Canomodine would not be able to do business with any entities connected to the trade union movement. Ecob did not notify John Rothwell that the ban was in place. However, it soon came to light.

Early on 13 May, Rothwell asked one of the station workers to go to Nyrang Creek silos, about 11 kilometres west of Canowindra, to purchase and collect 12 tonnes of wheat. The grain was desperately needed to help feed the station's flock as the Canowindra district, like most of the state, was in the grip of drought. Canomodine needed about 27 tonnes of grain per week to feed its flock. The ewes were also starting to lamb and needed extra energy to feed their young and brace for the approaching winter.

When the worker arrived at the silos, he was told he would be unable to purchase any wheat. The staff informed him that the grain loaders had been instructed by the AWU not to load any wheat for Canomodine. (Nyrang Creek was part of a network of silos operated by the Grain Handling Authority. Some staff were members of the AWU.) The worker returned to Canomodine and reported the black ban to Rothwell.

Trade union black bans were relatively common during the 1970s and early 1980s. They were a heavy-handed means of trying to gain leverage over an opponent or intimidate them into giving some ground in an industrial dispute. Usually they were a last-resort tactic, implemented after all other options for resolving an issue had been exhausted.

However, if the AWU thought its black ban of Canomodine Station would in some way give it the upper hand in the emerging wide comb dispute, it was badly mistaken. The ban certainly made a very clear and strong statement to the state's pastoral industry – that the union would not, under any circumstances, tolerate the use of wide combs. But it also had the effect of giving the issue a prominence it had not yet enjoyed. All of a sudden, everyone in the pastoral industry was focused on wide combs.

John William Rothwell was a strong advocate of wide combs. He was convinced they could improve productivity and efficiency in the shearing industry without requiring a large capital outlay. Far from being silenced or intimidated by the black ban, he became more vocal. Within hours of learning about the black ban, he gave an interview to ABC radio in which he outlined his views and condemned the union ban. The following excerpts are from that interview.

Interviewer (Kerry Cochrane): Did that [the black ban] surprise you?

Rothwell: Yes, it did really, because I didn't think that they'd be prepared to starve sheep.

Interviewer: Now, of course, at Canomodine, shearers are using the wide comb, is that right?

Rothwell: During the shearing and crutching that we have just recently completed, the shearers did use wide combs and that would be the union's claim, yes.

Interviewer: What does it mean then in terms of feeding your sheep?

Rothwell: Well, at present we have sufficient wheat in the silos to feed till next Monday [18 May], and from that point onward we have no feed at all for the sheep.

Interviewer: Have you lost very many at this stage?

Rothwell: No, but I think that if we take our sheep off the feeding rates, we will have a lot of deaths immediately.

Interviewer: When you say immediately, would you say within two or three weeks?

Rothwell: That's correct.

Interviewer: Do you suspect that the unions might continue with this ban for some time?

Rothwell: Well, I'd like to think they wouldn't because it's going to mean the death of many thousands of sheep.

Interviewer: Coming back to the wide shears again, you're a firm believer in the use of wide shears in the industry?

Rothwell: Yes, I am, I believe it's one method of improving the efficiency in the shearing industry without any great capital cost.

Interviewer: So, despite the embargo on supplying you with drought grain, you're sticking there with those wide combs?

Rothwell: Well, I think someone has to, to help the industry improve.[4]

The ABC sought the views of the union to provide balance and put the case for the black ban. New South Wales branch president Charlie Oliver was interviewed by journalist John Cocroft during the same broadcast. The Welsh-born Oliver was a formidable man – a former member of parliament in Western Australia, a union stalwart and political heavyweight, who went on to become the president of the Labor Party in New South Wales. Oliver told listeners,

> Now this is a very serious issue. This station is in breach of the Pastoral Industry Award. They are deliberately breaching the Award and leaving themselves open to prosecution. The issue of course, is the use of wide combs which are illegal to shear sheep with. Now, they've been warned repeatedly that this will cause trouble in the industry if they breach the Award. Now they've done it deliberately, so they can expect trouble… Canomodine Station has deliberately flouted the law, they've deliberately flouted the wishes of the shearers, so we are bound to meet at Dubbo and decide what action will be taken. In the meantime, the union is bound to stand up for its rights in the industry and if necessary, use any means at its disposal. That's what's happened at Canomodine.[5]

And he showed little sympathy for the predicament John Rothwell now faced:

> Well, I mean, you know, that's his problem. He should have thought of that before he started to stand over everybody. I don't know the bloke at Canomodine, and I'm not very anxious to know him. Anyone that deliberately flouts the law and decides to take everybody on deserves everything he gets.[6]

The following week Rothwell was quoted in *The Land* newspaper, which at the time was widely read in the rural community and arguably the leading farming publication in Australia. He again used the opportunity to spruik wide shearing gear, saying,

> We have the ridiculous situation of the wool industry actively looking for alternative means of shearing. Yet in wide gear we have a method of merely changing combs, cutter and fork in the handpiece resulting in an increase of up to 40 head a day for each shearer. It is a genuine way to help the industry yet the AWU refuses to recognise it.[7]

The same article also quoted Robert White, who said,

We shear more sheep in a day with less effort, the grower gets the job done quicker and cheaper and the sheep are not damaged as much, which means fewer losses off-shears. Every other industry in Australia has improved in some way or another in the past 50 years, except the shearing industry. Where applicable, the use of wide shears should come as a freedom of choice and as for the AWU's claim that wide gear would affect the whole basis of payment in the shearing industry, I think it's garbage.[8]

It seemed White really was shaping up for a stoush. And the AWU was preparing to oblige.

2

Dubbo Meetings Set the Tone

The discovery that Robert White's shearing team was using wide gear at Canomodine that autumn activated an AWU resolution that had been passed by the union's pastoral workers in Dubbo six months earlier. On Sunday 26 October 1980, during a meeting at the Dubbo Civic Centre that lasted almost three hours, members resolved 'that immediately there is evidence of illegal wide combs being used in shearing operations a stop work meeting of all members in the industry be called'.[9] In light of this resolution, and the wide publicity generated by the Canomodine black ban, the union organised a meeting to discuss the escalating issue of wide combs. On 27 May, Ernie Ecob wrote to all pastoral committees throughout the state, notifying them that a stop work meeting would take place in Dubbo on Monday 1 June 1981. 'A large attendance is expected from all parts of the state,' he wrote.

As it turned out, the meeting attracted 290 pastoral workers (mostly shearers). Several other states were monitoring the wide combs issue, so a handful of shearers travelled from as far as Dalby and Longreach (Queensland), Mount Gambier and Naracoorte (South Australia) and Mildura (Victoria). Most people travelled to Dubbo the day before to be ready for the 10.30 a.m. start. Some, from the local region, drove to Dubbo that morning. The meeting was again held at the council-owned Civic Centre in Darling Street, a few blocks east of Dubbo's central business district. The Civic Centre was often used to host large community meetings and conferences. Charlie Oliver chaired the meeting. Other officials present from the New South Wales branch included Ernie Ecob and Mick O'Shea, and organisers Tom Anderson, Laurie 'Bluey' Rodwell, Fred McInerney and Bill Keightley.

According to the minutes of the meeting, Ecob was first to address the shearers. He read excerpts from the 17 May article in *The Land* about the Canomodine black ban then condemned Robert White for his comments in the article, saying he was merely 'boasting and promoting his contracting business'. According to an ABC radio report the following day, Ecob told the audience there was a lot of evidence that wide combs were detrimental to the wool industry.[10] He said he had recently received messages of support from a few old-time shearers who remembered back to the mid-1920s, when graziers first sought the ban on wide combs. Ecob expressed suspicion of the LGPA, saying although the organisation's official stance was that members would not break the Award, clearly there were some graziers who supported the use of wide combs. He suggested the LGPA was developing a plan to try to break down shearers' working conditions.

Charlie Oliver then spoke and was fervent in his condemnation of the wool growers and shearers who had been caught using the unlawful wide combs. (Often at meetings Oliver would give impassioned monologues about the union's proud history and traditions and the need for shearers to honour and uphold these traditions. Indeed, at the meeting of 26 October 1980 referred to above, he outlined the development of trade unionism in Australia starting from early colonisation and progressing to the present day. It was a nightmare for the minute-taker Cec Newton, requiring five and a half foolscap pages of single-spaced type to summarise.) According to the minutes, Oliver referred to the owners of Canomodine and Millambri together with White's shearing team as 'contemptible conspirators' who had joined forces 'for an evil purpose' and 'committed the most repulsive act of scabbery in the history of the industry'.[11] He went on,

> This miserable minority have flouted decisions made by union members at properly constituted union meetings. In spite of the

Award prohibition, illegal wide combs were used in shearing operations. This crime was committed after repeated warnings and with a full realisation of the consequences of this detestable act. This crime must be exposed in the highest councils of the trade union movement. The whole weight of the trade union movement must be mobilised to prevent this immoral, unprincipled, minority group of industrial misfits from profiting from their crime.[12]

The meeting congratulated AWU members at the Grain Handling Authority's Nyrang Creek silos 'for their support in this vital struggle to prevent the ruthless massacre of the shearer's right to an established and proper standard of working conditions'. At first glance these minuted statements appear to be grossly exaggerated or embellished. However, taking into account the mood of the shearers, the statements highlight the degree of hostility and anger they were feeling.

A seven-point motion received unanimous support at the meeting. Essentially, the shearers voted to continue black bans; enlist the help of the New South Wales Trades and Labor Council to enforce any bans; publicise in *The Australian Worker* (the union's newspaper) the names of any shearers or sheds caught using wide gear; and continue negotiations to try to resolve the dispute (on the basis that wide combs would not be tolerated). If the dispute could not be settled peacefully by 1 August, the shearers planned to go on strike.

Ecob spoke on ABC radio the following day to explain to listeners the key outcomes of the meeting.[13] During the interview he outlined several reasons why the union was opposed to wide comb shears. He said wide combs were being used by 'a number of graziers who are endeavouring to try and break down the shearing industry and cause a restructuring of the industry'. He said shearers were concerned that a formula used to determine industry pay rates would be 'interfered with' if comb sizes were changed and this would invariably lead to lower pay rates. He also claimed that wide combs led to more second cuts (short portions of wool caused by a shearer making two blows over the same area) and skin cuts to the sheep and resulted in greater costs to the wool grower. 'Admittedly you may be able to shear a few more sheep [with wide gear] but the loss to the grazier is greater because of skin cuts and also skin pieces removed,' he said.

Ecob, a one-time apprentice umbrella maker and former shearer, made it clear the union would act decisively if it caught any shearers using wide combs. He said the affected properties 'would be declared black banned indefinitely' and those bans would extend to the movement of grain to and from the property, the handling of wool from the property by storemen and packers at wool stores, and the loading of wool at shipping ports by waterside workers. However, he also tried to downplay the significance of the problem by claiming it was restricted to 'just a few ratbag graziers who think they will save themselves a few shillings' but said, 'in the long run they will be paying more'.

The Dubbo meeting reinforced the union's enmity towards wide combs and put both wool growers and 'rebel' shearers on notice that breaches of the Award would result in potentially lengthy and costly sanctions. Oliver, Ecob and the handful of organisers at the meeting must have left Dubbo feeling reasonably confident that a major dispute would be averted. The union had 'flexed its muscles', as it had done many times in the past, and would surely get its way.

However, there were two telling and unreported aspects of the Dubbo meeting that were going to come back to haunt the union. The first was the notion that the wide combs issue could be peacefully resolved (in the union's favour) within two months. That was a gross miscalculation. The second was even more significant. During the meeting, members voted on and unanimously endorsed a statement that was to underpin the union's position during the next few years. It read,

> The members of the union in attendance at this historic stop work meeting declare their *implacable hostile opposition* [emphasis added] to any individual who provides wide combs or carries or uses wide combs or connives to introduce wide combs to shearing

operations in breach of the Pastoral Industry Award. The members in attendance at this meeting call on all union officials and union members to dedicate themselves to resisting this unscrupulous assault on the members of the union in the pastoral industry and the shearers in particular.

Interestingly, the union maintained its *implacable hostile opposition* to wide combs throughout the unfolding dispute. It refused to budge or compromise in any way from this original position. And ultimately the union's immovability led to its spectacular downfall.

Cumnock shed 'assault' triggers meeting

The meeting of pastoral workers in Dubbo on 26 October 1980, at which shearers voted to stop work if the union received any evidence that wide combs were being used in New South Wales, was dominated by discussions about the alleged assault of an AWU organiser. The incident occurred when Mick O'Shea and Bluey Rodwell travelled to Cumnock on the morning of 7 October 1980. It was a Tuesday, the day after the Labour Day long weekend. O'Shea had travelled from Mudgee, a bit more than an hour's drive east of Cumnock, while Rodwell was based in Peak Hill, a short drive to the north-west. O'Shea could not recall whether the two men met in Peak Hill or Yeoval, just north of their destination. However, Yeoval, which is best known as the childhood home of one of Australia's favourite poets, A.B. (Banjo) Paterson, was the logical meeting place. From there, O'Shea recalled the pair travelled in Rodwell's Ford panel van to a local wool growing property, Tenanbung.

A few days previously, the AWU had been tipped off that wide comb shearing equipment would be used at Tenanbung's two-stand shed. The 1,600-hectare property, which had Goobang National Park on three of its four boundaries, had been owned and run by Allan Watt since 1940. Although it was only a small shed (about 4,500 sheep), O'Shea and Rodwell had been dispatched to inspect it. At this stage the union was determined to stamp out the wide gear issue before it could gain traction.

Allan and his wife Betty had asked Robert White to help with the shearing that year. The other shearer was a local man who the Watts had contracted for years. Allan met Bob White when he visited a neighbouring property where White was shearing. White was planning to do the shearing himself. However, he badly injured his leg on the long weekend. 'It happened on the dance floor at Lyndhurst [a few kilometres south of Mandurama] on a Saturday night. He was just dancing around with his wife Gayle…he was a bit of a lair,' Allan said. White arranged for his close friend John Schick to take his place. The two men had met while shearing in Western Australia during the mid-1970s. Schick ran a contract shearing business on New Zealand's north island. At short notice he flew to Australia and travelled straight to Cumnock to shear at Tenanbung.

The two organisers were, in many regards, polar opposites. Rodwell had a reputation for being a fiery character who could become quite aggressive during shed inspections and, for that matter, at other times too. O'Shea, on the other hand, was known for his composure; he was amicable and generally well respected. What happened during the shed inspection remains a point of contention. Rodwell claimed to have been viciously assaulted; Watt emphatically denied that any such attack took place.

According to Allan Watt, the organisers walked into the shed while he was working the woolpress. 'They walked in behind me and went up on the stand to Schicky and said, "Have you been using wide combs?" It was merry hell. "What's he doing using wide combs?" I was getting a bit stirred up. Then he wanted to see if I had got them to sign on. I said, "They are signed on." I went and got the paper that showed they had signed on,' he said.

John Schick, who was using wide gear and did not have a union ticket, remembered Bluey Rodwell coming up onto the stand. 'From memory I was halfway through shearing a sheep and he [Bluey] pulled me out of gear and said, "What are you doing?" and of course I put it back into gear and kept going. He pulled me out of gear again and I said something like, "You touch that cord again and you are going to wear it".' Schick said Rodwell moved to pull him out of gear again, 'and that's when Watty poked him and he went down in a screaming heap, but he wasn't hit hard or anything, he was carrying on as if he had been shot'.

Watt said he 'touched him on the stomach' and remembered Rodwell 'jumped back and went crook and everything else, said I jumped him… I said, "Don't worry, if I had wanted to, I would have made a mess of you." That's all that was ever done.'

O'Shea did not witness the exchange. 'I went outside to get something from the car and when I came back Bluey was holding his face. "I've just been jobbed," he told me. He was going to take action but dropped the matter when he cooled down. He was a pretty tough old footballer,' O'Shea said. (Rodwell had played for the Peak Hill Roosters in the state's Group XI rugby league competition during the early 1950s and was a member of the club's 1951 first grade premiership winning team.)

Schick remembered it as a 'rather comical' incident. 'After the organisers left, Watty put the radio on and said something like, "I bet we'll hear about this incident on the news within the hour." Sure enough the news came on, "Union rep assaulted in Cumnock shed",' he said.

The incident was widely reported in the central west media. Dubbo's *Daily Liberal* newspaper quoted Ernie Ecob as saying,

> Mr Rodwell went to the property and in the process of carrying out his investigation, he was brutally and physically attacked. It was advised that he see a doctor. The whole controversy surrounding the use of wide combs is becoming serious. A full report concerning the use of the combs and the subsequent attack on our union organiser will be presented to the state-wide meeting of Australian Workers' Union employees in the shearing industry when we meet in Dubbo on October 26.[14]

The matter was reported to police, and an officer from the

Cumnock station visited Tenanbung to question Watt and Schick. No charges were laid. However, the incident and its subsequent reporting in the media added to the growing tension in the industry and set the mood for the AWU meeting in Dubbo later that month. In promoting this meeting, Ecob wrote a circular on 23 September 1980 to all members employed in the pastoral industry. In it, he warned,

> The union has been advised that 2,000 persons, non-union members, will be imported into New South Wales from Western Australia to force the use of wide combs. Members, all the struggles of the past hundred years will be sacrificed if this invasion succeeds. This may be the last opportunity to defend your future.[15]

The source of the advice about there being a planned 'invasion' was never explained. But irrespective of the veracity of the claim, it had the desired effect – most shearers were now angry and wanted the wide combs issue dealt with once and for all.

3

Two Key Unionists

Two AWU officials were to play a more prominent role throughout the wide comb dispute than all other members – Ernie Ecob and Charlie Oliver. Although it was the rank and file members who voted on key decisions, Ecob and Oliver carried considerable sway and influence and it was their leadership that helped determine the direction the union took during the early 1980s. Both men were powerful and persuasive figures who started out as friends and loyal allies then fell out and became bitter enemies before being reconciled once more.

Ernie Ecob (1930–2000)

It seems that even as a child, Ernie Ecob had an affinity for the underdog. His younger brother John recalls Ernie's primary school years at Maclean on the New South Wales north coast:

> …he was always a very vocal person, and always looking after the underdog, always; if someone was the underdog, Ernie would be fighting for him. He would get himself in all sorts of trouble fighting for the bloke who was being put down.

Ecob's early school years were fragmented, as his father Russell, a Baptist minister, moved Ernie and John from school to school in the Maclean and Lawrence communities, just north of Grafton. Russell Ecob was unhappy with the teachers at some schools and with the treatment of his sons at others, where they were bullied daily. 'The kids at Lawrence Public School ganged up on us because we were the pastor's kids. And we used to get chased home every afternoon after school. It became quite difficult,' John said. In 1944, Russell moved his family inland to Armidale, where Ernie had three years of high schooling. Two of these years were in the classroom of a teacher who spent most of his time reading the *Sydney Morning Herald* newspaper while the children were left unsupervised. 'He had a two-year gap in his education and he never picked up. There was nothing wrong with his intelligence but it's just that he had that gap,' John said. The family then moved to Sydney for Russell to take up an appointment at Hurstville Baptist Church, and Ernie finished his schooling at Mortdale.

Ernie was born in 1930 to devout, evangelical Christian parents in Dubbo, where Russell Ecob was the town's first Baptist minister. In fact, as a founding member, Russell had helped construct the church building. He too had been born into a Christian family – on the mission field in Uganda where his father, an Anglican minister from England, had served as a missionary. Ernie had three siblings, John, who was two and a half years his junior, Gavin (seven years) and Lois (11 years). The children were brought up in a strict but loving Christian home 'where the gospel was preached', said John. To illustrate this, he recalled the following incident:

> I remember once, just as a young lad, at Maclean on the north coast…it was a very wet night, and nobody turned up [to church], so Mum said, 'Ernest, would you like to preach?' And he got up and he preached. He would have only been about nine.

However, when he finished school and became more independent, Ernie shelved his faith and focused more on work, sport and his social life. He got a job in the city assembling umbrellas, and began playing rugby league, which he had taken up in Armidale. This meant he was spending most weekends, Saturdays and Sundays, playing football and socialising at pubs after the games – he did not have time for church. After a couple of years, in 1949 when he was aged 19, Ecob and a mate decided to leave the city and move to the country. Ecob's mate had family connections who farmed near Nyngan, roughly halfway between Dubbo and Cobar. However, soon after they arrived, Ernie had a row with his mate and they parted company. Ernie sought rural work wherever he could find it and ended up rabbiting and droving before he was offered a learner shearer's stand in a shed near Coonamble, where he eventually settled. He met his future wife Joan Farrell there – they married in 1951 and were later to raise five children. Ernie built his own house in Coonamble – he felled the trees needed for the timber, milled the timber and completed the project almost entirely by himself. Decades later, his brother John, who was a structural engineer, designed a holiday house for Ernie's family at Forster on the New South Wales north coast. Ernie built this house too.

While based in Coonamble, Ernie became at best an average shearer but a very active member of the AWU. Mick O'Shea, who grew up in Coonamble and was an AWU organiser during the wide comb dispute, remembered him as 'a terrible [sic] hard worker; he wasn't such a great shearer, but he certainly supplied the labour'. But it was in the shearing sheds where Ernie found his voice and his leadership came to the fore. 'Wherever he was, Ernie was always the spokesman, he had a big voice, he was a strong personality, he was a leader wherever he went, he was a natural. And in the shearing shed, if there was a dispute on, Ernie was the spokesman. And the union recognised this and [in 1964] they appointed him as the organiser for the north-west corner of New South Wales,' John Ecob said.

John recounted an interesting story about Ernie's wife Joan, who was raised a Roman Catholic but became a 'born-again' believer. At Hurstville Baptist Church in Sydney, where Russell Ecob was the minister for 13 years including most of the 1950s, there was a long-time member of the congregation, a Mr Mitchell, who was a railways worker. When he retired, Mr Mitchell became eligible for free railway travel throughout New South Wales, so he developed his own Christian ministry in which he would pack an overnight bag and a stash of Christian tracts then travel by train to a country town. While there, he would door-knock as many of the locals as he could and hand out and explain the content of the tracts – trying to convert his listeners to Christianity. John said that on one such occasion during the mid-1950s, Mr Mitchell visited Coonamble, and

> ...he came to Ernie's house, Ernie was away shearing, and Joan came to the door and he led her to the Lord on the doorstep...he didn't even know who she was. And he said to her, 'What's your name?' She said, 'Joan Ecob.' He said, 'You're not Ernie's wife, are you?' He could not believe it, that he had led Ernie's wife to the Lord. Because we had been praying for him. When Ernie came home, she told him that she had become a Christian and Ernest knew what that was all about because he had been brought up under the sound of the gospel. So he said, 'Well we better start both going to church.'

However, according to John, although he became a regular churchgoer, Ernie did not rekindle his faith until much later in life, when at age 59, he was eventually 'converted' and became a changed man. Certainly, during his career as a union organiser and New South Wales branch secretary, it seems there was little evidence of Ecob being a devout religious man. For most of his working life he was far more committed to the AWU and its members than the Church and its members. He was described by many as being a difficult man to deal with; he could be prickly and confrontational, sometimes aggressive and hostile. Mick O'Shea knew Ernie very well and says, '...he was an aggressive bloke there is no doubt about that, but at that particular time, in his era, you could be aggressive, but you could not be like that today, no way. He certainly didn't back away from a fight.' Paul Houlihan, who was the industrial director of the National Farmers' Federation during the dispute, was less complimentary:

> ...he was part of that wonderful tradition of the AWU – he was a great hater, a great, great hater, a seriously great hater. And mad as a cut snake. I don't really know what he was fighting against, I've never really understood what it was that he was fighting against,

except that he saw it somehow or rather as a point of principle by the New South Wales branch of the union to somehow toughen up the union. They were going to water; Ernie saw this as a means of imposing some rigour and discipline in the membership.[16]

The 1956 shearers' strike and its impacts

It is likely that Ecob's 'hatred' stemmed, at least in part, from events that took place during the mid-1950s. In 1956, when wool was still Australia's principal export commodity, there was a bitter strike in the shearing industry over pay rates. The union knew trouble was ahead when farmer groups began agitating in 1954 for a cut to the shearing rate on the basis that the wool industry was continuing to descend from its early 1950s peak. (At this time, shearing was a lucrative vocation, with good shearers earning twice the national average wage for men.) Graziers argued a downturn in wool prices following a boom associated with the Korean War meant they could no longer afford to pay shearers as much as previously. (An agreement had been struck between wool growers and the union in 1949 that shearing rates should be loosely tied to movements in the wool price.) In November 1955, the Queensland industrial court approved a 10 per cent cut to the shearers' rate of pay, which at the time was £7/14/3 (seven pounds 14 shillings and threepence) per 100 sheep. (Woolgrowers had pushed for a 15 per cent cut, while shearers had sought a 7.5 per cent increase.) Queensland shearers voiced their disgust at the ruling by striking from 1 January 1956.

The strike spread to New South Wales, when in February 1956, the then Commonwealth Court of Conciliation and Arbitration slashed the rate for shearers in the federal Pastoral Industry Award to £7/1/6 (seven pounds one shilling and sixpence) per 100 sheep – 11s 7d (11 shillings and seven pence) or 8.2 per cent less than the AWU had sought.

The strike became violent and eventually embroiled other unions, including those representing railway and maritime workers, who refused to handle 'black' wool. It lasted some 10 months in Queensland and six months in New South Wales. In the end, the union claimed a major victory as the old shearing rates were reinstated. The mateship and spirit of the shearers who held out and refused to shear at the new, lower rate became legendary within the AWU. Key aspects of this historic struggle were portrayed in the acclaimed 1975 Australian film *Sunday Too Far Away*.

Ernie Ecob was among the hundreds of shearers who refused to shear, except at the old rate, and as a consequence struggled to find regular work. The Ecobs ate a lot of home-grown vegetables and rabbits during that period. The hardship that he and his fellow workers endured for much of 1956 had a profound impact – most significantly, it exacerbated the historically strained and antagonistic relationship between wool growers and shearers (see chapters 7 and 8 for more details on this) and it enhanced the camaraderie and mateship of the union 'family'. For Ecob in particular, it helped to shape his uncompromising, hardline approach as an AWU official and explain his utter disdain for wool growers, of whom he later said, 'They have always been bludgers and parasites. You get the odd good cocky but there are too many who are hungry and demand more sweat from the worker.'[17]

Ecob becomes an organiser, then secretary

Following the strike, Ecob continued shearing and was a shed floor delegate for the union until 1964, when he was appointed a full-time organiser. Another candidate stood for the position but Ecob won through with the support of the powerful Charlie Oliver, who at that time was the New South Wales branch secretary. It was the beginning of what proved to be a tumultuous relationship between the two men. Ecob's new role was essentially to look after the needs of the union's pastoral industry members throughout the vast north-west region of the state. At that time, shearers could not work without being financial members of the union (unless they were learners), so union membership was strong, and the role required extensive travel, often to very remote areas. In her obituary for Ernie Ecob, Dr Marilyn Dodkin, an Australian Labor Party activist and historian, summarised the key leadership changes within the union that led to Ecob becoming the New South Wales branch secretary and Ecob and Oliver falling out with each other:

> At great risk to himself, Ecob, then an elected organiser, supported Oliver when he lost control of the union in 1969. The Oliver team regained control in 1973 and Ecob was elected branch president. In July 1980 Ecob became branch secretary when Reg Mawbey resigned, and the Ecob family moved from Coonamble to Sydney. Later Oliver turned against Ecob and supported left-wing challengers. This was a blow to Ecob, who had been loyal to Oliver, but the two men were reconciled, on Ecob's initiative, before Oliver died in 1990.[18]

The wide comb dispute was just beginning to unfold when Ecob moved to Sydney to take on the union's state secretary role. The new position would be a significant test for him professionally, but he certainly rose to the challenge. During the next few years, he was to become a powerful figure in the trade union movement and was very much the public face and voice of the state's shearers during the dispute.

Charlie Oliver (1901–1990)

For roughly three decades, Cecil Thompson (Charlie) Oliver was one of the most influential figures in Labor Party politics in New South Wales. His sway came largely through the control he exercised over the New South Wales branches of the AWU and the Australian Labor Party. Oliver was born in Wales in 1901 to Scottish parents – his father was a grocer and tea merchant in Bangor. He left school at 13 to work on a farm, but he left after a couple of years to work in a steel factory as an iron pickler to support the British war effort. Pickling involved using acids to remove impurities from the surface of the steel. In

Oliver's case, steam from the acids used in this process damaged his front teeth.[19] Following the Great War, Oliver and his brother Jack migrated to Australia.

Charlie ended up in Western Australia, in the remote goldfield town of Meekatharra (Aboriginal for 'place of little water'), inland from Geraldton in the state's mid-west. It was there, while working as a miner, that he joined and became active in the AWU, first as a union delegate and later, during World War II, as an organiser. In 1931, at Midland Junction on Perth's eastern outskirts, he married Ray Lord, the daughter of a grazier who he had met while doing a stint of rural work including fencing. In the mid-1940s, Oliver was elevated to secretary of the AWU's mining branch, a position that was to be a stepping stone into state politics – in December 1948 he successfully contested the seat of Boulder in a by-election and, although he was re-elected in 1950, his real passion was working for the AWU. So the following year he headed east after being appointed secretary of the union's New South Wales branch. Oliver left his wife and son in Kalgoorlie and rarely saw them again – he lived alone in a modest home in Miranda in Sydney's south. Later in his life, he was quoted as saying, 'There's no place for married life in the union or politics – not the way I played it.'[20]

Oliver had an imposing physical presence – he was 183 centimetres tall (about six foot two inches) and solidly built. Although he had only a very basic education, he became an avid reader and a workaholic who was known for his sharp negotiation skills. And while he had never been a shearer, he was to play a key role in the 1956 shearers' strike, particularly in the aftermath, where his negotiating skills came to the fore. He took on the difficult task of placating embittered members who in many cases had had to watch on as 'scab' workers took their jobs. He also sought to help re-establish peace and stability in the pastoral industry after black bans were lifted through negotiations with grazier groups.

Throughout the 1960s, Oliver was president of the New South

Wales branch of the Labor Party, a position he stepped down from in 1970. Concurrently, up until 1969, he was also the secretary of the New South Wales branch of the AWU. Throughout the wide comb shearing dispute, Oliver was president of the New South Wales branch of the AWU. He was never far from the many bitter infights and power struggles that plagued both the AWU and the Labor Party during the 1970s and 1980s. His falling out with Ecob, following the wide comb dispute, coincided with a time of significant internal strife in the AWU's New South Wales branch. Oliver is reported to have said at the time,

> I blame myself for these troubles in the union. I said to [the then New South Wales Industrial Relations and Technology Minister] Pat Hills soon after I got Ernie Ecob that job [as New South Wales branch secretary], 'I've made a blue. I've put a yobbo in as secretary.'[21]

However, as the wide comb dispute was unfolding during the early 1980s, Ecob and Oliver were perhaps at their zenith. Together, they made a formidable team. Both men had come through the 1956 shearers' strike emboldened by the union's victory and confident that it would again prevail.

4

The Infiltration of Wide Combs

A significant agricultural land development in Western Australia beginning in the late 1950s was the key driver for the steady 'infiltration' of wide gauge shearing combs into Australia. This at first seemingly obscure connection was explained succinctly by Paul Houlihan when he addressed the H.R. Nicholls Society in August 1988. The society was formed in 1986 to promote debate about and reform of Australia's industrial relations system. To some critics it was more about 'union-busting'. Former Australian Prime Minister Bob Hawke gave the society's profile an unintended boost when he labelled its members 'political troglodytes and economic lunatics'. The late Victorian trade union official John Halfpenny went even further, describing the society as 'the industrial relations branch of the Ku Klux Klan'. (He and *The Age* newspaper, which reported the comments, were subsequently sued by several of the society's senior office holders, including the former treasurer Peter Costello. The matter was settled out of court.)

Houlihan told his audience that Western Australia had achieved 'one of the most successful "new land" developments in Australian history' during the late 1950s and early 1960s after Department of Agriculture scientists discovered that a large-scale phosphorous deficiency in the vast tracts of land in the state's south-east could be fixed by using fertilisers.

The opening up of the Great Esperance sand plain country by the introduction of trace elements led to a situation, where in a period of some 20 years, Western Australia moved from running about 10 per cent of the nation's sheep flock to something approaching 40 per cent the nation's sheep flock. This dramatic increase in sheep numbers in Western Australia far outstripped the availability of either local shearers or shearers from other parts of Australia who were prepared to travel to Western Australia to shear this vast flock. Consequently, shearers from New Zealand commenced travelling to Western Australia in order for them to get work and for the flock to be shorn. The important thing…is that they brought with them the so-called wide comb. Interestingly those combs were made in Sydney.[22]

Rory O'Malley, an economic historian who converted his PhD thesis on Australia's shearing industry into a book, *Mateship and Moneymaking*, provides more details about the rapid growth of the wool industry in Western Australia.

The west's 11 million sheep in 1950 were dwarfed by the 53 million in New South Wales and approximately 100 million in the eastern states overall. However, it was beginning to catch up. The west had one sheep for every five in New South Wales; fifty years earlier it had only been one in ten. By the 1960s Western Australia was on a remarkable growth curve and by the mid-1970s supported over 30 million sheep. New South Wales, meanwhile, had slipped from a peak of 70 million to 55 million (and was still falling). The wool industry overall was increasingly in the grip of the profit squeeze, but aggressive state assisted agricultural development created quite different results in the west.[23]

But it was more than job opportunities that drew shearers across the Tasman Sea during this period. As well as there being plenty of work, it was quite lucrative, when the exchange rate was factored in, for New Zealand shearers to work in Australia. 'The West Australian shearers were simply overwhelmed, there were not enough Australian shearers,' Paul Houlihan said. 'New Zealand shearers working out here were getting paid much more than they would be paid in New Zealand. It was like Christmas.'

As it turned out, an unusual aspect of the operation of the federal Pastoral Industry Award made Western Australia an even more attractive destination for New Zealand shearers. The Award covered all states except Queensland, which had its own award dating back to 1911. However, in Western Australia there was an irregularity that severely restricted the application of the Award. Historically, the employer organisations that were respondents to the Award had very limited memberships, and there was no related state legislation binding all pastoral employers to the Award. The AWU moved in January 1980 to rectify this anomaly by asking the Australian Conciliation and Arbitration Commission to bind all pastoral industry employers in the state to the Award – a request known as a 'roping-in' application. However, the Farmers' Union of Western Australia Industrial Association opposed the application. On 1 July 1980, Commissioner Pauline Barnes ruled that the Farmers' Union should be bound to the Award. However, she reserved any decision on whether the clause prohibiting wide combs should be included in the roping-in. This ruling maintained the status quo in relation to wide gauge shearing equipment – with the commission planning to determine the matter at a later date.

In practice, this major limitation of the Award in Western Australia meant that shearers who were not members of the AWU were beyond the reach of the union and could not be prosecuted for breaches of the Award or penalised for breaking union rules. The union effectively had no power in the state. New Zealanders, and of course any other shearers, knew they could use wide gauge combs with impunity – all the union could do was voice its disapproval.

Patsy Adam-Smith, author of *The Shearers*, which many people consider to be the definitive history of the Australian shearing industry, wrote an article for the former weekly newspaper *The National Times* in 1983, in which she highlighted the prevalence of New Zealand shearers in Western Australia during the previous decade or so. 'In shearing parlance, Western Australia, as far as shearing is concerned, is known as, "the Third Island of New Zealand". There are 700 New Zealand shearers in the southern wool-growing areas of that state at present all using wide combs,' she said.[24]

Shearing industry concerns

During the late 1970s, Dave Hollis, a shearer and staunch member of the AWU based in Wanneroo in Perth's northern outskirts, was becoming increasingly concerned about the large number of New Zealand shearers he was encountering in the state's shearing sheds and by what he perceived as a corresponding breakdown in Award conditions. He wrote to the Western Australian Department of Agriculture on 2 April 1980 seeking information about the state's shearing industry and any data relating to the number of New Zealanders involved in the industry. The department's response, which was written on 15 April under the signature of A. Ingleton, confirmed the anecdotal evidence that there was a large presence of New Zealand shearers in the state's south-east. Ingleton said the department had no firm figures but 'sources in the great southern and Esperance area estimate 600–1,000'. The department also confirmed the state's desperate shortage of shearers was expected to continue into the early 1980s. It estimated there would be some 34.2 million sheep to be shorn during the 1980/1981 season. Using data from a shearing survey census conducted during the 1971/1972 season, the department knew that more than two-thirds (69.5 per cent) of the state's shearing took place between July and November, with most (18.8 per cent) occurring during September. Based on the assumption that shearers shore on average 110 sheep per day and worked 22 days per month, Ingleton estimated that during the busiest shearing month, 2,656 shearers would be needed to meet the demand.

A couple of months later, Hollis visited New South Wales, where he attended a shearers' meeting in Dubbo on 22 June. Ernie Ecob invited him to report on the situation in Western Australia. Hollis explained some of the information the Department of Agriculture had provided him with and emphasised the strong New Zealand presence. He said that New Zealand contractors with about 1,000 New Zealand shearers were breaking down rates of pay for shearers, shed hands, woolpressers, and cooks. He said the AWU only had 257 pastoral industry members in Western Australia, well short of the 2,656 shearers that were needed at the peak of the season. Even if the estimate of 1,000 New Zealand shearers was accurate, there was still a significant gap between the number of shearers needed and the number available. Some of this gap, of course, was filled by shearers from the eastern states. Hollis, who later became a union organiser in Western Australia, also told the Dubbo meeting that there were only about 30 non-union shearers in the west who were using narrow gauge gear. He warned members to be vigilant to ensure that the deterioration in the industry did not spread to the east.

Following this meeting, Reg Mawbey, who was secretary of the New South Wales branch of the AWU immediately before Ernie Ecob, wrote to the union's national secretary Frank Mitchell to highlight Hollis's concerns and the state of the shearing industry in Western Australia. Mitchell, who was the son of a farmer, a former shearer and union organiser, and a former Royal Australian Air Force serviceman, was national secretary of the AWU from 1972 to 1983. Although he was in a fairly prominent role and would be expected to deal closely with the media on behalf of the union, Mitchell had a dislike for journalists and only ever gave one interview in his capacity as national secretary – to ABC radio's *AM* program in July 1976, in which he spoke on the federal government's proposed changes to wage indexation guidelines at that time. In his four-page letter, which was dated 23 June 1980, Mawbey wrote in part,

> Mr Hollis is a shearer who is endeavouring to earn a living in the industry in Western Australia, but because he tries to obey the Pastoral Industry Award and adhere to strict trade union principles he finds he is faced with extreme difficulties earning a living because of the high content of scab element in Western Australia who have captured the industry by non-observance of

the Award and trade union principles... You will agree the number of shearers who are members of the union in the industry is deplorable compared to the number of shearers and shearing personnel engaged in the pastoral industry in West [sic] Australia... The shearing industry in West [sic] Australia is in a shocking, deplorable state of affairs and the union in West [sic] Australia has to accept the blame for allowing the shearing industry to deteriorate to such a low level. The conditions in the industry in West [sic] Australia are below the raddle days of the shearing industry practised in the 1800s.[25]

Mawbey asked that his letter and a copy of Hollis's report be tabled for discussion at the next meeting of the AWU Executive Council, which was scheduled for 10 July. His letter clearly had the desired effect. Following the Executive Council meeting, Mitchell wrote to all branch secretaries warning them of the threat of wide combs and urging them to remain vigilant. The council had passed the following resolution:

> That where a branch of the union becomes aware that pulled or wide combs are being used or other breaches of the Award are occurring, that the Branch Secretary shall be authorised to take action to have bans applied by AWU members and/or members of other unions on the handling of livestock or produce on properties where the offences have occurred. That where prosecutions are possible that steps be taken immediately by the Branch Secretary to prosecute both the employer and the employee.

Union branches were put on notice. The union was determined to do everything in its power to prevent the spread of wide comb shears to the eastern states. However, it was an uphill battle. A small but growing portion of the New Zealand shearers who were working in Western Australia during the late 1970s and early 1980s started to pick up sheds in the eastern states. Of course, some of them brought with them their wide gauge shearing equipment. However, there was also another 'enemy' for the union – a small number of eastern states shearers who were wide comb proselytes: they had travelled to the west for work and discovered the 13-tooth combs the New Zealanders were using. Most were content to use the wide gear in the west, where the industry was unregulated, but would revert to narrow gauge gear in their home states to comply with union requirements. However, a handful believed the wide gear was so superior to the standard gear that they were prepared to defy the union. Robert White was one of those proselytes.

5

A Tale of Two Brothers

Mount David barely rates a mention on most maps of New South Wales. It's the best part of an hour's drive south of Bathurst, on the western slopes of the Great Dividing Range and just over 1,000 metres above sea level. It was there, on a mixed farm running sheep and cattle and growing potatoes, that Robert White grew up during the mid-1940s and 1950s. Robert had four siblings, including his elder brother Peter, who was also a shearer. Peter was also to play an important role in the wide comb shearing dispute – as an AWU organiser. Although the two brothers were close during their childhood and teenage years while growing up on the family farm, their friendship ended when Robert started advocating for the introduction of wide combs. This was a position that Peter, as a staunch unionist and later a union employee, could not accept. Their friendship never recovered, and they remained bitterly divided at the time of Robert's tragic death following a farm accident in 1986.

Shearing careers

Although both Peter and Robert were to become highly accomplished shearers, their paths into the industry were quite different. Peter remembered shearers coming to the family property and him as a youngster being invited to try his hand at shearing the odd sheep. 'Eventually it got that way that I could shear a few sheep,' he said. His first shearing job was shearing a neighbour's flock – the neighbour didn't have a shearing shed so he contracted Peter to shear his 600 sheep in the Whites' shed. A few years later, the neighbour built a single-stand shed and for the next 30 years or so, Peter continued to shear his flock, which grew to about 3,500. 'I got into shearing from there…got in with a local contractor, and then got a few cocky sheds,' he said. The contractor had a run around the Rockley and Bathurst areas. He later joined another contractor who worked further afield, with runs in the Tibooburra, Bourke and Cobar areas of north-west New South Wales.

Robert's entry into shearing was not quite so smooth. He started shearing in 1969 and although he picked up a bit of work in New South Wales, he was unable to find regular work. Frustrated, he wrote to shearing contractors in three states seeking a job, but they all replied that he could not shear enough sheep. He later saw an advertisement seeking shearers to work in Western Australia. It had been published in *The Australian Worker* which, according to the minutes of an AWU meeting in Dubbo, was 'established as an organ of working class thought'.[26] He corresponded with the advertiser, Kevin Sarre, who was to become one of Australia's greatest shearers. White told an Australian Conciliation and Arbitration Commission hearing about his move to Western Australia in the early 1970s,

> He [Sarre] told me that in Western Australia they had the Tally-hi coaching system going where they had instructors teaching you to shear. If I was prepared to go over there, they would give me a job. As soon as I got the letter I immediately went to Western Australia.[27]

Sarre (1933–1995), who was from Lockington, Victoria, was a five-time Australian shearing champion who shore a record tally of 346 in one day at a station near Penshurst in Victoria in October 1965. He once swapped from his dominant right hand and shore left-handed for a day – and still notched a tally of 200. Sarre developed the Tally-hi system for the Australian Wool Board in 1963 to be an industry standard method of shearing.[28] It saved roughly 30 seconds per sheep, compared to other shearing techniques used at the time. The system (or variations of it) is still used today.

Robert spent about six months with the Tally-hi instructors, a period that included dedicated coaching as well as on-the-job training and general shearing work, before he signed on with a contractor. It was during this period that he was first exposed to pulled combs. During the commission hearing referred to above, Robert described that experience:

> I never even heard of a pull comb or wide comb or anything before I went to Western Australia…another contractor had an advertisement in the paper, and above the Award payments. I rang him up and he gave me a job. I did one day [of shearing], and I was still using narrow combs, and on the Sunday the contractor rang me up and said to go down to his place. When I went there he was in the process of pulling some combs; in other words, you pull them out [the outside teeth] and make them wider. I asked him all about them and he told me you can shear more sheep with them, and I said, 'Pull a few for me and I will give them a try.' … I went into his team then and began to use wide-pull combs.

Robert spent three months with this contractor, then had several more months of training in the Tally-hi shearing method.

It was later, while he was working with another contractor, Dennis Beck, that Robert was first exposed to wide comb shears. Beck had been to New Zealand and had brought back some wide combs. However, they were not designed to shear dense-woolled merino sheep – they were more suited to coarser-woolled crossbreeds. 'After a long time, we eventually found out if you ground the comb right down, so it was nearly flat, it would enter the merino wool,' Robert told the commission. But they were still far from ideal.

About this time, during the early 1970s, Robert was involved in a tractor accident in Western Australia and badly injured his back. Doctors told him he would never be able to shear again. However, after some two years out of the industry, he started shearing once more, first in New South Wales and then back in Western Australia, where he resumed working for Beck. Among the other shearers employed by

Beck were two New Zealanders, who introduced Robert to the Sunbeam-branded Hustler, Fine Wool and Top Flight wide combs. He told the commission that with some slight modifications out of the packet – the teeth had to be 'thinned out' and the back of the comb also had to be ground down – 'they did a perfect job'. He said, 'From then I just used nothing else but Hustler, Fine Wool and Top Flights.' And in the early 1980s, when he moved back to his home state for good, he gradually started to use them in local sheds, initially in the Oberon area south-east of Bathurst, against both the Award conditions and the union rules.

Bathurst committee formed

Peter, meanwhile, was becoming increasingly involved in the AWU. He first joined the union when he started shearing in 1955 and was a paid-up member until he retired in 1996. However, during the early 1970s, he and several colleagues from the Bathurst area started to take a much greater interest in issues affecting the shearing industry and began attending union meetings in Dubbo. Issues such as wage rates, travel allowances, accommodation standards and taxation reform were regularly debated in meetings during the mid to late 1970s. In 1973, with a growing number of Bathurst shearers taking an interest in such issues, a local committee of the union was formed. Peter served as the committee secretary for the next 10 years. It was in his capacity as the Bathurst AWU Pastoral Committee secretary that Peter wrote to the union's New South Wales branch in November 1981, expressing concern at the growing prevalence of the use of wide comb shears in the central west. He was, in effect, informing on Robert, who was the main contractor in the area who was using wide gear. Earlier that year, Robert and his team had been caught using wide combs while shearing at three Canowindra district properties. And in July the previous year, he had publicly goaded the AWU – telling *The Land* newspaper that he planned to continue using wide comb shears because they were more efficient and easier to use. 'They say the wide blades cannot be used on all sheep,' he was quoted as saying. 'I haven't found a sheep yet that the blade doesn't suit. The wider blades have been in use in Western Australia since 1970, and 98 per cent of the state's sheds now use them. Between 80 and 90 per cent of sheep in Western Australia are now shorn with wide blades.'[29] In the same report, White went on to taunt the powerful Charlie Oliver, who had been interviewed on ABC radio earlier that month about the emerging wide comb dispute. Oliver told listeners,

> I would say 10 or 20 years ago, a wide comb was unheard of in Australia, but they have been introduced from New Zealand in recent years. The New Zealand shearer comes over here and he brings his comb with him. Well, of course, he did not get away using it for many years, but it has gradually worked in until in places like Western Australia they have practically an open go. My understanding in Western Australia, the industry is completely disorganised. The statistics say there is about four-and-a-half thousand employed in the industry included in which would be two-and-a-half thousand shearers. In the union, which in New South Wales is fully organised, the industry is fully organised, but in Western Australia out of that workforce a man came to Dubbo a fortnight ago and told a meeting there that there were only about 257 people in the union that worked in the pastoral industry so you can imagine the state of chaos that is there… I will assist any shearer to resist the intrusion of wide combs into the industry.[30]

Asked what would happen to shearers who were using wide combs, Oliver declared, 'We will turf him out of the industry…he has no place in the industry of New South Wales. The practice they use in South Australia, they go to the shed, smash all the combs up and in some cases turf the bloke out of the industry.'

Robert White, referring directly to Oliver's threat to 'smash up the combs' of wide gear users, was reported in *The Land* as saying, 'He can start by breaking mine.'[31] As if that wasn't enough, during the same interview he further incited the union by claiming that its organisers needed to 'get out of the pubs and into the sheds where they should be'.

Ernie Ecob responded to the Bathurst AWU Pastoral Committee's letter on 23 November and said, in part,

> We have made investigations and we only know of some [wide comb shearers] in the Oberon-Bathurst area and Roberts [sic] team in the Mandurama area and that he is doing sheds at Yass, Coonamble and Crookwell, but we have not found out till after the sheds have been completed this year. I have arranged that an organiser will be in your area within the next week, so I hope the [union] shearers will give him all the assistance that is required, especially as to where they are shearing.

Knowing that Peter and Robert were brothers, Ecob signed off with a sympathetic acknowledgement of Peter's predicament: 'Hoping that we can have your problem settled in the near future.'[32]

Although he was a vocal wide combs advocate, Robert was also a member of the union, having signed up in 1970. He maintained his membership and indeed told the Australian Conciliation and Arbitration Commission that a strong, organised union was needed in the industry: '… I am not trying to weaken the union. You have to have a union. But as far as weaken it, no way in the world.'[33]

Peter became even more involved with the union in 1984, when he was appointed an organiser, initially for the central west region based in Bathurst. However, he later had a stint in Canberra and when Bluey Rodwell retired in 1987, Peter moved to Dubbo to take over from him, covering the vast western and north-west areas of the state, as far as Cameron's Corner. Reflecting on his relationship with Robert, he said, 'When Robert went to Western Australia we had a couple of run-ins and we were never very close from then on…yeah, we didn't get on.'

6

Preliminary Research Trials

Australian wool growers enjoyed an extended period of profitability during the 1950s and 1960s, compared to many other agricultural producers. Both sheep numbers and wool production increased and this was indeed the era in which Australia 'rode on the sheep's back'. However, underlying concerns arose during the 1960s about the trajectory of the wool price – since peaking in the early 1950s boom, the price and subsequent profit levels had been in steady decline. These concerns proved justified when in 1970 wool prices plummeted, triggering the federal government's intervention in the market through various price support schemes. The most significant of these was the Reserve Price Scheme, which was set up in 1974 to provide growers with a guaranteed minimum price for their wool. The scheme was administered by the Australian Wool Corporation (AWC), which had been established the previous year as the key industry body to facilitate research as well as wool marketing and promotion. The corporation was funded through a levy paid by wool growers. The Reserve Price Scheme worked by the AWC purchasing all the wool that did not achieve the agreed floor price at auction, then selling it later when the demand and price were more buoyant. However, during the late 1980s and against the advice of many agricultural economists, the federal government gave the AWC greater powers to adjust the floor price. Through a combination of optimism and greed, the floor price was artificially inflated, creating an unsustainable market. The scheme's inevitable and spectacular implosion occurred in January 1991, when the AWC had more than 4.6 million bales of wool stockpiled. Leading Australian wool grower and author Charles Massy describes the AWC's collapse with a conservative estimate of $9 billion of debt as 'the biggest corporate disaster in Australian history in terms of losses generated by a single corporate or statutory business entity'.[34]

In terms of wool industry research, the focus up until the early 1970s had been mostly on achieving improvements to sheep breeding and wool production, as well as the packaging and processing of the wool fibres. Following the collapse of the wool market in 1970, there was a much greater industry focus on reducing production costs and, as a consequence, the focus of industry research bodies switched to wool harvesting. Some important technical improvements were made to shearing machinery in the early 1900s and shearing methods were refined over the years – for example, the Tally-hi shearing method. However, before the 1970s there had been only minimal changes to the technology used for the shearing process and very little research on wool harvesting. This new focus led to the establishment in July 1973 of the Australian Wool Harvesting Program (AWHP), which was under the control of the AWC. The program was charged with developing new and improved methods of shearing, as well as examining methods to reduce shearing costs and minimise the arduous nature of the job.

Funding for this program had to be approved by the Minister for Primary Industry, who in the early 1980s was Senator Fred Chaney. Senator Chaney (Liberal, Western Australia), in answer to a 'Dorothy Dixer' from Senator Peter Rae (Liberal, Tasmania), told parliament on 3 March 1981 that a total of $7.526 million had been allocated to wool harvesting research during the period 1972/73 to 1979/80.[35] Funding had increased from a minuscule $111,000 in 1972/73, peaking at $1.499 million in 1977/78. Senator Chaney told parliament that the program was

>   ...largely in response to the recognition by the industry and research bodies that a potential future problem could be emerging in relation to increasing costs of shearing and decreasing

availability of adequately skilled shearers. While most early developments were related to seeking to modify and improve the existing shearing system and some promising work still continues in this area on improving the life of shearing combs and cutters, the main thrust of the wool harvesting program is now towards novel methods of wool removal such as chemical (and/or biological) and/or automated wool harvesting methods. These novel systems are undergoing intensive scientific and engineering investigations and trials to determine technical feasibility and provide data on which future assessments of likely commercial viability can be made.

The wool industry slump during the early 1970s was a time when many shearers left the industry. Although there were signs of a recovery again by 1973, there was little indication that shearers were returning to the industry. Wool industry researcher and controller of the AWHP, Alan McDonald Richardson, noted in July 1973,

> The trouble is however, that good professional shearers are already in short supply and that young shearers are not coming forward in sufficient numbers. Because shearing is such a strenuous occupation, because it generally requires long periods away from home, and because for many it is only a seasonal occupation, it is no longer as popular as it was in times of less-full employment and a less-affluent society.[36]

Richardson quotes Commonwealth census figures to highlight the shearer exit – there were 9,046 shearers in 1961 when the national sheep flock numbered 163.6 million, while a decade later, in 1971, there were only 6,373 shearers and 178.5 million sheep. (This equates to one shearer for every 18,000 sheep in 1961, and one per 28,000 in 1971.[37] It does not, however, include part-time shearers who mostly worked in other industries.) He also pointed out,

> Wool harvesting is a costly, labour-intensive area of wool production. Because of this it is particularly prone to cost increases. But also because of this it is very likely to be amenable to cost reduction, or at least to cost containment by the

introduction of modern methods and equipment to increase labour productivity... There is clearly, for the two reasons of high labour intensity and high cost content, a strong case of adequately planned and funded research and development work in the wool-harvesting field.[38]

Shearing represented a significant cost for wool growers. Figures from the late 1970s suggested that it constituted about 22 per cent of the total harvesting, marketing, handling and transport costs of wool.[39] Although, as Senator Chaney explained to federal parliament on 3 March 1981, most of the industry research carried out during the 1970s was on 'novel' methods of wool harvesting, there were several relatively small-scale projects that focused on the most basic tools of the shearing process – combs and cutters.

The first such project took place during the mid-1970s. Alan McDonald Richardson, on behalf of the AWHP, wrote to David Trebeck, the then executive officer of the Australian Woolgrowers' and Graziers' Council (AWGC) on 12 November 1976, regarding the results of this project. (The AWGC was an industry association representing farmers and graziers. It operated from 1919 to 1979, when it merged with several other industry bodies to form the National Farmers' Federation.) In the letter, Richardson provided the following details:

> As you are aware, the Australian Wool Harvesting Program, in connection with its work on the development of new and improved methods of shearing, has been experimenting for some time with the use of wide shearing gear. The gear used has included the 3-inch wide comb of various tooth configurations as used in New Zealand, and the various 4-tooth New Zealand cutters; and also, an experimental 4-inch wide comb and 5-tooth cutter of our own design and construction. Combs with bent or 'pulled' teeth have not been included in the investigations.
>
> ... Our experiments to date have been purely qualitative, and no comparative trials of shearing tallies or of shearing quality have been attempted, either as between wide and narrow gear or as

between Australian and New Zealand sheep. Our findings at this stage are confined to a subjective appraisal of the suitability and effectiveness of wide gear for shearing Australian merino and crossbred sheep.

There seems to be a body of opinion that it is not possible, or at least very difficult, to shear the Australian merino with wide gear without excessive skin cuts to the sheep and/or second cuts in the wool. The alleged reason for this is the dense wool and the relatively folded and wrinkled skin development of the merino compared with New Zealand breeds. …but we have found that wide gear presents no real problem with any form of shearing, conventional or otherwise, of any part of the merino. On the contrary, in the hands of skilled shearers, it enables fast shearing of high quality to be carried out.[40]

Based on these qualitative results, the AWHP proposed a series of comparative trials of wide and narrow-gauge equipment in early 1977 to quantify what increase in tallies might be possible from using wide combs and the relative quality of the shearing achieved from using both wide and narrow combs. Although the proposed trials did not eventuate the following year, the AWC funded a series of trials that were run by the Western Australian Department of Agriculture in 1978/79.

The Western Australian trials

In October 1979, five of the department's researchers published the findings of their preliminary investigation into the performance of wide combs.[41] The study compared the performance of conventional combs, in both standard (64 mm) and widened (pulled to 73 mm) form, with two New Zealand wide combs (76 mm and 86 mm) and an Australian prototype wide comb (86 mm) designed specifically to use with merino sheep. (The narrow 10-tooth combs were used in combination with a three-tooth cutter, while the wider 13-tooth combs were used with four-toothed cutters.)

The researchers, led by R.J. (John) Lightfoot, established two matching experiments at separate sites – the Merredin Agricultural Research Station and Wongan Hills Agricultural Research Station. The Merredin project ran during October 1978 and involved 150 medium-wool merino ewes. This flock was in full wool and carried a light infestation of grass seed and medic burr. The Wongan Hills experiment was carried out during February 1979, using 150 medium-wool merino wethers. The sheep were in full wool, with the fleeces heavily infested with grass seed.

Three professional shearing instructors were used to shear the sheep. They had a combined total of 24 years' commercial shearing experience and 23 years in employment as professional instructors, but none had previously used wide combs. The results showed a progressive reduction in average shearing times as the comb width increased. The 73 mm, 76 mm, 86 mm (Australian prototype) and 86 mm (New Zealand) combs produced mean shearing times six, seven, 14 and 14 per cent faster than the standard narrow comb (64 mm) respectively. Taking into account differences in results between the sites (attributable to the types of sheep shorn) and the individual shearers' times, the researchers concluded that, based on an average shearer using 64 mm combs and turning out 130 sheep per day, there was the potential for an increase of 18 sheep per day with 86 mm combs. The economic benefit of this increase would vary considerably between sheds. In their report, the researchers wrote,

> In a four-stand 'owner-class' shed shearing 4,000 sheep and employing casual shed labour, the time for shearing could be reduced by about one day. If the traditional shed labour force could cope with the faster rate of wool flow, economies in labour could be realised. With larger sheds, however, assuming the traditional shed labour force is efficiently employed, any reduction in the duration of shearing may be offset by the need to employ additional shed hands.

The study did identify one disadvantage – there was an increased incidence of second cuts. Using the average of 5.7 grams more second cuts for the two widest combs, the researchers calculated a potential economic loss of about 0.8 cents per sheep, or about $24 for a flock of 3,000 sheep. 'While not to be ignored, such losses seem comparatively minor compared with potential economic gains through faster shearing,' they said in their report. Interestingly, they also found that the two widest combs 'may reduce the number of skin cuts on the sheep, and coincidently the incidence of skin pieces in the fleece'. The researchers said this could help reduce the incidence of diseases such as cheesy gland, which can be spread by shearing cuts.[42]

It was clear that any speed advantage from wide combs would vary between shearers and flocks. But it was also important to note that these gains had been made by shearers with no previous experience using wider combs, and it was quite likely that their times and tallies would have improved with practice. The researchers recommended that more research be carried out, identifying the need for larger-scale testing under full commercial conditions with a wide range of sheds, shearers and sheep. This recommendation was one of the key arguments used by the LGPA in an application it made in May 1980 to the Arbitration Commission to approve industry trials of wide combs. The researchers also could see substantial benefits arising from the ongoing development and refinement of wide comb designs, to combine and improve on the best features of the two 86 mm combs used in their research. Even though this preliminary research had demonstrated that wide combs offered a potential 14 per cent improvement in shearing times over standard gauge combs, the recommendation to proceed to full commercial trials was never implemented.

7

Colonial History Provides Important Context

To make sense of the way the wide comb dispute unfolded, it is necessary to delve into Australia's past. Events that occurred a century or so earlier, especially during the two decades leading up to Federation in 1901, help explain the bitter and protracted nature of the dispute. The economic and social conditions that existed in Australia's colonies during this period also provide an important context for understanding the turbulent relationship that existed between pastoralists and shearers. The historical information presented in this chapter is not intended to be comprehensive – it aims merely to provide some background to key events that led to the development of the Pastoral Industry Award, which will be discussed in the next chapter.

Following the discovery in 1851 of payable gold deposits at Ophir, just north of Orange, Australia enjoyed almost four decades of economic prosperity. Although the boom was fuelled mainly by the ensuing gold rush, other industries including wool contributed significantly to the extended period of strong economic growth and development. In fact, for large chunks of this period, wool eclipsed all other industries as Australia's largest export earner. For example, 'In 1886 wool exports were valued at £12.9 million, gold at £3 million and all other Australian exports at £4.9 million.'[43] Skilled labourers were in high demand and a prosperous working class emerged. Many large cities and regional centres experienced a building boom. Melbourne in particular benefited during these years, experiencing what became known as the Land Boom in the 1880s and growing to become Australia's largest city for a time. Colonial governments helped underpin the economic expansion by investing heavily in infrastructure, especially railways. (By the end of the 1880s, the railway service in New South Wales employed almost 10,000 workers and was the biggest employer in the colony.) Strong foreign investment, particularly from Britain, injected capital and confidence into the colonial economies. Many historians mark this period as a time when Australia's colonies emerged from their pioneering past to attain a level of economic independence, maturity and security.

However, as the 1880s drew to a close, there were signs that an economic slowdown was looming – asset and commodity prices were shrinking and there was increased pressure on borrowers. By the early 1890s, the economy had not just hit the brakes, it had skidded to a stop and the gear lever was in reverse. In what was to become a recurring theme, the major banks had been overzealous in approving loans, many of which had been used to fund speculative investments in real estate and pastoral properties. Historian Geoffrey Blainey points out that

> By the mid-1880s the annual interest owed by many individual sheep stations equalled one-third or even one-half of the value of the annual wool clip, and five years later the lower wool proceeds of many stations could not even meet the interest owed to the city finance houses.[44]

The contraction in the economy (and property values) meant a large number of loans could not be repaid. Bankruptcies rose. Many companies, large and small, failed. Foreign investment dried up. Unemployment rose rapidly. Panic set in as depositors sought to withdraw their life savings – producing runs on several banks in 1892 and early 1893. Eventually, in April and May 1893, the banking system largely collapsed – many banks suspended trading and closed. Australia's colonial economies tumbled into depression, as did many countries in other parts of the world at this time.

Before Federation, Australia's six colonies had no formal social security system to support the unemployed or disadvantaged in society. There was much hardship and misery as the effects of the depression stretched to the turn of the century. At the start of 1895, just as the economy was beginning to show signs of improvement, another disaster struck. Drought took hold of most of eastern Australia and held it firmly in its grip until 1903.[45] The Federation Drought, as it became known, remains one of the most severe droughts experienced in Australia since European settlement. It devastated rural towns and communities at a time when they were still battling to recover from the depression. Crop yields were slashed, as were livestock numbers. Sheep flocks in the eastern colonies halved during this period, while cattle numbers declined by more than one-third. (In New South Wales, the sheep flock dropped from 57 million in 1894 to 26.6 million in 1903.) Paddocks across the country turned to bare ground; then in many areas the topsoil blew away too. Many landowners lost everything. Faced with no livestock or topsoil, they were unable to pay their debts and simply walked away from their farms. The drought peaked in severity during 1902, when in New South Wales all businesses (except pubs) closed on 26 February for a day of prayer for rain. In December that year, the drought broke in Victoria. It broke in New South Wales and Queensland during 1903.

The social divide

During colonial times, pastoralists were also known as 'squatters'. Monaro district grazier Charles Massy begins his forensic account of the decline of the Australian wool industry, *Breaking the Sheep's Back*, with an insightful summary of the early colonial 'squattocracy':

> This exclusive group of landowners became politically powerful, with close connections in government, the legislature, and big business. For this influential group the English system of landed power, wealth and social position was successfully replicated. The squatters ruled their vast estates like lords and expected to be

called 'Sir' or 'Mister'; they had teams of servants, along with city homes in Toorak, Bellevue Hill and Adelaide Terrace, from where they retreated into their mock-London clubs.[46]

This is a widely accepted view. Research economist Alistair Watson sheds more light:

> The wool industry has occupied an important position in Australian political and social history. From the earliest times of European settlement, the larger wool growers were politically, economically and socially powerful. In fact, the term pure merino was used in the 1820s to describe those who wished to exclude former convicts from their society.[47]

In general, pastoralists viewed shearers as second-class citizens – they were unsavoury, reckless itinerants; the dregs of society. And they were treated as such. Living conditions for shearers ranged from appalling to primitive. There were certainly no luxuries. The following is a description of the conditions that shearers could expect during the mid to late 1800s:

> The accommodation at this period was very bad. The huts were usually built of slabs without any windows, and the floor was the bare ground. The bunks were built in tiers around the walls and the dining table ran down the centre. The fireplace at which everything was cooked was at one end of the hut. Sanitation in many cases was unknown and, where it was provided, it was of the most primitive nature.[48]

Typically, landholders would supply rations to the shearing team for an agreed but heavily inflated amount. One estimate suggests shearers ate, on average, about 20 pounds (nine kilograms) of meat, mainly mutton, per week.[49] However, kitchens or cooking facilities were often ill-equipped, posing a major challenge for the team's cook.

Despite poor conditions, shearers were relatively well paid in the late 1800s. They worked a six-day week and, depending on their tally, could pocket from £3 to £6. (Most other rural workers such as stockmen, shepherds and shed hands earned much less: the average wage for unskilled labourers at that time was seven shillings a day – just over £2 for a six-day week.)[50] It should also be noted that blade shears were used up until the late 1880s. More accomplished shearers could record daily tallies of 80 to 100 sheep. And merino fleeces during this era weighed significantly less than they do now – livestock breeding programs over many decades have produced animals with much denser and heavier fleeces than during this era.

One downside of the relatively good pay was the itinerant, uncertain nature of the work. When they cut-out at one shed, shearers would move on to another in the hope of securing more work. Often, they walked long distances between sheds and towns, carrying nothing but a swag and a few belongings. Mark Hearn and Henry Knowles, in their detailed history of the AWU, *One Big Union*, provide an account of a shed hand, Syd Fernandez, who worked in the Broken Hill district in the early 1900s:

> In 1906 he walked 285 miles to work two sheds. In 1907 he hoisted his swag over his shoulder again and walked 390 miles, then walked south to the Mildura region – another area where he regularly found work – and, when sheds cut-out down there, tramped back to Broken Hill. In total, he estimated that he walked 980 miles in 1907–08.[51]

While this example may be extreme and from the early post-Federation years, it highlights the plight of many shearers and rural workers during the late 1800s. Some shearers had the luxury of a horse and a small number had sulkies, which provided for the colonial equivalent of car pooling. In some areas, it was possible to make use of paddle steamers. Irrespective of their mode of transport, the reality for most shearers was extensive travel with no guarantee of work. Inevitably, some wandered the countryside for days or weeks before they were back on the board plying their trade.

The poor view pastoralists had of shearers was reciprocated; shearers had an abiding disrespect for and mistrust of their employers.

They perceived them to be arrogant, harsh, overbearing, and often unreasonable and unfair. Pastoralists treated others, particularly shearers, with disdain. Some routinely docked a shearer's wages for what they deemed to be substandard work. (Wool growers would mark sheep they considered poorly shorn with a red ochre, a practice known as 'raddling', and marked animals would not count towards a shearer's tally.)[52] In many cases, the quality of the work was perfectly acceptable; the pastoralists were simply trying to save money. However, there was no effective recourse for penalised shearers. This perceived social divide and mutual disrespect caused decades of friction between the two parties.

A fraction too much friction

During the trying economic times immediately before the Federation Drought, pastoralists, like other business owners, were looking for ways to save money to make their businesses more viable. They started a push to drive down the pay rates of their workers. However, about the same time, shearers had begun their own push – for improved pay and conditions. They had witnessed workers in other industries, particularly mining, achieve various gains. So, for the first time, shearers were demanding, in an organised way, a greater share of the wealth that had been flowing from the wool industry. They were doing this through trade unions.

The first trade unions in the colonies were established during the 1830s. They were seen by members as offering an opportunity to exercise some influence over the terms and conditions of their employment, particularly wages. By the start of the 1890s, there were trade unions representing shipwrights, boatbuilders, cabinetmakers, compositors, stonemasons, miners, maritime and waterside workers, and tailoresses. In the shearing industry, several small unions were formed in 1886, including the Bourke Shearers' Union, the Wagga Shearers' Union, and the Australian Shearers' Union, which was based at Creswick, near Ballarat in Victoria. The following year, these three organisations merged to form the Amalgamated Shearers' Union of Australia (ASU), with a combined membership of about 9,000 shearers. A concerted effort to grow the membership through the employment of organisers paid dividends – by the end of 1888 the union had 16,000 members and by the end of the following year, roughly 19,000 shearers were on the books. The ASU quickly became the voice for shearers in New South Wales, Victoria and South Australia. A much smaller but equally vocal union represented shearers in Queensland. The Queensland Shearers' Union (QSU) was founded in January 1887 with about 900 members. By 1889, membership had stretched to about 3,000. The Queensland union strongly resisted several approaches from the ASU to consider amalgamating. (Ironically, a series of mergers resulted in both unions eventually becoming part of the one organisation, the AWU, in 1904.) In 1890, at the ASU's annual conference in Bourke in north-west New South Wales, members voted to refuse to work with non-members of the union. The logic of the decision was twofold – it aimed to encourage union membership and to make it harder for pastoralists to employ non-union labour.

The same year at two intercolonial pastoral industry conferences, which were held at Melbourne on 7 November and Sydney on 22 December, wool growers decided to ignore any previous agreements they had made with unions and shearers. They also determined to cut wages and conditions, and use non-union workers through what were known as free labour contracts – an arrangement that allowed them to employ whoever they wanted to and pay those workers at rates they determined. This would mean the men they employed in their sheds were not subject to union rules. While pastoralists called such employees 'free labourers', the union called them 'scabs' or 'blacklegs'. This new regime was to be introduced for the 1891 shearing season. Shearers in both Queensland and the southern colonies stridently opposed the plan. The fractious relationship between pastoralists and shearers was about to boil over. In fact, it boiled over twice in quick succession during the early 1890s.

8

Two Key Strikes

The strife started in Queensland on 5 January 1891. About 120 shearers and farm labourers had gathered at a station called Logan Downs, near Clermont, inland from Rockhampton, seeking employment at the station's shed. The station was one of several owned at the time by the Fairbairn family, who were prominent among Victoria's colonial elite. It was managed jointly by brothers Charles and Frederick, both graduates of the Geelong Church of England Grammar School and Cambridge University, and both fervently anti-union. Frederick read out the terms of the contract by which they were prepared to hire the assembled workers. It was based on the standard free labour contract drawn up by pastoralists at their intercolonial conferences in the previous months – meaning the workers' pay rates and rights would be significantly diminished. The free labour contract 'lowered wages by 15 to 33 per cent and disregarded the eight-hour principle. Furthermore, it gave the pastoralists the right to retain a man's wage until the end of the season, when the money could be forfeited if the labourer were deemed to have breached the new rules.'[53] At this time, shearers were earning a minimum of 30 shillings per week plus keep.[54] Not surprisingly, the shearers refused to sign the agreement and when the Fairbairns would not negotiate, they went on strike.

They were joined almost immediately by shearers who had been employed on the Aramac district stations Vindex and Oondoroo. Word spread quickly and very soon shearers at other stations in central

Queensland joined the strike. During the next couple of months, 22 'strike camps' were formed in various towns in the region, including Clermont, Wolfgang Creek, Capella, Springsure, Emerald, Tambo, Winton, Blackall, Hughenden and Barcaldine, which became the headquarters for the protest. The shearers made it clear they would only return to work if they were guaranteed a continuation of the existing pay rates, the protection of their rights and entitlements, and just and equitable agreements. The affected pastoralists, who were all affiliated with the Pastoral Employers' Association of Central and Northern Queensland, met on 13 January and made some slight revisions to their proposed contract. They gave shearers two weeks to accept the offer and begin work. However, the shearers' terms were still not met, and they continued the strike. In late January, after they had 'called the bluff' of the shearers and failed to secure any workers, the pastoralists began to seek 'free labourers' to work in their sheds.

They did not have any trouble finding willing workers. With the help of colleagues from Victoria and with a guarantee of six months' work, they initially organised for about 200 unemployed men to travel north to work on the properties in the central highlands district. The men boarded the ship *Derwent* in the port of Melbourne on 3 February and disembarked a week later at Rockhampton. In anticipation of strife, the pastoralists had asked the Queensland government to provide police protection for the workers. The government acceded and extra police were stationed in the towns near where the strike camps had been established.

Queensland's then premier, Sir Samuel Griffith, was at meetings in Tasmania and New South Wales (where he was attending the National Australasian Convention in Sydney) for the first three months of the strike and did not arrive back in Brisbane until 13 April. When it came to taking sides, Griffith's administration had no hesitation in backing the pastoralists. However, as the dispute dragged on, the premier was critical of both parties – the pastoralists for their obstinacy in refusing to negotiate and the unionists for demanding that only union shearers be employed in the sheds. He said on 21 March 1891 via telegram from Sydney,

> I think that the claim of the Unions that none but unionists shall work is absurd and can never be conceded but I think that the refusal of the pastoralists to meet the unionists and state their views to them in fair discussion is equally unreasonable and is in the existing state of things a most lamentable event, the consequences of which it is difficult to foresee the end.[55]

Tension escalated during autumn as both parties refused to compromise and repeatedly antagonised each other. The pastoralists brought in more and more 'scabs' and the unionists, who numbered almost 8,000 across the 22 camps, tried to intimidate them and impede their free movement.[56] The unionists, many of whom were armed throughout this period, also sabotaged properties, starting grass fires that destroyed valuable pasture, crops and fences. In some cases, shearing sheds were also burnt down. Trying to keep the peace was a steadily expanding number of police officers – the government appointed special constables and deployed military forces to the region to try to maintain law and order. At times, central Queensland seemed to be on the brink of a civil war. Remarkably, although there were numerous assaults and violent altercations, no lives were lost.

Demoralised by the regular influx of 'scabs' and facing hunger and financial ruin, the shearers conceded defeat in mid-June and called off the strike. Although the QSU was supporting the strike camps through a fighting fund, its resources had been steadily dwindling and it could no longer afford to finance the protest. (When the strike started in January, the QSU had £5,000 available, but by the beginning of June it had been reduced to just £270.)[57] Other factors also served to limit the effectiveness of the strike. The timing was unfortunate, from the shearers' point of view, as the bulk of the shearing in central Queensland took place during winter – only about 20 per cent of the sheds undertook early season shearing.[58] This gave the pastoralists an extended period during which they could continue the dispute, knowing there was a buffer before it would start to have any major impact on their enterprises. The dispute also occurred at a time when there was an abundance of unemployed workers who were available to the pastoralists.

During the dispute the Queensland police had arrested and charged numerous union leaders and prosecuted them under an archaic conspiracy law. The men were convicted and sentenced to jail for terms of up to three years. The intervention of the Queensland government played an important role in containing the stand-off and helped give the pastoralists the upper hand in the dispute. However, it came at a cost. One estimate suggests there was a £2 million drain on the colony's treasury to supply the extra police and military personnel needed and to prosecute the union leaders.[59]

Henry Lawson captured the mood of the striking shearers in his poem 'Freedom on the Wallaby', which was written in May 1891 following a march in Barcaldine involving more than 1,300 strikers, many of whom were carrying the Eureka flag and protesting their plight at the hands of the pastoralists. There was a genuine fear at the time that the colony could descend into civil war. The poem first appeared in the Brisbane *Worker* newspaper. The final two stanzas read,

> So, we must fly a rebel flag,
> As others did before us,
> And we must sing a rebel song
> And join in rebel chorus.
>
> We'll make the tyrants feel the sting
> O' those that they would throttle;
> They needn't say the fault is ours
> If blood should stain the wattle!

The 1894 strike

By 1894, the depression had brought the economies of colonial Australia to a standstill. There was a large number of unemployed people looking for work, many of whom, despairing of securing employment in the cities, travelled to the country in the hope of finding at least some opportunities. Wool prices were also a victim of the depression, falling significantly during the early 1890s. In 1889, wool was valued at 11¼ pence per pound. By October 1893 the price had dropped by almost one-third to 7¼ pence.[60] Most wool growers, although far from down and out, were starting to feel the pressure as the general economic malaise spread to commodity prices.

In the aftermath of the 1891 dispute, representatives of the pastoralists and QSU met in August and formed a new agreement that was due to be reviewed again in 1894. However, the terms were very much in favour of the victorious pastoralists, with the vanquished shearers forced to agree to 'open' sheds (non-union labour and conditions) and reduced pay rates. Another important post-strike development in Queensland was the merger of the QSU with the Queensland Labourers' Union to form the Amalgamated Workers Union of Queensland. The new organisation had about 5,300 members at the start of 1893, with branches in Longreach, Hughenden and Charleville. In the southern colonies, the ASU had amalgamated with the General Labourers' Union, which represented shed hands and bush workers, to form the Australian Workers' Union in February 1894. It was not an altogether smooth process, with the founding president of the ASU, William Spence, resigning and storming out of the Sydney conference at which the amalgamation vote took place. However, the newly formed union, which had a combined membership of 30,000, began its expanded role with a fresh resolve to challenge the power of the pastoralists.[61]

In April 1894, the pastoralists began notifying the AWU that the 1891 agreement would no longer be honoured. Rates would be cut for the current season, from 20 shillings per hundred to 18 shillings for blade shearing and 16 shillings 8 pence for machine shearing.[62] As well, the new terms as proposed by the pastoralists included the following clause: 'It is hereby distinctly understood and agreed that the person in charge of the shed, on behalf of the employer, shall be the person to decide all questions arising under this agreement and that his decision upon on questions shall be final and conclusive.' The AWU found this clause particularly galling, as it effectively gave station owners complete freedom to ignore or dismiss any legitimate complaint or concern on the part of shearers.

Once again there was growing tension in the pastoral industry as a stand-off ensued over wages and conditions. Despite attempts to negotiate, neither side would give ground and the shearers called a strike in June. This strike was to be shorter but more intense and violent, as well as more widespread (affecting Queensland, New South Wales and parts of South Australia and Victoria) than the 1891 strike. During the next few months there were several extremely violent acts, which included, for example:

> The burning of a woolshed at Ayrshire Downs Station near Winton in Queensland on 3 July by some 20 armed striking shearers. The strikers fired shots at two station hands who tried to extinguish the fire.

> Between 50 and 60 strikers storming and attempting to burn the woolshed and workers' huts at Kallara station near Bourke in New South Wales in mid-August. Police who were guarding the property fired shots at the retreating shearers and there was no major damage.

> The sinking of the paddle steamer *Rodney* on the Darling River near Pooncarie, New South Wales, on 26 August. The steamer had been carrying a cargo of 45 'scabs' from Wentworth to Tolarno Station, as well as general merchandise to Wilcannia. The strikers boarded the vessel while it was moored for the night, offloaded all the passengers and crew, then set the steamer alight and let it float downstream. (This incident remains the only recorded act of piracy on Australia's inland waterways.)

> Fifty strikers from a camp at Wilcannia set out in late August for the nearby Grassmere Station woolshed, where they had heard 'scab' shearers from New Zealand were working. The men attempted to storm the workers' huts and as they did, two

(William McLean and John Murphy) were shot by police who were on hand to protect the workers. Both men survived, but 'Billy' McLean died 18 months later as a result of an injury to his chest that he received during this incident.

About 20 striking shearers were involved in a shoot-out with police and station hands at Dagworth Station north-west of Winton in Queensland on 2 September. About 100 shots were fired. During this incident the strikers set fire to the woolshed, destroying the shed and some 140 lambs that were penned inside ready for shearing the next day. The following day, one of the strikers, Samuel Hoffmeister, was found dead next to a waterhole a short ride from the station. The details of how Hoffmeister died remain shrouded in mystery. However, it is generally accepted that Banjo Paterson's iconic bush verse, 'Waltzing Matilda', which was written during the January after these events, is based on the strikers' attack on the Dagworth shearing shed and Hoffmeister's subsequent death.

Hundreds of striking shearers were arrested during the three-month protest, with many charged with the offences of 'unlawful assembly' and 'riot' and many sentenced to jail terms. Patsy Adam-Smith in her epic history *The Shearers* lists at least six sheds that were destroyed by fire between June and November 1894 and estimates they were worth a total of £15,000.[63]

As was the case in the previous strike, the shearers' unions struggled to maintain financial support for their members. The strike petered out in September in Queensland, where it was costing the union about £500 per week to fund the strike camps.[64] However, it lingered another couple of weeks in the southern colonies before it was called off. Once again, the unionists had failed to persuade the pastoralists to compromise in any way, although the pastoralists' victory was not quite so resounding on this occasion – there were numerous woolsheds in New South Wales where the station owners maintained the previous pay rates and conditions throughout the dispute. And any 'victory' for the pastoralists had come at a significant cost – the quality of shearing was much poorer, there had been expensive delays, and hiring 'free labourers' involved many extra expenses.

Although the 1891 strike failed to achieve its objectives and the 1894 strike was largely ineffective, these events proved to be a turning point. Following their demoralising defeat in 1891, the shearers were left with a sense of being powerless; of having no political voice. Their disenfranchisement became the trigger that eventually led to the formation of the Australian Labor Party.[65] The need to seek representation and a voice through the political process was only reinforced by the outcome of the 1894 strike. Having failed through direct action to effect any significant change in pay and conditions for their members, the shearers' unions decided to change tactics – they switched their focus to the ballot box.

9

The Pastoral Industry Award

There were widespread social and economic divisions in Australia at the time of Federation – a legacy, in part, of the preceding turbulent decade. The economic depression combined with several brutal industrial disputes (not limited to the wool industry) and a severe drought had exacerbated many deep divisions that were entrenched in colonial society. However, as Federation edged closer, there was a growing sense of unity and hope among ordinary people that as well as addressing big picture issues such as trade, defence and immigration, the new national government would also deal with social justice issues and help create a fairer society.

Given the events of the 1890s, it was no surprise that one of the first significant issues to be debated in the fledgling Australian parliament was how best to handle and resolve industrial conflicts. To try to engender a more peaceful and stable industrial relations environment in the new century the government legislated in 1904 to form the Commonwealth Court of Conciliation and Arbitration. The Arbitration Court, as it was known, was to play a significant role in modernising and civilising Australian workplaces by acting as an independent umpire when major disputes arose between employers and workers, and by providing a safety net of minimum wages and employment conditions for workers.

Battered by the decade-long recession and Federation Drought, the wool industry was in steep decline at the turn of the century. Nationally, sheep numbers roughly halved to 54 million between the early 1890s and the end of the drought.[66] (Most of these sheep were in New South Wales, which pastured 62 million sheep in 1891 but just half that number at the time of Federation.)[67] With a rapidly dwindling wool clip, shearers and other pastoral workers were forced to look for opportunities in other industries. This in turn had a major impact on the AWU's membership, which more than halved from 30,000 when it was founded in 1894 to an estimated 14,000 in 1902, when the drought was at its worse. However, two years later, coinciding with the enacting legislation for the Arbitration Court, the union received a major boost. The Amalgamated Workers Union of Queensland agreed to a merger proposal, swelling the AWU's membership to 30,000 and making it the largest trade union in the country. The following year, the AWU was registered under the Commonwealth Conciliation and Arbitration Act 1904.

Two industries were most affected by the industrial turmoil that beset the 1890s – the maritime industry and the shearing industry. The first two awards established by the Arbitration Court covered these industries. The second, the Pastoral Industry Award, came into effect in 1907 and guaranteed shearers a minimum rate of pay (24 shillings per hundred sheep shorn) as well as various minimum working conditions that had been agreed between wool growers and the AWU. For the first time, the union had a formal, legislated mechanism through which it was able to negotiate pay rates and working conditions on behalf of its members.

Handpieces, combs and cutters

A mechanical handpiece used for shearing is essentially an industrial version of the electric hair clippers that were once used exclusively by barbers but nowadays are readily available as a general consumer product. Frederick Wolseley developed and refined the handpiece during the mid-1880s while working at his Euroka Station near Walgett in north-west New South Wales. Before moving to Euroka, the Irish-born Wolseley hobnobbed in Melbourne, where he had been a long-time a member of the Melbourne Club. In 1883 he was a pallbearer at the funeral of the former Melbourne commissioner of police, Captain Frederick Standish.[68] Although an avid inventor, Wolseley had few practical engineering skills and relied on several associates to bring his ideas and designs to reality. After his handpiece was patented in 1887 as the Wolseley Sheep Shearing Machine, Wolseley set about demonstrating the machine throughout the eastern colonies and in New Zealand, promoting it at every opportunity. At one such demonstration in Melbourne, the mechanical shears were used to shear three sheep that had just been shorn by a skilled shearer using traditional blade shears. The result was that an extra two and a quarter pounds of wool were removed from the trio (three-quarters of a pound per animal). This demonstration helped to convince many pastoralists that the new technology would provide them with a quicker, more efficient and ultimately more economical means to harvest their wool clip. The mechanical handpieces were first used commercially at Dunlop Station near Louth, about 100 kilometres south-west of Bourke in north-west New South Wales in 1888, where 184,000 sheep were shorn in the 40-stand shed. Eighteen other stations installed mechanical shearing equipment that year and within a few years most wool growers throughout the eastern colonies had adopted the new technology.

The two main components of a handpiece are the comb and cutter. When the Pastoral Industry Award was developed, the comb consisted of 10 pointed steel teeth protruding from a flat base or heel. The heel had two holes through which the comb would be screwed into the 'comb bed' of the handpiece. The comb was a non-moving part, no more than two and a half inches (64 mm) wide as measured between the tips of the two outside teeth. It was designed to separate the wool fibres and position them along the teeth so they could be severed as the shearer moved the handpiece through the fleece. The cutter, which had three stubby prongs with sharp, bevelled edges, was designed to oscillate across the cutting surface of the comb, slicing the wool fibres as it moved back and forth approximately 6,500 times per minute. The cutter was positioned under a set of forks such that the centre of the cutter corresponded to the centre of the comb. This allowed for an even to and fro movement of the cutter across the comb from one side to the other. Combs and cutters required regular grinding to keep them sharp and each shearer would thin and shape the teeth to his own liking and specifications to ensure the smooth operation of the handpiece.

Wide gauge and 'pulled' combs

Wide combs, or broad gauge combs as they were originally known, appeared during the decade after Federation. They had 13 teeth, were roughly 20 mm wider than the standard gauge combs and were paired in the handpiece with a four-pronged cutter. It seems that in a bid to ensure all shearers were using the same gear and to minimise any potential disharmony about different equipment being used within each woolshed, the AWU intervened to support the more accepted, narrower gauge combs. Rory O'Malley in his history of the Australian shearing industry during the twentieth century, *Mateship and Moneymaking*, records some details of the meeting at which the union restriction was introduced.

> While there is no evidence of widespread controversy (over broad-gauge combs), the subject came up at the Annual Conference of the AWU in 1910. A resolution asking for a restriction was moved by A. Dawson of the Central Division. The argument was that the wide comb was unfair. Equally, Dawson indicated that many would like to use them. A speaker from Bourke warned that 'there [is] a good deal of feeling' and that they 'should be discouraged'.
> … The debate was brief and unheated but it did result in a new union rule: No shearer shall use a broad gauge machine unless all other shearers employed in the shed are supplied with similar machines.[69]

In maintaining their gear, shearers routinely tweaked their combs and applied slight modifications that they felt improved overall performance. They could, for example, adjust the arc of the bevel that existed on the tip of each tooth – a short, round bevel suited open woolled sheep, while a longer, pointier bevel was more effective for denser woolled sheep. There were, however, limited opportunities to make any major changes to the manufacturer's standard comb design. Perhaps the one exception related to the bending or 'pulling' of the outside teeth of the comb, a practice that seems to have developed as a furtive way of overcoming the union-imposed ban on wide gauge combs. Shearers used various techniques to bend the teeth, but the end result was a comb that gave the shearer's handpiece a slightly wider cut, while using the standard three-pronged cutter. However, both wool growers and the union looked down on this practice.

Variations to the Award

Shearing combs have been subject to various legal restrictions in terms of width and tooth design since 1926, when the first of several amendments was made to the Pastoral Industry Award. The summary below outlines significant applications and changes that have been made to the Award relating to shearing comb width:

> 1926 (10 January) – Wool growers applied to the Arbitration Court seeking a restriction on the use of 'pulled' combs. They were concerned that these combs caused excessive damage to the wool and to the sheep. The AWU opposed any such restriction.

> 1926 (10 June) – Mr Justice Powers, the then President of the Arbitration Court, handed down his decision. He said the employers' concerns were serious and inserted a new clause into the Award that read, '*The shearer shall not without the consent of the employer use any comb wider that the standard size of two-and-a-half inches, nor shall he use any double bent teeth comb.*'[70] It should be noted that this ruling, which was to come into effect from the following year, did not represent a total ban – it gave shearers a

qualified licence to use non-standard gauge gear provided the employer consented to such use.

1927 – The AWU applied to have the prohibition against 'pulled' combs lifted, while wool growers supported its retention. Mr Justice Dethridge accepted that double bent combs tended to 'injure sheep and ridge wool', and so concluded, 'I shall allow the prohibition to remain in the agreement.'[71]

1936 – Wool growers applied for a further restriction on the type of combs that could be used, seeking a ban on combs with a longer tooth on the lower side or wider space between the last two teeth on the lower side. Mr Justice Dethridge granted the application, saying, 'I think the risk of injury to the sheep or the fleece is increased by the use of such combs by some shearers although probably not in the hands of all. The employer may consent to such combs being used, but I think he should have the right to prohibit them if he desires to avoid that risk.'[72]

1938 (9 September) – By the consent of both wool growers and the AWU, Mr Justice Dethridge removed the clause that gave employers discretion to allow non-standard combs to be used for shearing. (Employers were concerned that the conditional ban was ineffective because unless they specifically expressed their opposition to pulled combs, shearers could interpret their silence on the issue as tacit consent to use them.) The relevant clause was revised to read, '*The shearer shall not use any comb wider than two-and-a-half inches between the points of the outside teeth.*'[73] This absolute ban was to come into effect from 1 August 1939.

1948 – The AWU sought to vary the agreement so that employers (as well as shearers) would be liable for any breach of the prohibition on non-standard combs. Commissioner Donovan granted the union's application and the relevant clause was changed to read, '*A shearer shall not use nor shall the employer permit a shearer to use any comb wider than two-and-a-half inches between the points of the outside teeth.*'[74]

1967 – Wool growers tried unsuccessfully to have the discretion clause reintroduced into the Award through a variation of the relevant clause to read, '*Unless the employer so permits, no shearer or crutcher will use any comb wider than two-and-a-half inches between the points of the outside teeth.*' This claim was made pending further investigations into the possible use of wide combs. At the request of the wool growers, this claim was placed on a reserved list to be considered at a future hearing.[75]

1969 (December) – The AWU sought and obtained the deletion of the reservations clause.

Shearing comb specifications outlined in the Award then remained dormant for more than a decade, before they became an issue once more in 1980. On the morning of Wednesday 14 May, Edward 'Ted' Cole, an industrial officer with the National Farmers' Federation, and Ian Arthur Manning, his counterpart with the LGPA, met in an office on the sixth floor of the association's headquarters at 56 Young Street, Sydney. Cole was nearing the end of his career, most of which had been spent with the Australian Woolgrowers' and Graziers' Council working in industrial relations. He was well regarded in agri-politics. Manning, the great-great-grandson of James Rutherford, one of the driving forces behind the success of Cobb & Co., was also making a name for himself as an advocate for the state's farmers. He had a reputation for being highly organised and meticulous – something of a perfectionist. Manning was a forensic researcher who documented just about everything and kept copious and detailed records. He was to play a key role in the industrial case that the two men were about to initiate.

The pair spent a couple of hours finalising an application – tweaking the wording to make sure it conveyed precisely the intended meaning. Manning was not certain, but he was fairly sure, that Cole then hand-delivered the application. He would have walked out of the association's office and headed south several blocks to the Queen's Square Law Courts building in Macquarie Street, where he filed the application in the Sydney registry of the Australian Conciliation and Arbitration Commission (ACAC).[76] The application sought to have a sub-clause to Clause 32 (which covered comb widths) inserted in the

Award that would allow wide combs to be used in 'field research trials' under the auspices of the Wool Council of Australia, provided the AWU was notified in advance of the details of any such trials. This seemingly innocuous application was to have far-reaching consequences – it eventually morphed into a much broader application to have the Award's shearing comb width restriction completely removed. The LGPA had just opened a large can of worms.

10

The Arm Wrestle Over Trials

When the LGPA lodged its trials application with the Arbitration Commission, it was conscious that what it was proposing represented a monumental shift in the pastoral industry. Even testing wide combs for research purposes was a highly sensitive issue. At the time, wide combs had been outlawed for more than 50 years and any move towards legalising them would be pushing against not only a defiant and powerful trade union, but also against tradition and the weight of history. With this in mind, the LGPA was careful to emphasise that it was merely advocating formal trials and it would not proceed with any such trials without the support of the AWU. It stressed that it wanted to work cooperatively with the union to try to identify the most efficient comb design for Australian shearing conditions. The trouble was, however, that the union was not interested in field trials, or indeed, anything to do with wide combs.

Diplomacy and defiance

In its field trials application, the LGPA sought to have a sub-clause inserted into Clause 32 of the Award, which defined the width restriction for shearing combs. The subclause read,

> Sub-clauses (a) and (b) of this clause shall not apply to shearing where the use of different combs is being investigated in field research trials under the auspices of the Wool Council of Australia. Provided that prior to the commencement of any shearing in such trials, the Secretary of the Union shall be supplied with details of the shed name, district and proposed starting date for each such shearing.

The application was made on the basis that the Australian Wool Corporation's qualitative research during the mid-1970s (through the Australian Wool Harvesting Program) had found there could be substantial benefits to wool growers and shearers from comb design changes; the Western Australian Department of Agriculture had recommended full-scale field trials of wide combs; and given wide combs were emerging as an industry issue there was a need to test all combs (even those banned by the Award) to identify and promote the most efficient combs. However, within weeks of the trials application being lodged, the AWU had rejected the proposal and resolved to oppose it in the Arbitration Commission. Still, Ian Manning was treading carefully when he was asked about the application during an ABC radio interview in June 1980. He said although the LGPA did not need the support of the union to pursue the matter in the Arbitration Commission, '…we feel that because it is a sensitive matter we do not particularly want to confront the AWU over the issue at this stage'.[77]

In July 1980, the Arbitration Commission decided to join the issue of field trials to an outstanding matter relating to the question of whether or not Clause 32 of the Federal Pastoral Industry Award (dealing with shearing comb width restrictions) should apply to Western Australia. Proceedings were then adjourned to allow the AWU and the LGPA to hold discussions about field trials. Soon after this decision, Charlie Oliver was interviewed on ABC radio and he made it clear that the AWU did not want to have anything to do with wide combs. 'I will assist any shearer to resist the intrusion of wide combs into the industry,' he said.[78] Later during the same broadcast, Ian Manning was still treading carefully but stressed that the objective of the trials was merely to obtain an objective assessment of the performance of wide combs. He said,

> …at this stage it is our prime objective to first of all establish what the facts are on the use of wide combs. We understand and fully appreciate that there has been a prohibition on the use of combs wider than two and a half inches since 1926. Now you do not just

walk in and change 50 years of history overnight without first of all having a thorough look at the changes that are proposed and in these changes I might add we are not only going to be looking at the width of combs but we are also going to be looking at other parameters such as the shape of the combs and…the thickness of the combs… There are a number of parameters of comb designs which will be looked at in these trials in order to establish the most efficient comb for shearing sheep in Australia.[79]

He expressed some confidence that the AWU would agree to take part:

I would certainly be disappointed if we could not convince the AWU of the need for further investigations…we have had discussions with various officers in the Federal AWU, they appreciate our position and there is absolutely no indication from them that they are not going to continue to cooperate.[80]

About a week after this interview, the AWU's Executive Council reinforced the union's tough stance towards wide combs. It passed the following resolution at its 10 July meeting:

That where a branch of the union becomes aware that pulled or wide combs are being used or other breaches of the Award are occurring, that the branch secretary shall be authorised to take action to have bans applied by AWU members and/or members of other unions on the handling of livestock or produce on properties where the offences have occurred. That where prosecutions are possible that steps be taken immediately by the branch secretary to prosecute both the employer and the employee.

Later that month, Manning and Richard McEvoy, who was the head of the New South Wales Rural Industry Training Committee, a group responsible for overseeing the training of shearers and shearing shed staff in the early 1980s, devised a detailed set of guidelines for the proposed field trials of shearing combs. A copy was sent to the AWU. The pair suggested the trials be run by a national committee chaired by the president of the Wool Council of Australia (who at the time was Ian McLachlan) and made up of representatives from the WCA and the AWU.[81] Once the trials were completed and the data evaluated, they proposed,

> The Committee's report and recommendations will be the basis for conferences between the AWU and employer representatives. These conferences will endeavour to draft Award variations to promote in the shearing industry use of combs in accordance with this recommendation.

Tensions, and the dispute, escalate

Soon after these guidelines were prepared, the wide comb dispute intensified when 48 shearers and AWU officials met at the Amoco Hall in Orange on 21 September. The meeting was prompted by Robert White's provocation of the union as reported in *The Land* newspaper on 17 July. Essentially, White had publicly stated that he was going to defy the union and continue to use wide combs. Officials at the Orange meeting included New South Wales branch president Charlie Oliver, the recently appointed branch secretary Ernie Ecob (who was less than three months into this role) and organisers Mick O'Shea and Tom Anderson. The union could not ignore White's challenge to its authority. So, in a bid to try to silence him, union members voted to black ban White and anyone who worked with him, as well as any properties where he worked. The shearers expected the wide comb issue to be discussed at the next union meeting, which was planned for Dubbo on 26 October 1980. (This was the meeting in which the alleged assault of Bluey Rodwell at Cumnock in early October was discussed.) White attended this meeting and was given a fairly hostile reception. However, he gave an assurance that the upcoming shearing at the Canomodine shed near Canowindra would proceed according to Award conditions.

Mindful of the growing tension in the state's pastoral industry, the LGPA carried a reminder to its members in the 31 October edition of its magazine, *Livestock and Grain Producer*, that employers would be in breach of the Pastoral Industry Award if they permitted their employees to use shearing combs wider than 64 millimetres.

In November, shearers meeting at Naracoorte in the south-east of South Australia, endorsed several resolutions that were passed by their New South Wales colleagues at the 26 October meeting in Dubbo. Allan Begg, the AWU's South Australian branch secretary, addressed 51 shearers at the Kincaid Hotel on Sunday 2 November. Begg had attended the Dubbo meeting the previous Sunday. He updated members on developments in the dispute in New South Wales. The members then passed several resolutions, including the following: 'That the members of this union in attendance at this meeting pledge themselves to resist at all costs the breaking down of working conditions in the industry which includes the use of wide combs and pulled combs.' They strongly opposed any relaxing of Award conditions to allow for field trials and noted that the introduction of wide combs would completely downgrade all existing conditions in the pastoral industry; lead to employers applying for a decrease in the rate per hundred; and lead to the phasing in of weekend, overtime Monday to Friday shearing and eventually shorten the length of the shearing season.

Meanwhile, in New South Wales, Robert White and his team began shearing at Canomodine in early November. White's every move was now under union scrutiny, so it was inevitable that local organisers would inspect the shed. They did, but without incident and the shearing was completed with no reported breaches of the Award. The following month, the AWU convened a meeting of its Pastoral Committee to discuss the problem of wide combs. The committee was chaired by Edgar Williams, a former shearer and long-time Queensland state branch secretary. The membership comprised Frank Mitchell (national general secretary), Errol Hodder (a Queensland organiser and state branch executive member who became state branch secretary when Williams retired in May 1982), Ernie Ecob, Ian Cuttler (the Victorian state branch secretary), John Butler (Tasmanian state branch secretary) and Gil Barr (Western Australian state branch secretary). The committee met at historic Macdonell House in Pitt Street, the site of the union's headquarters for many years. Built in 1914, the eight-storey building was named after Donald Macdonell (1862–1911), who worked his way up from shearer and unionist to Labor Party member, one-time federal Minister for Agriculture and general secretary of the AWU. Henry Lawson had met Macdonell as a shearer near Bourke in the early 1890s and following Macdonell's death wrote the memorial poem 'Donald Macdonell'.

Frank Mitchell began the day one proceedings on Monday 8 December with a summary of all the key developments that had taken place in relation to wide combs. He said the committee needed to assess the union's position in light of these developments and matters currently before the Arbitration Commission, including the LGPA's field trials application. An unrelated item on the agenda took up most of the afternoon session, so discussion on the wide combs matter resumed the following day. Most of the state secretaries (Begg, Ecob, Cuttler and Butler) opposed any trials of wide combs being carried out. Barr gave details of the situation in Western Australia where there was extensive use of the wide gear, and he too said he opposed the application for field trials. The two Queenslanders, Williams and Hodder, said there had been no evidence of wide combs being used in Queensland. However, organisers had been instructed to be vigilant to ensure they did not infiltrate the industry. The committee made two significant recommendations to the union's Executive Council: 'That the union proceed to argue for the inclusion of Clause 32 (restricting shearing comb widths) of the Pastoral Industry Award in the roping-in Award covering the Farmers Union of Western Australia Industrial Association'; and 'That the union opposes the introduction of wide gauge gear in the pastoral industry'.

Although the LGPA had managed to place wide combs on the agenda of the pastoral industry, the union had not budged in its opposition to formal field trials. The LGPA was hoping the following year, 1981, would provide a breakthrough.

11

The Stalemate Continues

The Four Seasons Hotel in Macquarie Street, Hobart was the venue for the 95th annual conference of the AWU in late January 1981. As expected, the key item on the pastoral industry agenda was the wide comb dispute. In his report to delegates, national secretary Frank Mitchell conceded, 'Whilst the branches have devoted much energy to trying to stamp out wide gear the practice does not seem to be abating to any significant degree.' By this stage, the union's Executive Council had endorsed the Pastoral Committee's pre-Christmas recommendations regarding wide combs. Mitchell provided delegates with a sobering assessment of the year ahead:

> …1981 looks like being a very important year in respect to the pastoral industry, as a number of vital issues will face the union and will ultimately have to be determined. I refer in particular to the issues of wide gear and non-union membership of shearing employees, both of which are inter-related. It is important that the union receives the full support and cooperation of members if we are going to combat the difficulties that lie ahead and protect this most important Award.

Field trials take back seat

As it turned out, wide comb field trials took a back seat for most of the first half of the year. Other issues emerged in the pastoral industry. The National Farmers' Federation, the recently formed peak lobby group for the nation's farmers, grabbed the spotlight in February with a call for a complete overhaul of Australia's arbitration system. The federation said that although it agreed in principle with a system where wage rises were based on productivity increases, across the board wage rises did not always suit primary industries because the capacity of employers to pay varied greatly with seasonal and trade conditions. Ted Cole, who had only recently retired after a 25-year career as the industrial director of the Australian Woolgrowers' and Graziers' Council (which became part of the National Farmers' Federation), went as far as calling for a Royal Commission into the arbitration system. He said the system was devised earlier that century when there was a need for a fairer wage system. However, it had become outdated and was delivering outcomes that many employers simply could not afford. He said a revamped system was needed to cure the nation's crippling 'union disease' and suggested a Royal Commission might be the best way to go about reform.[82]

A couple of months later, as this debate was still taking place, Robert White and his team were caught shearing with wide gear at Canomodine Station. The fallout from this incident dominated the pastoral industry for several months and made it difficult for the LGPA to push the field trials proposal. The union had resolved during a stop work meeting in Dubbo on 1 June to pursue a 'peaceful settlement by negotiations with all interested organisations' by 1 August, otherwise its members would go on strike. Following up on this resolution, Ernie Ecob contacted LGPA chief executive officer John White and industrial director Ian Manning in mid-June to discuss the dispute. He asked that the LGPA put in writing that it would not proceed with field trials until it obtained the consent of the union. White and Manning agreed to do so and to encourage LGPA members to continue to observe the wide combs ban, provided the AWU agreed not to stage strikes or implement black bans and to participate in 'constructive discussions' on the proposed field trials.

A week later, on 22 June, Manning sent Ecob a letter confirming the terms of the 'peaceful settlement'. (Before mailing the letter he rang

Ecob and read the contents of the letter to make sure both parties had a clear understanding of the terms of the agreement that had been reached.) The following month, LGPA members endorsed the agreement during the organisation's annual conference in Sydney. In doing so, they also passed a resolution: 'That LGPA continues to seek, by negotiation, Australian Workers' Union consent to variations in the Pastoral Industry Award which would permit the conduct of field research trials on the use of different combs.' Ecob was subsequently invited to make a statement on the LGPA's weekly radio program *Agristock Review*, which was broadcast on commercial stations all over New South Wales. It was the first time in 23 years that an AWU official had been invited onto the show. Ecob confirmed the peaceful settlement, said there would be no shearing strike the following month (as had been planned if no peaceful settlement was reached) and reiterated the union's opposition to wide combs.

Peaceful settlement fails

However, within weeks the peaceful settlement was in tatters. On 1 August 1981, the *Central Western Daily* newspaper in Orange reported on the agreement and quoted Ernie Ecob as saying the AWU would never consent to wide comb field trials taking place. This prompted a letter from Ian Manning on 20 August, seeking an assurance from Ecob that the union would still participate in field research trials. He warned that unless the union cooperated on this issue, 'I can no longer guarantee that the LGPA will not review its policy without further notice.' Ecob did not take kindly to the tone of the letter, replying on 9 September with his own warning to the LGPA, who he accused of going back on its word. He sought a meeting with Manning to 'determine the future of industrial relations with your association. I shall await your reply and suggest a time and date if you desire to arrive at an agreement for industrial peace in the future,' he wrote. He did not mention the issue of field trials.

Rockdale black ban

Later that month, Robert White's team was shearing at Rockdale near Canowindra when an AWU organiser inspected the shed. White and his team were shearing with standard gauge narrow gear in accordance with the Award. However, the property owner's young son reportedly told the organiser the shearers had been using wide combs and 'they took them off yesterday'. This led to the property being black banned, with organisers Mick O'Shea and Bluey Rodwell visiting the shed to inform the owner, Phillip Wythes, of the ban and to record details of the wool brand (to pass on to storemen and packers at the Yennora wool store in Sydney). Although the shearing was completed without further incident, the dispute was about to escalate dramatically.

Ian Manning became aware of the Rockdale black ban on 26 September and he immediately contacted Ernie Ecob to try to have the ban removed. However, Ecob refused, saying the ban had been imposed because the Rockdale wool had been shorn by 'scabs'. Paul Houlihan, the NFF's industrial director, intervened and contacted Frank Mitchell, who simply referred the matter back to Ernie Ecob. Frustrated, Houlihan contacted the Arbitration Commission on 28 September and sought an urgent relisting of the field trials matter. The commission consented to the request and the matter came before Commissioner Ian McKenzie the following day. After hearing evidence from several witnesses, including Robert White, Phillip Wythes and Jack Rodman (the wool classer at the Rockdale shed), the commissioner ordered the AWU to lift all black bans (on properties and contractors) and organised a compulsory conference on field trials for both parties in Sydney on 7 October.

Commission ruling misreported

Unfortunately, several prominent media outlets misinterpreted these orders and mistakenly reported that the commission had ordered all bans on wide combs to be lifted.[83] However, it was the mistake in *The*

Land that was most concerning, as it was considered authoritative when it came to rural affairs. Ian Manning noticed the mistake early on Thursday 1 October, when he picked up a copy of the paper at Sydney's domestic airport about seven a.m., not that long after that edition had rolled off the press. He was preparing to fly to Orange then drive to Canowindra to attend an LGPA conference. Realising the gravity of the mistake, he adjusted his schedule. When he landed in Orange, he immediately contacted the local ABC radio and Midwest Television (now Prime7) stations to arrange to do interviews to clarify the commission's ruling and to try to make sure LGPA members and the wider community knew the wide comb ban was still in place. As a follow-up, and to reinforce this message, the LGPA issued a media release the following day (2 October) to the wider media emphasising that the commission's ruling related to the lifting of bans on properties and shearers, not wide combs.

The AWU did not accept that the misreporting of the commission's orders was unintentional. Ecob and Oliver co-signed a circular to all pastoral industry members on 6 October, in which they said, '*The Land* article is cunningly designed to lead members in the pastoral industry to believe that it is legal to use wide combs.' On the same day, the AWU's federal office contacted the Arbitration Commission seeking an urgent relisting of its claim to extend the wide comb ban to Western Australia. The following day, just before the compulsory conference was due to start, representatives from the NFF and LGPA received legal advice from a barrister to the effect that Clause 32 of the Award (restricting comb widths) was unenforceable.

During the conference, which Commissioner Ian McKenzie chaired, Ernie Ecob produced a letter dated 6 October stating that union members were planning to meet in Dubbo on 1 November to discuss the wide combs and black bans issues. He also stated the AWU was still opposed to field trials of wide combs. The NFF and LGPA, however, had had enough. Paul Houlihan asked the commission to rule directly on whether wide comb field trials should proceed, as the union was refusing to negotiate over the matter. (This was a step up from the farmer groups' previous position, which sought a variation in the Award to allow trials to proceed with the consent of the union.) Houlihan warned that unless the union lifted its black bans and consented to the commission hearing an application about field trials, he would hold a press conference and announce that Clause 32 of the Award was unenforceable. The union, however, held its line and insisted it would not lift any black bans until the issue was discussed by members in Dubbo on 1 November. (This was despite the commission having already ordered it to lift the bans.) The hearing was a bit like two heavyweight boxers squaring off before a bout – there was plenty of brash talk but the real fight hadn't started. Despite various threats, both parties came away still locked in a stalemate. The matters were adjourned for hearing on 27 October.

The following week, Ian Manning told *The Land* that the LGPA still wanted trials to proceed with the union's approval. However, as if to emphasise that the organisation's patience was not infinite, he said if the union continued to stonewall on the issue, 'wool growers may be better off to take a punt on the inevitable increase in wide combs use'.[84]

In mid-October, Manning checked with the New South Wales branch of the Storemen and Packers' Union about the status of the Rockdale black ban. The then secretary Don Green confirmed the ban was still in place and would remain so until Ernie Ecob authorised its removal. A few days later, on 20 October, Manning wrote a four-page letter to Ecob providing a detailed outline of recent events in the dispute and the LGPA's position in relation to wide combs. He warned that unless the union lifted its black bans, the LGPA would object to the commission hearing the union's application to extend the wide combs ban to Western Australia, which was set down as part of the 27 October matters. The LGPA was clearly losing patience with the union.

On 22 October Manning was quoted in *The Land* once again, this time claiming the AWU was 'pig-headed and bloody-minded' for refusing to consent to the trials application being heard in the commission. However, he said that despite its frustration the LGPA would persevere with its quest to establish the proper legal framework needed for wide comb trials to proceed. Wool growers were in a bind: they needed the union to be on side for trials to proceed, otherwise the industry would descend into chaos.

12

Mission Impossible

During mid-October 1981, key representatives of the LGPA and NFF were becoming increasingly dismayed at the union's lack of compromise on the issue of wide combs. They decided a fresh approach might help break the impasse. Ian Manning contacted Ernie Ecob and Charlie Oliver and invited them to a lunch with Paul Houlihan and himself to discuss the wide comb dispute. It was an attempt to reach some common ground, mend strained relationships, and prevent the dispute from worsening and the pastoral industry plunging into industrial turmoil. Both men accepted the invitation, but on the day, Sunday 25 October, only Oliver turned up. Ecob apologised, saying he had to attend to an urgent matter relating to the Builders Labourers Federation.

The lunch was held at Edna's Table, which became a renowned Sydney eatery during the 1980s. It was run by brother and sister team Raymond and Jennice Kersh, who became pioneers of the bush tucker food movement in Australia. The restaurant was named after the siblings' mother, who for many years ran the all-night canteen at the Hunter Street headquarters of the *Sydney Morning Herald* newspaper. Manning later recalled a slightly unnerving moment when Oliver put his hand on Manning's forearm, looked him in the eye, and said something to the effect of 'If you and I work together, we could move mountains.' During the luncheon, Oliver made it clear he was strongly opposed to wide combs but suggested the wool grower organisations advocate for 'the use of any combs that shearers could use in a good and workman-like manner' rather than focusing on 'wide combs'. Houlihan and Manning agreed to issue a statement to this effect, and in return Oliver agreed to try to end the campaign of black bans when shearers met in Dubbo on 1 November. Both parties agreed to seek an adjournment of the 27 October hearing in the Arbitration Commission.

Wool Council enters the fray

The day after the luncheon meeting, the Wool Council of Australia stepped into the fray, warning that the wool industry was losing patience with the AWU. The council's president, Ian McLachlan, said that unless the union immediately consented to the conduct of field research trials on wide combs, there would be an inevitable escalation of the wide combs dispute. However, McLachlan appreciated the sensitivity of the issue and said wool growers would not proceed to wide comb trials without the consent of the union. 'For 18 months wool-grower organisations have tried without success to persuade the union to accept the reality of the wide comb issue and their patience with the AWU on this matter is almost exhausted,' he said. 'If, contrary to the views of many of its own members, the union refuses to adapt to the issue, wool growers will have no alternative but to advocate that shearers use any comb which allows them to shear in a good and workman-like manner.' McLachlan expressed concern about this 'open slather' approach to shearing comb use, but said if the regulation of shearing combs perpetuated an inefficient means of shearing, wool growers and shearers were justified in trying different gear to identify the tools that best suited their individual requirements.

Although the 27 October commission hearing was adjourned without incident, the 1 November shearers' meeting certainly did not go as Oliver suggested it would. Rather than putting an end to the black bans, the 90 shearers present effectively agreed to intensify the bans. They voted to reinforce the existing bans and to extend them to any property owner who employed Robert White or any shearer White had employed. The union was effectively trying to squeeze White out of work, and out of the shearing industry altogether. The shearers passed a resolution in relation to the Rockdale black ban, that it would only be lifted if Phillip Wythes gave a written undertaking to the union that he would not employ anyone who had used or intended to use wide combs. Wythes said he could guarantee that he would only employ shearers who agreed to abide by the Award, but he could not provide an assurance about the future intentions of his shearers in regard to using wide combs. The ban, therefore, remained in place.

The day after the Dubbo meeting Ernie Ecob wrote to Ian Manning to confirm the bans on Rockdale Station and Canomodine Station were continuing and to provide details of the resolutions that had been passed. He ended the letter with the following statement:

> I would advise that in the best interest of those of your members that have in the past employed White that they should give serious consideration to engaging shearers who have not been employed by White or worked with him; if this is achieved no doubt a peaceful working relationship should be gained in the pastoral industry.

About this time, Robert White wrote to Charlie Oliver asking that, '…in the interests of unity among shearers', the union stop refusing to renew his membership; lift the bans it had imposed on him; adopt a positive attitude towards the use of wide combs; and organise shearing sheds more effectively. The handwritten, five and a half page (A5) letter was undated, but Ernie Ecob replied on behalf of the union on 26 November. White also said, 'To date the unions [sic] effort to throw me out of the industry have [sic] been unsuccessful and I am confident the campayne [sic] against me will not succeed apart from creating needless animosity between shearers.' Ecob's reply was slightly disjointed, as if he was so fired up he did not know what to say next. He started by writing, 'At first when I read your letter I thought it a waste of time for me to reply, but on second thoughts I feel that I should.' He went on, 'If it is the attitude of you and the men that work with you to try and promote the use of wide combs then you can forget everything as it is totally against the Award. As for the use of wide combs in Western Australia it has been brought to our notice that for the first time in a few years graziers are advertising for shearers with the Award combs as they have learnt of the damage to the sheep.' This was a claim repeated several times by the union. However, no evidence was ever presented to support it. Robert White gave evidence to the Arbitration Commission in December 1981 that these advertisements had nothing to do with the quality of shearing – rather, they were placed by contractors who employed union members who would only work with narrow gauge shearers.[85] Ecob finished the letter with the following statements:

> I would suggest that if you want to be equal with all other shearers that you and your shearers give some indication of such and are willing to put in writing that you will abide by the Award Rules and Policy of the Union. If this is done then it can be discussed at a meeting of the rank and file as they are the ones whom you are defying, not me. All you have done is give Mr Ian Manning all the support he requires, not to those whom you expect to work for you or those others that have to toil in the industry.

The Victorian development

As the AWU and New South Wales wool growers were locked in a tussle over trials, an interesting development occurred south of the border. Shearers meeting in Bendigo on 8 November voted to cooperate with wool growers to conduct field trials. It was completely unexpected – an anomaly that the union worked frantically to overturn. The motion was moved by Brian Clarke, a second-generation shearing contractor from Eaglehawk, a picturesque former gold mining village on Bendigo's western outskirts.

Clarke was a union member and a stickler for upholding Award conditions and provisions. However, he was also keen for the industry to progress and had an open mind about new technology and anything that would allow him to do his job better. He first came across wide combs when he took on some New Zealand shearers. 'They would work for me at times, and they would bring the new wide gear and I would have to say, "no you can't use that". They didn't use it, but I had a chance to look at it a bit,' he said.

About a fortnight before the Bendigo meeting, a local farmer asked Clarke to visit his property. The farmer had engaged five local shearers to shear his flock and they were all using wide gear and were not union members. The farmer's daughter was a Melbourne solicitor and had warned him that he could be prosecuted for allowing the shearers to use wide combs. The farmer wanted Clarke's advice. Clarke told the shearers that if they wanted to use wide gear they needed to attend an upcoming shearers' meeting in Bendigo and vote to support research trials, which were being debated at that time. The shearers agreed to do so and to encourage other local shearers they knew who were using wide gear or interested in trialling it to also attend. 'There were about 45 [shearers] turned up without tickets…they paid for a ticket at the door, and joined the union,' Clarke said.

As soon as proceedings were under way, Clarke moved a motion calling on the union to negotiate with the Victorian Farmers' and Graziers' Association to organise field trials of wide combs. Someone immediately seconded the motion. The chairman tried to reject the motion but Clarke knew proper meeting procedure meant that once the motion had been moved and seconded, it had to be debated and voted on. He insisted the motion be put to the vote and given the strong presence of wide comb supporters, it was passed. This defiant resolution was an embarrassment to the union, which up until then had presented a united national front opposing wide combs. Having a small branch in central Victoria calling for trials to proceed was extremely damaging.

Union officials immediately organised another meeting for a week later to have the resolution overturned and made sure they had sufficient staunch unionists present to vote it down. This episode was to have serious repercussions for Clarke, who subsequently became the target of a union smear campaign.

As the Victorian branch of the AWU was rushing to have Clarke's resolution overturned, the Wool Council of Australia and the LGPA were trying one final time to pressure the union into giving ground on trials. On 13 November, both organisations delivered an ultimatum to the AWU that unless it ended its black bans by 24 November, consented to the trials application being heard in the commission, and agreed to cooperate with the trials if the application was approved, the trials application would be substituted with an application to remove Clause 32 and replace it with 'No shearer or crutcher shall use, nor shall the employer permit him to use any comb, the width or design of which, in the opinion of the employer hinders the employee from shearing or crutching in a good and workman-like manner.' The AWU's Executive Council met four days later and rejected the ultimatum. Paul Houlihan recalled the frustration of trying to get the union to agree to trials:

> …we put a proposal to the Commission that there would be trials, but we only wanted this if the union was going to be involved in the trials. The union said they did not want to be involved in the trials. It was an extraordinarily difficult thing to deal with – you could not compromise because the people on the other side of the table would not touch it; they wanted nothing to do with it.

Time to act

It was clear to the farmers' organisations that there were no options left other than to carry out the threat that had been outlined in the ultimatum. On 19 November, just two days after the AWU Executive Council rejected the ultimatum, Houlihan wrote to the Arbitration Commission to give notice that at the next scheduled hearing of the wide comb matters, on 1 December, the LGPA would withdraw the trials application, which dated back to 14 May 1980, and substitute it with an application to replace Clause 32 with its non-width-restricting 'workman-like manner' clause. A few days after this letter was mailed, Ian Manning telephoned Ernie Ecob and invited him to attend a demonstration of wide comb shearing at the Sydney Showground on 2 December. Ecob declined, however, saying he understood the process of shearing sheep. About the same time, shearers in Victoria, Western Australia, South Australia and Tasmania voted to strike for one week to protest the growing use of wide combs. Although the level of support was difficult to establish, *The Land* reported on 3 December that more than 3,000 shearers were involved in the strike. As these shearers were striking, the LGPA and NFF were preparing their case on behalf of wool growers for the Arbitration Commission hearing. On 1 December, the LGPA withdrew its trials application and sought to have the width restricting Clause 32 removed from the Award. This application was joined to the AWU's application to extend the wide comb ban to Western Australia and the matters were adjourned to the following day for hearing.

After 18 months of trying, the farmer groups now realised that introducing wide combs into the pastoral industry through negotiation was 'mission impossible'. It would now be up to an independent umpire to examine the case and rule on the matter. It was, however, going to be a longer and more gruelling case than anyone ever imagined.

13

Why Oppose Wide Combs?

It is only fair to assume that a trade union representing pieceworkers would be eager, or at the very least open, to investigate a new technology that could enable its members to increase their output. In such circumstances, the union would normally make every effort to encourage the testing, development and adoption of the technology – given the potential economic benefit to its members. After all, unions only exist to look after the interests of their members. However, in the case of the AWU and the 'new' technology of wide combs, this did not happen. The union's response to the LGPA's invitation to be involved in trials to assess the performance of wide combs was somewhat ambiguous. On the one hand, union leaders gave assurances to the LGPA that the union was keen to be involved. However, officials were also issuing public statements questioning the need for any trials. It seems the union was stalling, while trying to placate the LGPA. Behind the scenes, however, the AWU was maintaining its *implacable hostile opposition* to wide combs.

On 28 July 1980, not long after it had lodged its trials application, the LGPA contacted the AWU with a proposal on how a series of wide comb trials could be independently managed and assessed. The association tried to reassure the union that the proposed trials were not 'a half-baked or underhand attempt to introduce wide combs' and that the association had an open mind as to which equipment, wide or narrow gauge gear, would prove best.

The union's arguments against wide combs

At various times the AWU outlined several reasons for its reluctance to trialling wide combs. Soon after the trials application was lodged, the union claimed that wide combs caused too much damage and were too hard to push through the sheep's fleece. Speaking on ABC radio about the LGPA application, Ernie Ecob said in response to a question about the potential of shearers to earn more money using wide combs,

> Well, I don't think it is the money issue, tests have been proven… that there is more loss to the grower, second cuts, skin pieces and that with the use of wide combs. In New South Wales you have got harder cutting sheep and (shearers) would have bunged up wrists and so forth, which would bring about a lot of chaps being on compensation.[86]

The second cuts and skin cuts to sheep were economic issues, while the potential for shearers to incur wrist damage because of the extra force required to push the wider comb through the sheep's fleece was a health and safety issue.

Mel Johnston OAM, a retired shearer who grew up at Gallymont, near Carcoar in the New South Wales central west, was called by the AWU to give evidence in one of the many Arbitration Commission hearings relating to the wide comb dispute. Johnston won dozens of shearing competitions – he was awarded the Australian Shearer of the Year title by the Canberra Agricultural Society in 1978; he won the inaugural Queensland Diamond Shears Competition at Longreach in 1980; and went on to win the World Shearing Title in Denver, Colorado, in 1985. He was inducted into the Shearers' Hall of Fame in March 2013, and later that year was awarded the Medal of the Order of Australia for his services to the shearing industry. As well as being an outstanding shearer, Johnston was a devout unionist and refused to use wide combs. On one occasion, he tried to explain to the Arbitration Commission the difficulties of shearing a wrinkly merino sheep with a wide comb. He later recalled,

I explained to them in court with a glass and a cigarette pack. How can you shear something round with a flat surface?... And [with] the 64 millimetre [comb], you had a big chance. I've seen sheep shorn with wide combs that look like weatherboard houses running around the paddocks, you couldn't believe it...the ridges on them because when you run that [wide] comb like that, you are going to leave wool there [creating ridges], but if you take that [leftover wool] off, that's where the second cuts come in.

Later, during the national strike called by the AWU at the height of the wide comb dispute, Johnston used the following analogy to try to explain to journalists the difficulties of using wide combs: 'A wide comb is like pushing a three-metre wide lawn mower through tough grass.'[87] Interestingly, wide comb shearer John Schick, from Matata on New Zealand's North Island, used a similar analogy to condemn narrow gear: 'Using narrow combs is like trying to sweep the floor with a toothbrush.'

Charlie Oliver later reinforced these objections, but introduced a slightly nuanced argument – the need for all shearers to be on an equal footing. Shearing is an extremely competitive vocation. In each shed, shearers vie with each other to be the 'ringer' or 'gun' – the shearer with the highest tally. In this environment, it is important that all equipment is the same so that the only distinguishing feature is the individual skill of each shearer. Oliver told ABC radio listeners in July 1980 that shearing combs needed to be uniform:

> The shearer does not want to be pushing a big wide comb through the sheep and where his earnings are based on his average number of sheep that are shorn it was an important part of his conditions that the combs should be regulated, that they should all be shearing with the same type of comb so that no one gets an advantage over someone else. Then the other point about it, of course, is that the producers, that is the wool grower, he wants his sheep shorn closely, he does not want any second cuts and very few farmers who have good flocks of sheep would allow their sheep to be shorn with wide combs because of this short wool, second cuts.[88]

During the same program, however, Ian Manning was interviewed and expressed confidence that the proposed trials of wide combs would proceed. He was asked if the LGPA would be able to convince the union to support the trials. 'I would certainly be disappointed if we could not convince the AWU on the need for further investigations, it would be most disappointing. In fact, if the AWU would not cooperate in the trials, I think it is fair to say at this stage, that we have had discussions with various officers in the federal [branch of the] AWU, they appreciate our position and there is absolutely no indication from them that they are not going to continue to cooperate,' he said.

In September that year, AWU organiser Mick O'Shea warned that wide combs would lead to a breakdown of Award conditions. He said this was what had happened in Western Australia following the steady infiltration of wide gear in that state and there would be widespread industrial unrest in the eastern states if wide combs were legalised.[89] The following month, Keith Begg, a union stalwart and accomplished shearer from Orange, introduced another union objection to wide combs. He told ABC radio listeners that the introduction of wide combs would inevitably lead to reduced pay for shearers. He was quoted as saying, '…if they introduced wide combs it would mean that the rates of pay would be attacked by the LGPA'.[90] This was the first time the union had publicly argued that the wide combs posed a financial threat to shearers' earnings.

The following year, Ernie Ecob started adding the threat to shearers' pay rates to his list of objections to wide tooth combs. He warned, '… the [shearers' pay] formula is based on the number of sheep they shear and it has been set at 480 sheep a week or 90 sheep a day…everything is based on that and if you start interfering with… changes in the size of combs then you are going to have to start changing your formulas.'[91] The implication was that if wide combs were permitted, there would be moves to adjust the formula used to calculate pay rates for shearers and ultimately those rates would be reduced. There was, however, no evidence that this would occur. And both the LGPA and the NFF had made it clear they had no intention of attempting to interfere in any way with shearers' pay rates. In fact, in a bid to dispel this assertion by the union, the LGPA provided a written undertaking to both the Arbitration Commission and the AWU that it would not attempt to reduce shearers' pay rates or increase their work hours. However, it did not stop the union repeating the claim. In early December 1981, the LGPA organised a shearing demonstration using wide comb shears at the Sydney Showground. While speaking to the media about the demonstration, Ian Manning told reporters that the AWU's claim that wide combs would ultimately mean less pay for shearers was simply untrue. He referred to the 1956 shearers' strike to support his position. 'In 1956, when the wool bonus payment scheme was due to come out of the rates of pay for shearers, wool growers unsuccessfully sought to have the rate for shearing reduced, and we say that if wool growers ever had merit for reducing the rate of pay, it was then. They tried, they failed and they're not likely to go into another no-win situation again,' he said.[92]

About the same time, AWU organiser Mick O'Shea spoke out publicly against trials. When asked during an interview why the union was so opposed to trials, he said, 'Well, they've had trials for about 14 years in Western Australia, and they're using them over there flat out so why the heck would anyone want to press on with trials when they've already trialled them for years?'[93] The implication was that the use of wide combs in Western Australia had somehow demonstrated their unsuitability. However, rather frustratingly, the interviewer didn't ask the obvious question, why would shearers use combs for that length of time if they were no good?

A few weeks after this interview, Ernie Ecob wrote a letter to Robert White in which he claimed, 'As for the use of wide combs in Western Australia, it has been brought to our notice that for the first time in a few years graziers are advertising for shearers with the Award combs as they have learnt of the damage to the sheep.'[94]

The following week, Ecob wrote a circular to union members, in which he outlined another general objection to wide combs: 'The resentment of members of the union to any breaking down of Award conditions has been expressed on numerous occasions at meetings.'[95]

Later on in the dispute, in early 1983, Ecob was even warning that wide combs would increase costs for wool growers. He told the *Stock and Land* weekly newspaper, which circulated in Victoria, south-east South Australia and Tasmania, that the introduction of wide comb shears would remove equality between shearers; increase workers' compensation payments; and result in the shearing pay rate formula being increased from 480 to 525 sheep a week. (It is not clear how Ecob derived this new figure.) He went on to warn that wool growers would face extra costs if wide combs were approved, as they would need to supply twice as many handpieces to ensure their shearers could choose between wide or narrow gear, and they would need to employ more rouseabouts to process the quicker throughput of sheep.[96] So it seems that as the dispute escalated, the focus of the union's objections to wide combs gradually expanded – from the initial claim that they caused excessive skin and second cuts and were too hard to push, to a concern that they posed a threat to pay rates, to the much broader fear that they would bring about a breakdown of Award conditions in general, and eventually to increased costs for the wool growers.

Hodder summarises the union's concerns

Perhaps the most detailed and coherent explanation of the union's opposition to wide combs was compiled by Errol Hodder, the former Queensland Branch Secretary of the AWU (1982–88). Hodder started his working life as a woolpresser during the mid-1950s and went on to become a shearer and union organiser. Following his role with the Queensland branch of the AWU, he served as the union's federal secretary (1988–1991) and was then appointed a commissioner of the Australian Industrial Relations Commission (1991–2003). In 1983, at the height of the wide comb dispute, Hodder wrote a paper which was published in the *Queensland Digest of Industrial Relations* in which he outlined several reasons why the union was so strongly opposed to wide combs.[97] He asserted that the main argument against wide combs was the potential for wool growers to use increased daily shearing tallies as leverage to reduce the shearers' rate of pay. Hodder put it this way: '…graziers could use tallies from individual sheds to seek a review of the average number of sheep shorn per week as used in the shearers' formula. This could result in a reduction of the rate per hundred sheep shorn.' The key modifier in the above statement was the word 'could'. As explained above, wool growers had provided a written guarantee that they would not seek such a review. And higher daily tallies meant their flocks would be shorn quicker. A briefer overall disruption from shearing would allow them to focus on other aspects of their business.

Hodder listed four other key concerns, which were all mentioned at various times by officials such as Ecob, Oliver and O'Shea. They were injuries to shearers, injuries to sheep, injuries to the fleece and deregulation of the industry. He said,

> The use of wide combs increases the incidence of back injuries, wrist and elbow injuries and tendonitis among shearers because of the increased mass of wool a shearer lifts with his comb, and the unsuitability of the wide combs for the heavy Australian merino fleeces. This would ultimately reduce the number of men able to bear this heavier workload; it would reduce the working life of those shearers able to use the wider combs and it would increase the cost burden on employers through higher workers' compensation insurance.

In relation to injuries to sheep, he said evidence from Western Australia indicated that wide combs caused up to 20 times more skin cuts to sheep than narrow gear. Where precisely this evidence came from is unclear. If it was from wool growers, it is not clear why they would engage wide comb contractors if wide gear was producing this result. His argument about injuries to fleece asserted that wide combs caused more ridging and second cuts. 'In some respects the use of the wide comb is analogous to the use of a tractor-based slasher to cut the lawn of a suburban house. The quality of the job is nowhere near the quality obtained from the use of a conventional lawn mower,' he said. The contrary view was that in the hands of shearers who had had some experience with wide combs, fleece damage was actually less than with narrow gear. Hodder also warned that the industrial chaos of the deregulated shearing industry in Western Australian would spread to eastern states if wide combs were legalised.

A voice of reason?

On 26 October 1980, almost 200 shearers from all over New South Wales met in Dubbo to discuss a range of issues, including the alleged assault on Bluey Rodwell during a visit to the Cumnock district property Tenanbung earlier that month. This was the meeting that set in place the trigger for a stop work meeting immediately any evidence came to light of wide combs being used in New South Wales. Another interesting development occurred during this meeting – a shearer who was a loyal unionist and not a 'rebel' wide comb shearer, spoke out in favour of trialling wide combs. That shearer was James 'Percy' Thompson, who was from Gulgong, near Mudgee. Thompson was later to become well known in the region through his role as a Mudgee Shire councillor (now Mid-Western Regional Council), which included a stint as mayor, and as a country horse trainer. He ran his horse training business from a small property at Mebul, west of Gulgong. In his younger years he performed contract shearing work throughout New South Wales and Victoria.

Thompson was keen for the union to use the wide comb issue to negotiate better working conditions for members. He told ABC radio the day after this meeting that he could see an opportunity for the union to push for a shorter working day for shearers. He said,

> I was in favour [of wide combs]…if we could get the hours cut down, to make it a better industry for the shearers, with their long hours, they work 40 hours a week with the narrow gear to earn their money. If graziers were interested in introducing the wider

gear, if they worried about young chaps not coming into the industry, not enough learner shearers, if they made it less hours where the work was not so strenuous on the shearer they would be working for less hours and earning the same amount of money that we are earning today. There should be a lot more shearers coming into the industry.[98]

He said it might be possible for shearers to work a 30 or 35-hour week with wide gear and maintain their weekly tallies but reduce the physical strain on their bodies.

Thompson's proposal was essentially ignored during the union meeting. The only reference to it in 10 pages of minutes states, 'James Thompson spoke of the use of the wide combs but to work a six-hour-day in exchange.'[99] The irony is that Thompson's plan, or at least a variation of it, almost certainly would have worked. Both the NFF and the LGPA, the organisations that prosecuted the wide combs case in the Arbitration Commission, were more than willing to make trade-offs on working conditions to have wide combs approved – a position later confirmed by Ian McLachlan. Had the union sat down at the negotiating table, it could have gained several improved working conditions for its members. However, the AWU was simply not willing to negotiate.

14

The Toughest Job of All

The AWU's unswerving opposition to wide combs was even more difficult to fathom considering the nature of the work its pastoral industry members performed. As former wool classer and author Hazel Riseborough says, 'There're not many jobs like shearing any more, where people take a towel to work to wipe the sweat off their brow.'[100] Of all professions involving physical labour, shearing has been widely regarded as being the toughest and most draining.[101] However, it has only been in recent years that the physical effort involved in shearing has been able to be accurately quantified. Several physiological studies have revealed just how much energy goes into a day's shearing. And the results have astounded even the researchers – it turns out shearers are the elite athletes of blue-collar workers.

The job description

To appreciate the significance of the results of this research, it is necessary first to consider what shearers do day in, day out, and some of the associated health and safety risks they face while doing their job. During the years of the wide comb dispute, a normal working day for shearers comprised four two-hour runs, starting at 7.30 a.m., 10 a.m., one p.m. and 3.30 p.m., with breaks at 9.30 a.m. (half an hour), noon (one hour for lunch) and three p.m. (half an hour). This 40-hour week had been in place since 1944 and still operates today. During these eight hours each day, shearers have to catch a sheep from a nearby holding pen, then lift and drag it along the board to their stand where they must position the animal while moving it and restraining it as they shear different parts of the animal's body. With adult wethers typically weighing 65 to 70 kilograms, sometimes more, it requires considerable physical exertion to control a compliant animal so it can be shorn, let alone a non-compliant one. For shearers who tally 200 sheep, the simple act of pulling sheep from the holding pen to their stand involves dragging as much as 14 tonnes each day. The following descriptions provide a hint of what shearers have to endure for eight hours each day. Wool industry researcher Alan McDonald Richardson summarised the role as follows: 'Shearing involves heavy physical labour and the maintenance for long periods of a back-wearying, doubled-up posture. A special physical skill is also required to continually restrain the sheep and to position it in relation to the shearing handpiece.'[102]

During the Arbitration Commission's 'showground hearings', wide comb advocate Robert White gave detailed evidence about the process involved in shearing different types of sheep with different types of combs. The following excerpt also sheds some light on the physicality of the work. Speaking about using a wide comb to shear the neck and shoulder of a merino wether, White told the commission,

> The wider the blow up the neck and you can see where you put that blow in, and with the narrow comb on long wool sheep, it is hard to see. It is recommended by the coaching systems to have three blows but I practically only ever have two blows so you can cut down one blow and you have the weight of the sheep on your legs. He is leaning away from you, and that is one of the hardest parts because you have to pick up the sheep with one hand to clean the front leg... You can more or less do it in one blow down, and you save one blow and you can lay your sheep down and you have got no weight until you finish the long blow... You go to the finish and you have virtually got to pick up your sheep again and the big heavy weight, all the strain is on your back and you have to lift him up with one arm. And when you get down to the shoulder you go back to the point of balance of the sheep and you can virtually balance him there and there is no weight, but until you

do that you have got a lot of [the] weight of the sheep on your left shoulder and back.[103]

And during the subsequent health and safety inquiry into wide combs, champion shearer Dick Duggan provided the following insightful description of the job he excelled at:

> … Shearing is a terrible job. It is a back-breaking, hard job, and the only thing that keeps men going is the will and the competition to be in front or catch the bloke just in front of you, or make sure the bloke behind you does not get past you. That is what the whole thing is about, shearing…we slave, shearers slave. They are completely competitive and that is the thing. You take away the competitiveness and the job will break.[104]

It has long been said that Australia's economy once 'rode on the sheep's back' but a more accurate colloquialism might be that it 'rode on our shearers' back-breaking work'. Certainly in terms of modern workplace health and safety codes, shearing oozes injury risks. Just about every aspect of the job raises warning flags – lifting and dragging heavy, live animals; twisting, turning and restraining them; working while doubled-over, stooping and bending; controlling a vibrating, steel-toothed cutting implement; using it to defleece an animal that often wants only to escape; and finally corralling and pushing that animal through a narrow chute. Then, repeat this process up to 200 times a day; usually in a stinking hot tin shed. What could go wrong? Well, plenty. Unfortunately, shearers have been way over-represented when it comes to workplace injuries.

A study presented to the annual conference of the Ergonomics Society of Australia in November 1997 quoted Worksafe Australia compensation data from 1992/93 to show that shearers suffered injuries at a rate six times the workforce average.[105] The researchers, led by John Culvenor, found, 'Shearers made 150 claims per 1,000 workers per year (incidence), compared with the average of 26 claims. The comparison of *claims frequency* shows a similar relative magnitude;

shearers made 1,000 claims per million hours whereas the average was 17 claims.'[106] The research also found,

> While greater in relative number, shearing injuries also take longer to rehabilitate and are therefore more costly. Data reported by Worksafe Australia (1995) indicate an average cost of shearing injuries of $9,500; 70 per cent higher than the average of $5,600. Recently obtained data from the Victorian WorkCover Authority detailing 1,098 injuries to shearers...between September 1985 and August 1997 show an average cost of $26,000; 140 per cent greater than the overall mean of $11,000 (September 1985 to December 1996). The greater cost of shearing injuries seems mainly due to the lengthier rehabilitation. Victorian data show that shearing injuries averaged 180 days rehabilitation whereas the all-industry average is about 90 days.
>
> Shearing injuries are confined to a few areas of the body. Both the national and Victorian data show that about 50 per cent of shearing injuries affect the arms (shoulder, upper arm, elbow, forearm, wrists, hands and fingers), 20 per cent the back, and 10 per cent the knee. The data for days compensated and cost are different as back injuries involve lengthy rehabilitation. The average period of rehabilitation for a back injury (which constitute 44 per cent of days compensated) as shown by the Victorian data is approximately one year. Back injuries constitute about 50 per cent of the cost, arm injuries about 25 per cent and knee injuries about 10 per cent. Injuries to the back, arm and knee therefore constitute 80 per cent of claims, days lost and cost.

Although this research relates mainly to the early 1990s, almost a decade after the wide comb dispute had ended, it does include some Victorian data from the mid-1980s. Data relating to shearer injury rates from the years of the wide comb dispute are hard to come by, but a study published in *The Australian Journal of Physiotherapy* in 1986 provides some insight into the prevalence of back injuries during the early 1980s.[107] This study examined the incidence of back complaints among shearers in Western Australia, through a survey of 32 shearers carried out in 1984, during the tail end of the wide comb dispute. The sample size was small as the research was undertaken as a pilot study to promote further research in this area. The results showed 90 per cent of respondents (29 out of 32) currently had moderate to severe lower back pain or had suffered from lower back pain recently. The researcher, Gisela Gmeinder, a physiotherapist at the Royal Perth (Rehabilitation) Hospital, also carried out a series of observations of shearers to determine how much time they spent in different positions as they shore each animal. Extrapolating this information to an eight-hour day, she found shearers spent an average of six hours four minutes (76 per cent of their work time) with their back bent over and knees straight or partly flexed; one hour four minutes (13.4 per cent) half-kneeling, and 52 minutes (10.6 per cent) walking to and from the pen to catch another sheep. Most of the shearers who experienced back pain said it had developed within six to 10 years of them taking up shearing. And most said their back pain increased during shearing. Of the 29 shearers who suffered back pain, 21 had sought medical treatment, 18 had never missed work because of the problem and only one had missed work for more than one week, indicating most chose to continue working even while they were in pain. The study also used data from the State Government Insurance Office in Perth, which showed that the lower back ranked fourth as the site of injury among shearers insured. Gmeinder said,

> While injuries to this area [the lower back] represented 12 per cent all claims made, they were responsible for 65 per cent of all working time lost and 57 per cent all compensation paid. Between 1982 and 1983, $98,664.20 was awarded for lower back injuries to shearers in Western Australia.

This study was too small-scale to draw industry-wide conclusions. However, a few years earlier, in 1979, renowned New Zealand physiotherapist Robin McKenzie began what was to be a five-year study investigating lower back pain among New Zealand shearers. He never completed the study, due mainly to difficulties tracking the participants, but the initial results showed lower back pain was almost universal among the shearing population.¹⁰⁸ So it seems, from the limited research available in this area, that shearers suffer a disproportionately high incidence of back pain and injuries – due almost certainly to the demanding physical nature of their work.

The strength and stamina of shearers

During the late 1990s, a team of researchers set out to measure for the first time how physically demanding it was to shear sheep. Led by David Stuart, a lecturer in exercise physiology at the University of South Australia, the team used a range of physiological assessments as the basis for the study, including heart rate, oxygen consumption, and calorie and fluid loss. The measurements showed the shearers' heart rates and oxygen consumption readings were at levels consistent with labourers undertaking very heavy work. For example, the heart rate measurements were between 140 and 150 beats per minute. While many labourers reach this rate for brief periods, shearers essentially maintain this rate for their whole work day. But the most surprising result for the researchers came when calculating energy expenditure – on average shearers burnt about 21,000 kilojoules per day, more than a top professional in any code of football (about 17,000 kJ/day). The amazing thing with shearers is that they repeat this performance five days a week, whereas footballers recover, train and then build up to another game usually five to seven days later. The team's research was unpublished, but Stuart spoke about the study on ABC radio in early 2000. He said,

> We were staggered at what a demanding occupation sheep shearing is – in fact, I mean…I've never measured a Bolivian tin miner, they may work harder, but I'd say of anyone that's been actually physiologically assessed, these people are the hardest working people in the world.¹⁰⁹

Case study: Dwayne Black, champion shearer

Perhaps the most comprehensive study into the physical effort involved in shearing focused on the efforts of one man – champion shearer Dwayne Black. Born in New Zealand, Black grew up in Esperance in Western Australia. He started a business/law degree in Perth but dropped out of university to pursue a career in shearing. The change certainly paid off – he quickly developed to become a champion shearer with six world records to his name, mainly in endurance events. One of those records was achieved in 2005, when he spent nine hours shearing 513 merino ewes – surpassing the previous record by six. A team of researchers from the University of Western Australia was present that day, 4 April, at a shed near Kojonup, about 250 kilometres south-east of Perth. They monitored and assessed various measures while he was shearing during the first two-hour run, when he shore 112 sheep.

They reported Black's heart rate averaged 158 beats per minute – about 84 per cent of his estimated maximum heart rate. He lost 3.0 kilograms in weight and 5.5 litres (about 46 millilitres per minute) of fluids during the run, even though he drank 2.5 litres of water. The researchers said this rate of fluid loss was similar to that experienced by marathon runners. Factoring in breaks, the nine-hour event took place over 12 hours. During this time, Black lost four kilograms in body weight and even though he drank 12 litres of fluids, his total fluids loss for the day was 16 litres. Black's energy output was estimated at an astonishing 33,500 kilojoules, almost twice as much as a professional footballer burns up during a game. Based on the measures obtained, the researchers concluded the physical effort involved in achieving his record tally was more intense than the effort expended by top level footballers and ultra-marathon runners. And not only was it more intense, the effort extended over a much longer period than a football game. Just as Stuart's team had done a few years previously, these researchers concluded shearing was one of the most physically gruelling occupations of all.[110]

Although this research focused on a single elite shearer, the nature of the work is the same for all shearers and the physical effort and stamina required to shear hundreds of sheep, day after day, is simply staggering.

Doubly perplexing

Seen in the context of the toilsome nature of shearing work, the union's stance against wide combs was doubly perplexing. Shouldn't the union, purporting to represent the interests of workers who undertake the hardest physical labour you can do in any job, at the very least consider a new technology that could in some way relieve the physical effort required to do that job? Surely that would be in the interests of its members? These are workers who finish each day physically exhausted; who incur work-related injuries at an alarming rate. Many endure ongoing pain. They toil in a doubled-over posture more than three-quarters of each working day. And here is a simple, technological advance that will potentially allow its members to either use less energy and still shear as many sheep, and therefore earn the same amount, or to work just as hard and shear more sheep, and therefore earn more money. Given the potential benefits, investigating the potential of the technology would be a priority. Not in this case. The AWU maintained its *implacable hostile opposition* to wide combs.

15

Enter the National Farmers' Federation

During the 1970s, the agri-political landscape in Australia was a real hotchpotch. There were numerous organisations representing the nation's diverse agricultural producers and in some cases multiple organisations were vying to be the main voice of the particular agricultural industry they championed. The result was a disparate and largely ineffective representation of the overall interests of the farming sector, as organisations jostled with each other to attract the federal government's attention. However, towards the end of the decade there was a growing realisation that there needed to be a more cohesive approach to advocacy – one that would sideline self-interest and narrow, industry-specific agendas. And so, in July 1979 the National Farmers' Federation (NFF) was established to be a single, united voice for farmers and the farming community.

Groups amalgamate

The new peak lobby group was effectively an amalgamation of the Australian National Cattlemen's Council, the Australian Farmers' Federation, the Cattlemen's Union of Australia, the Australian Woolgrowers' and Graziers' Council, the Australian Wheatgrowers' Federation, the Australian Wool and Meat Producers' Federation, the Australian Vegetable Growers' Association, and the Australian Seed Producers' Association. Its main role was to advocate for the farming community at a national level on industry-wide issues such as industrial relations, market access and trade policy, improving productivity and competitiveness, natural resource management, biosecurity, animal health and welfare, and education and training. It should be noted that the NFF did not represent farmers directly – its members were the key farm industry organisations in each state, as well as other groups such as national commodity councils. However, farmers were affiliated with the NFF through their relevant state organisation. Also, from the outset the NFF took an apolitical approach to its operations to ensure it could work effectively with all major political parties and the government of the day. The organisation became influential and respected partly because of this approach. In delivering his opening address to the NFF's annual conference on 17 May 1983, just four years after it was founded, the then prime minister Bob Hawke told delegates,

> By putting forward on behalf of the rural sector a well-argued position which has regard to broader national economic issues, the federation does considerable service both to its members and the community as a whole… I respect the federation's professional approach to its role. That professionalism has given the farming community a respected voice near government.[111]

The times they are a changin'

Australia was at an economic crossroads when the NFF stepped onto the national agri-political stage. Events of the 1970s had shown the economy to be shabby and in desperate need of a makeover. It was, in the words of former governor of the Reserve Bank, Glenn Stevens, '… heavily regulated, suffering poor productivity growth, (and) sheltering behind high barriers to foreign competition'.[112] After almost two full decades of strong economic performance during the 1950s and 1960s, circumstances changed dramatically in the 1970s as almost all key performance measures turned for the worse. International economies and markets became much more volatile; many countries, including Australia, experienced a recession. Two international oil price shocks added to domestic inflationary pressures – between 1970 and 1979 Australia's consumer price index rose on average 10.7 per cent a year, producing a significant decline in the purchasing power of the Australian dollar during this period. Unemployment rose from about two per cent in the early 1970s to about six per cent in the late 1970s and Australia's comparative living standards (as measured by the gross domestic product per person) declined from fifth in the world in 1950 to ninth in 1973. During this same period the national average annual economic growth rate was 2.5 per cent, compared to 3.5 per cent for other OECD countries. Australia's key trading partners were the United States, major European countries and Japan, and the terms of trade index was declining as commodity prices fluctuated but generally decreased, while the cost of imports was rising. It was in 1974 that the nation's current account slid into deficit – it has still not returned to surplus. The wool industry also experienced a turbulent period during the 1970s – the national sheep flock peaked at 180 million in 1970, when Australia produced 890,000 tonnes of wool. However, the wool price plummeted during the early 1970s, and by 1974, when the Reserve Price Scheme was introduced, the national flock had shrunk to 140 million. The industry's decline was due in part to unfavourable seasonal factors but also an increasing demand for synthetic fibres. The reserve price provided some stability and there was a brief recovery in 1975, when sheep numbers increased to 150 million, but by 1978 the national flock was down to 135 million.

The dismal performance of the Australian economy during the 1970s exposed many underlying structural impediments to future growth and efficiency. These impediments included the fact that the economy was highly insular and regulated; local manufacturers generally were shielded from competition through a range of quotas, tariffs and subsidies; work practices in many industries were inflexible and in some industries trade unions exercised an unhealthy degree of power; many key government businesses operated as monopolies and were highly inefficient; and export industries such as agriculture and mining were heavily regulated.

It became apparent that major structural changes were needed to free up the Australian economy and make it more flexible, productive and competitive. Many other countries had begun this process – adopting more open and liberal economic policies to improve domestic performance and compete in the emerging global marketplace. And gradually, from the mid-1970s, the federal government began implementing a series of reforms designed to make Australia more productive and efficient. However, the underlying problems were of such a scale that it would take successive governments many years to phase in the changes necessary to turn the economy around.

When the NFF joined Canberra's legion of lobby groups, this reform process was just gathering momentum. It was clear that many more years of profound change lay ahead if Australia was to meet the economic challenges it faced. In this context, the NFF began operating at a crucial stage in Australia's economic transition, and with the farming sector standing to benefit greatly from a more open and liberal economy, the federation was determined to contribute to the restructuring process. This very clear agenda helped shape some important decisions and appointments during the organisation's infancy.

The NFF's inaugural industrial committee, which oversaw the critical area of industrial and workplace relations policies, comprised three men who were each to make an indelible mark on Australian agri-politics. They were the German-born businessman turned farmer Wolf Boetcher (founding chairman); Sir Sam Burston OBE, a Victorian grazier who was the president of the Australian Woolgrowers' and Graziers' Council immediately before it gave way to the NFF; and Ian McLachlan AO, a South Australian who was 42 at that time and a rising star in the wool industry. Born into a wealthy, prominent pastoral family in Adelaide and educated at the city's top school, St Peter's College, and Cambridge University, where he studied arts and law, McLachlan was chosen largely on the basis of the role he played on behalf of graziers during the live sheep export dispute the previous year.

The live sheep export dispute

In early 1978, a major industrial dispute erupted in Australia's live sheep export industry. It was to have a profound effect on the future of industrial relations for the country. David Trebeck, the then executive officer of the Australian Woolgrowers' and Graziers' Council, and later long-time senior official with the NFF and Canberra-based consulting economist, outlined the significance of the dispute during an address to the H.R. Nicholls Society in February 1989. He said, 'The 1978 live sheep export dispute marked the turning point in the handling of industrial matters in Australia...its importance as a precursor to many of the major industrial battles waged over the subsequent decade is difficult to overstate.'[113]

Australia's main market for live sheep exports was the Middle East. The industry started from scratch in 1960 and by the late 1970s had developed into a $300 million a year trade. However, as the industry grew, so too did the discontent of meat industry workers in Australia. The trade union representing those workers, the Australian Meat Industries Employment Union (AMIEU), was concerned that the increasing volume of Australia's live sheep exports was steadily eroding abattoir jobs – the processing work was effectively leaving Australia's shores along with the sheep. The union claimed that 16,000 abattoir jobs had been lost in the mid-1970s because of increasing live sheep exports. However, Trebeck dismissed this claim at the time and attacked the union, saying industrial disputes in the meat industry in 1977 alone had cost more than 262,000 work days – enough to employ roughly a thousand people for a year. The union wanted ratios imposed on meat exporters, requiring them to export either two or three sheep in carcase form for every one sheep exported live. Most exporters resisted, and tension continued to build.

On 19 March, frustrated at the lack of any concessions, the union called a strike and picketed the docks at Port Adelaide to try to prevent 30,000 Elders-owned sheep being held on Adelaide's outskirts from being loaded on the *Iran Cremona*, which was due to sail to the Middle

East. The farmers and exporters immediately countered by forming a combined livestock committee, under the chairmanship of Ian McLachlan. As you would expect from someone who had played first class cricket for Cambridge University and South Australia, McLachlan was an astute tactician. The committee passed a resolution on 23 March calling on farmers in South Australia to withhold their sheep from the market on the basis that the strike was distorting prices. The resolution was carefully worded so as not to put the committee or farmers in breach of the Trade Practices Act, which made it unlawful for a person to join with another person to hinder the supply of goods or services by a third person to a corporation and thus cause any loss or damage to that corporation. The same section of the Act (45D) was used successfully by Elders soon after to obtain a Federal Court injunction against the union. The logic of the committee's resolution was that if the meat processors could not access livestock there would be no work for their employees (that is, AMIEU members). It was an aggressive response. However, farmers rallied behind their affected colleagues and heeded the committee's call and almost immediately abattoirs were starved of the thing they needed most – livestock.

The dispute quickly spread to Western Australia, which was the main exporting state in the live sheep trade, and soon there were violent confrontations on wharves between farmers and union picketers. At the end of March, Bob Hawke, the then president of the Australian Council of Trade Unions (ACTU), stepped into the fray with an offer to halt the bans in return for an inquiry into the live sheep export trade. However, the farmers were having none of it, arguing that inquiries more often than not were a waste of time and resources. At this stage, the farmers moved to garner public support, organising a motorcade of more than 4,000 vehicles to converge on Adelaide's city centre, where they spoke with members of the public and handed out leaflets about the dispute. Although it caused traffic chaos, they received widespread media coverage and a great deal of public sympathy.

After several weeks, the backlog of sheep for loading at Port Adelaide had grown to more than 100,000. With stockfeed running out and the situation becoming desperate, the committee devised a covert plan, appropriately named Operation Sheeplift, to sidestep the blockade. It announced publicly that an empty live sheep carrier was being sent from Port Adelaide to Western Australia to collect a load of sheep for shipment to the Middle East. However, once clear of the harbour, the ship diverted north into the Spencer Gulf to Wallaroo, a small port on the eastern side of the gulf, south of Port Pirie and about 150 kilometres north-west of Adelaide. The committee had arranged for the stranded sheep in Adelaide to be trucked to Wallaroo, where they were loaded without incident onto the ship. Wallaroo was ideal because vessels could manoeuvre in and out of the harbour berths without needing tugboats – meaning tug operators would not be on hand to inform the AMIEU about what was happening. The union was taken by surprise and with its picket line breached, the stand-off soon came to an end.

At the time, the main participants in this dispute did not fully appreciate its significance. But looking back, it was clear that the farmers' victory in 1978 was incredibly important to the future of industrial relations reform in Australia. In the first place, it helped smooth the way for the formation of the NFF the following year – farmer groups at that time had tended to be fairly parochial, but this campaign had demonstrated the value of working together for a common cause. And secondly, it gave farmers and other employers the confidence that they could take on powerful trade unions and prevail. McLachlan was later to say, '…the live sheep dispute was certainly catalytic in changing farmers' attitudes as to what they could and couldn't do industrially.'[114]

Three industrial disputes during the following two decades were particularly significant: the wide comb shearing dispute; the Mudginberri abattoir dispute in the Northern Territory from 1983 to 1985; and the waterfront dispute of 1998. They reduced the power and influence of unions by doing away with compulsory unionism; exposed unions to massive fines for unlawful conduct; and freed up workplaces, making them far more flexible and productive. Interestingly, McLachlan was heavily involved in all of these disputes. He had emerged from the four-week live sheep export strike the toast of the state's pastoral industry. He was widely praised for his level-headed leadership and ability to make sound decisions under pressure – it was the start of what was to be a stellar career in agribusiness and politics.

In mid-1980, it fell upon the NFF's industrial committee to appoint an industrial officer for the organisation. Surprisingly, given the NFF's attitude towards unions, particularly at that time, McLachlan, Burston and Boetcher selected Paul Xavier Houlihan for the role. He had spent 10 years working for the Federated Clerks' Union – two as an organiser in Victoria, the rest as state secretary in Tasmania. Houlihan had grown up on a dairy farm near Koo-wee-rup, Australia's largest asparagus growing district, south-east of Melbourne. He started work for the NFF in Canberra on 1 December 1980. McLachlan was to recall later,

> Considering the National Farmers' Federation view of unions in the late '70s and early '80s, it is a wonder he got an interview at all. Despite his somewhat socialist views on a number of matters, he was obviously starting to consider things like productivity, export performance – we thought he might actually be on the philosophical turn, so to speak. In any case, he was our last chance, so he got the job.[115]

McLachlan and Houlihan were to become close friends. And both were to play key roles in the ensuing wide combs, Mudginberri and waterfront disputes. On the conservative side of politics they are lauded; on the left side, they are not.

16

Shearers Prosecuted

The AWU's 96th annual national convention was held at the Grand United Order of Oddfellows building in Castlereagh Street, Sydney. On Friday 22 January 1982, as the first week of the conference was drawing to a close, the New South Wales branch secretary Ernie Ecob interrupted proceedings to report some good news to delegates. A court case brought against five shearers for using wide comb shears in breach of the federal Pastoral Industry Award had just been finalised in the union's favour. This represented a major victory for the AWU and had vindicated its strict approach to policing the use of the banned wide combs, Ecob said. The outcome buoyed delegates and reinvigorated their collective determination to rid the pastoral industry of the 'scourge' of wide combs.

White's team in court

Earlier that day, Robert White and four of his team members had appeared before Magistrate Clive Werry in a special sitting of the Industrial Court in the 101-year-old Bathurst courthouse. The five shearers – White together with Adrian Ridley, Paul Woollaston, Cliff Healey and Frank Myers – were all due to be penalised for using the banned wide comb shears the previous year. Each had pleaded guilty to breaching Clause 32 (a)(i) of the federal Pastoral Industry Award, 1965, which provided that

> 32 (a) No shearer or crutcher shall use nor shall the employer permit him to use:

(i) Any comb wider than two and a half inches between the points of the outside teeth.

The breaches occurred in April, when White, Ridley, Woollaston and Healey were caught by AWU organiser Tom Anderson shearing with wide combs at Canomodine Station, and in May 1981, when these four men together with Frank Myers were caught by AWU organiser Bill Keightley using wide gear at the Millambri property near Canowindra. The prosecution was brought by the AWU's New South Wales branch through summonses to the shearers and the first hearing took place on 13 November, when all five men entered pleas of guilty. The LGPA did not fund the shearers' defence but it kept a close eye on proceedings given that the case was related to the broader industrial dispute over wide combs.

During the court proceedings in November, counsel for the shearers tried to argue a technical, legal point – that Clause 32 of the Award, referred to above, was a 'bans clause' under Section 33 of the Australian Conciliation and Arbitration Act 1904. Essentially, he argued that the clause outlawing wide combs was invalid because it constituted a restriction or limitation that hindered the performance of work in accordance with an award. Counsel sought to have the complaints dismissed on the basis that the federal legislation required any bans clause to be dealt with by a deputy president of the Australian Conciliation and Arbitration Commission. Counsel for the AWU, however, rejected this argument and submitted that the wide combs clause was merely one of many normal regulatory provisions contained in the Award. After hearing submissions from both sides, Mr Werry reserved his decision until 17 December.

When the matter returned to court the following month, counsel for the shearers immediately made an application seeking to have Mr Werry refrain from making a decision in the matter, on the basis that the LGPA had recently initiated proceedings in the Australian Conciliation and Arbitration Commission seeking to have the prohibition against wide combs removed from the Pastoral Industry

Award. However, the union's legal team opposed the application, arguing that the magistrate had heard the preliminary submissions and had an obligation to either uphold or dismiss the complaints. They also argued that it was the duty of the court to apply the law as it existed at that time, and that it was highly desirable for the issue to be resolved because of the continuing widespread publicity in the pastoral industry surrounding wide combs. Mr Werry favoured the union's argument and ruled that Clause 32 in the Pastoral Industry Award did not constitute a 'bans clause'. He convicted all five shearers of breaching the Award, however, he adjourned the matters until 22 January to determine the question of penalties.

When the matters returned to court in the new year, Mr Werry heard submissions from both legal teams about the appropriate penalties. He fined Robert White $250 (the maximum permitted under the union rules) for his role in allowing shearers employed by him to use shearing combs wider than those permitted by the Award. He fined Adrian Ridley, Paul Woollaston and Cliff Healey $150 each for using wide combs on two occasions. Frank Myers was fined $100 for breaching the Award once. He ordered that the fines be paid to Ernie Ecob in his capacity as secretary of the New South Wales branch of the AWU – a particularly galling outcome for the shearers.

Aftermath of the ruling

Frank Myers, who grew up on a farm between Bathurst and Hill End, said the consequences of the legal action led to him leaving the shearing industry within months of the court case being finalised. Myers had trained as a wool classer during the 1950s before later becoming a shearer. He was first exposed to wide combs during a holiday with his wife, Libby, in New Zealand in 1978. They visited the Agrodome Farm Show near Rotorua on the North Island, where Myers noticed something odd about the shearing demonstration – the shearers seemed to be going too fast. He went and spoke to them following the demonstration and realised they were using wide combs

– it was the first time he had seen them. Keen to see how they would perform, he brought some with him when the couple returned home. 'It made a big difference…it put me up at least 40 [sheep] a day without working. I didn't really want to be a gun or beat blokes I was shearing with. I just wanted to make it easier,' he said. Myers said once the court case ended and he was black banned by the union, he gradually moved out of the industry. He said although he had offers of shearing work at small 'cocky' sheds in the Bathurst district, he felt reluctant to put the farmers in a position where their wool and properties would be black banned by the AWU if they employed him as a shearer. 'Even though a few of them [local graziers] rang me up, I said, "Well, I can't do it because you blokes will suffer for it, they will black ban your wool for sure and you won't sell it,"' he said.

In the week after Mr Werry's ruling, both Ian Manning and Ernie Ecob were interviewed on ABC radio's *Country Hour* program to discuss the implications of the case. Manning said the ruling had vindicated the LGPA's position, which had consistently been to warn its members against allowing wide combs to be used on their properties in breach of the Award. '… As I've said, the Award is the Award. It is in breach of the Award for shearers to use wide combs or for employers to let their shearers use wide combs; they're both in breach of the Award if apprehended, and until such time as the Award is varied, we will have to repeat our warnings that people should adhere to the Award and that if they're not satisfied with the wide comb prohibition, well then they should get together with us and try and develop a consensus approach to work out how we might modify the prohibition,' he said.[116] Manning went on to say that it would be 'regrettable' if the union were to harden its attitude against wide combs following the ruling.

However, when Ernie Ecob was interviewed, he seemed to indicate that the union would, at the very least, be continuing its hardline approach. He said delegates to the union's annual convention the previous Friday (the same day the court ruling was made) had been involved in 'some very strong debates' about the use of wide combs and had decided to continue to 'take every step possible to stop the use and spread of the wide combs throughout Australia, including Western Australia'. Ecob again used the media to try to downplay the extent of the problem, suggesting a small number of rebel shearers were causing a disproportionate amount of strife in the shearing industry. He told listeners,

> The [AWU annual] convention has had reports from Western Australia where they [wide combs] have been in use for quite some time and the reports that we've got from the [Western Australian] Department of Agriculture…are in favour of the union's decision not to introduce or have introduced wide combs into the federal Pastoral Award. Also, there has been a growing demand for the use of the two and a half inch comb in Western Australia, where previously they were using combs of wider width in that state.

It is not clear what information Ecob had to back up this claim about the increasing demand for narrow gear in the west. He went on to say, 'The wide comb in New South Wales, from all reports that I have received…there's something like 12 to 15 shearers who are using it, most of those are New Zealanders and half-baked cockies' sons, who are only in it to try and disrupt the industry by causing industrial unrest.' Asked if it was worth the effort the union was going to if the problem was only minor, Ecob replied, 'Yes, for the harmony of the industry and the future of the industry, it's worth every bit of it.'

One important aspect of the proceedings against White and his team had created a quandary for the union – the economics of pursuing and prosecuting rebel shearers. The fact that any charges brought against shearers or wool growers for breaching the Award were treated as industrial matters, not criminal matters, meant the court had no discretion to rule on costs. In effect, all parties to any proceedings brought by the union would have to foot the bill for their legal costs. In the case against White and his team, the shearers each paid about $4,000 in costs, while the union's legal bill was estimated at more than

$10,000. Given that the maximum fine for any breach was $250, it was simply not economical to prosecute Award breaches. And legal costs would be significantly more in cases where shearers or farmers were to contest the charges and plead not guilty, meaning witnesses would have to be called to give evidence. Such matters could have dragged on for many months, increasing court time and legal costs.

Ecob told the *Country Hour* that although delegates to the annual convention had debated proposals to significantly increase the quantum of penalties as listed in the union rules, the consensus was that using black bans to target offenders would be far more effective. He said,

> …the discussions that have taken place at the convention are not in favour of increasing the fines, but to impose penalties on people who use or engage shearers who use or intend to use wide combs… This means black bans on their produce, such as wool and wheat and also asking the trade union movement not to allow materials on to the properties.[117]

So it was clear that although there was a legal avenue for the union to prosecute wide comb shearers, it was financially unviable to use this method of enforcement.

White and his four team members later lodged appeals against their convictions. They intended arguing several technical points about the validity of Clause 32 of the Pastoral Industry Award, as well as seeking reductions in their penalties on the basis that there was evidence that all shearing combs in use at that time contravened Clause 32 – meaning every shearer was in fact breaching the Award. This evidence was based on the findings of two researchers, Alistair MacKenzie and Bruce Field, who examined 28 different types of narrow gauge combs.[118] Both MacKenzie and Field were engineers with the University of Melbourne's Agricultural Science Department. However, MacKenzie was also a wool grower who had a property Hillside, at Ararat, north-west of Melbourne. He was described during the Arbitration Commission hearings on the wide comb dispute as 'an academic well known for his innovation aimed at progressing the wool industry'.[119] The combs were made by nine manufacturers and the researchers used packets of five combs for each different comb type, meaning they studied 140 combs in total. The researchers made detailed measurements of all aspects of the combs and found that 'no make of comb that was examined complies unambiguously with Clause 32 of the Award'. As it turned out, the appeals did not proceed and were later withdrawn, meaning the convictions stood.

17

The Sydney Showground Demonstrations

A peculiarity of the federal Pastoral Industry Award in the early 1980s was that its provisions did not apply to non-commercial shearing demonstrations. Paul Houlihan discovered this anomaly in late 1981, while scrutinising various aspects of the Award as part of his preparations for the upcoming Arbitration Commission hearings. And armed with this information, he and Ian Manning hatched what could really only be described as a devious plan. For the previous century, since 1881, the Sydney Showground at Moore Park in the city's inner south-east had been the venue for the Royal Easter Show – the annual showcase event of the Royal Agricultural Society of New South Wales. The show aimed to bring the bush to the city; to give city dwellers a taste of country life without the inconvenience of having to venture across the Great Dividing Range. And although in November 1981 the next Royal Easter Show was still several months away, Houlihan and Manning were planning a show of their own at Moore Park early the following month.

Commission hears arguments

Proceedings in the Arbitration Commission hearing into the unresolved wide comb dispute matters resumed in the Queen's Square law courts building in Macquarie Street, Sydney, on Wednesday 2 December 1981. Most of the morning session was taken up with preliminary, administrative matters. However, late in the morning, Houlihan applied to have the commission attend a wide comb shearing demonstration at the showground at Moore Park that afternoon. Following lunch, at two p.m., Commissioner Ian McKenzie heard submissions from both parties about whether or not the commission should sanction and be involved in the proposed shearing demonstration. The union strongly opposed the application. Peter Sams, who represented the federal branch of the AWU during these proceedings, argued the demonstration was a stunt and unnecessary. However, several months previously, Commissioner McKenzie had hinted there might come a time when a demonstration of the wide comb shearing equipment was needed. It seemed the time had come! The commissioner approved the application for a demonstration that afternoon, on condition there would be no members of the media present. Houlihan agreed to this condition. However, in doing so he was at best being disingenuous and, at worst, downright deceitful. Behind the scenes, he and Ian Manning had already organised for a shearing demonstration to take place for the media that morning, while preliminary matters were being heard in the commission a few kilometres away in the city. The pair had invited all the national television, radio and print media as well as key rural media outlets to attend. And given the controversial nature of wide combs and the heated debate they had been generating, there was a large media contingent present at the showground. For the city journos, it was an opportunity to expand their focus and file a slightly offbeat but topical story about the bush. For their rural counterparts, this was an important issue that warranted continued and detailed coverage.

Robert White demonstrates wide combs

By this stage, Robert White was on friendly terms with the key officials of the farmers' groups involved in the dispute. He knew Houlihan and Manning quite well and given that he had developed something of a profile as a vocal wide combs advocate, it was no surprise that he was chosen to be the shearer to demonstrate the wide gear at the showground that day – for both the media and the Arbitration

Commission. From the wool growers' perspective, the aim of the day was to show the commission that all breeds and classes of Australian sheep could be shorn professionally using wide combs. To do this, White was to shear 12 sheep under the watchful eye of accredited national shearing competition judge, Geoff Still, and two wool growers. The sheep were of different age, sex, breed and wool type.

Commissioner McKenzie suspended Clause 32 of the Award for the duration of the demonstration, which took place in the Agrodome. Although technically it was not necessary to do so, given the Award provisions, the effect of the suspension was to give an added assurance to all those involved in the demonstration that they could not be prosecuted for participating. Manning later recalled watching Robert White shearing during the demonstration for the Arbitration Commission and being concerned that he was going too slow. He felt certain the times would not be much quicker than typical narrow gauge shearing times, thus rendering the wool growers' industrial case pointless. However, White's wife Gayle, who was standing nearby with a stopwatch, pointed out how quickly he was actually shearing. The apparent 'slowness' came from White's incredible shearing technique – each blow was so smooth and seemingly effortless that he appeared to be going almost in slow motion, when in fact he was shearing very quickly.

The media demonstration

Earlier that day, White had performed an almost identical demonstration for the media. Every major outlet was represented and Ian Manning gave interviews to several journalists in which he emphasised the suitability of wide combs to shear all types of sheep in all sorts of conditions, gave assurances that wool growers would not use wide combs to try to erode shearers' pay rates, and said how disappointing it was that AWU representatives were not present to witness the demonstration. This comment in particular was to draw the ire of the union. He was quoted on the Channel 9 television news that evening as saying,

If wide combs can enable a shearer to shear an extra 20 sheep a day, and our view is that is at least a minimum for most shearers, that's an extra $16 a day that a shearer earns during ordinary hours and per week that's $80… So I can see no basis for the suggestion that the introduction of wide combs is going to lead to lower earnings for shearers.[120]

He told the Channel 10 news reporter,

In 1956, when the wool bonus payment scheme was due to come out of the rates of pay for shearers, wool growers unsuccessfully sought to have the rate for shearing reduced, and we say that if wool growers ever had merit for reducing the rate of pay, it was then. They tried, they failed and they're not likely to go into another no-win situation again.

He went on to say, 'We certainly have difficulty understanding their [the AWU's] opposition to our proposal to have trials, and quite frankly we're disappointed that the representative of the union is not here today to witness this demonstration.'[121]

Houlihan and Manning knew that staging the demonstration for the media would be highly provocative but they felt frustrated that the wide combs campaign had lost momentum. The union had refused to lift several black bans, it was not negotiating on the proposed trials, it was prosecuting Robert White's team of shearers and it had staged various stop work meetings and brief strikes to protest against wide gear. What better way to reinvigorate the campaign than to involve the national media? The following day, Thursday 3 December 1981, when the Arbitration Commission hearings resumed in the city, they must have felt like two naughty schoolboys who were about to face the principal.

All hell breaks loose

Unfortunately for Houlihan and Manning, Commissioner McKenzie had watched the television news the previous evening. So had Peter Sams, one of the union's legal representatives. So, when proceedings opened, the atmosphere in the room was highly charged. Sams immediately asked Commissioner McKenzie if he could make a statement, and was invited to do so. He showed little restraint:

> Yesterday, despite the union's opposition to the Commission granting the employers' request for a demonstration of the use of wide gear, the Commission, on its own motion, suspended Clause 32 of the Award for the period of the demonstration that we saw yesterday, and for that period alone... The AWU put to the Commission its dissatisfaction with the course being proposed and expressed a *prima-facie* position that the demonstration should not proceed in any event. Sir, the union in conformity with your request to attend the demonstration, despite our opposition…agreed to do so. We did so because we believe we were acting responsibly and honourably.
>
> However, it seems there is only one party in this dispute that has acted honourably and with integrity, because we had the situation last night that was witnessed across the nation of the most disgraceful, contemptible, orchestrated stunt that I have ever seen perpetuated in my experience with the pastoral industry. I refer to the disgusting abuse of propriety that we saw last night reported on national television. I happened to be watching the news program last night. When it came on I thought, 'This is impossible. There were no films being taken of the demonstration, there were no cameras when we were viewing the demonstration.' Then it clicked, because what had happened was the filming had taken place prior to the demonstration, in the morning.
>
> … The Commission has told the parties on numerous occasions that this is a highly emotive issue. The emotion engendered by the problem is not resolved or tempered by the blatant grandstanding that has been done and sanctioned by the LGPA and the employers in this case. Of course, we were treated to the spectacle of Mr Manning extolling the virtues of wide gear on television and expressing his complete loss as to why the union was not in attendance at the demonstration. That was patently false because we did attend the demonstration against our wishes, but we did so in compliance with your request… We say that the disgusting episode last night is an indictment on the employers

and does not assist one iota with the resolution of this dispute. In fact, as a result of last night, I believe the dispute has escalated.

… We are so appalled by this incident that I have been tempted to withdraw from these proceedings forthwith. Acting as reasonably as we do, we are not going to stoop to the levels that the employers have done in that episode last night… We certainly ask the Commission to severely reprimand whoever was responsible for this type of activity, which only seeks to exacerbate the situation and make it harder and harder to resolve this very complex dispute.[122]

You would think, given his role in organising the media demonstration, and in the face of such pointed criticism, that Houlihan might have been somewhat circumspect and contrite that day. However, the barrage of condemnation had little effect on him – he brushed it aside before returning fire:

… The righteous indignation that has been manufactured here for this occasion has got to be tempered in the light of why we are here, why we have the problems we have got, and why we are doing the things we are doing to try and get out of that problem. For Mr Sams to put on the performance that he did about the responsibility and the integrity of the union is simply laughable in view of the fact that bans you [Commissioner McKenzie] ordered to be lifted three months ago are still in place. The union directly responsible for placing those bans boasts about the fact that those bans will never be lifted. Yet we are castigated for being irresponsible!

The same people have got strikes in three states of the Commonwealth now on this issue that they pretend does not exist… The union concentrates on manufacturing righteous indignation to try and cover the fact that the union has not got a position to take on this issue. All the union can do, and all the union has been able to put to us and this Commission for three months, is the fact that the clause should stay in the Award, that the status quo should be retained. The fact that this status quo is the seed of the dispute that we have got is completely ignored.

The fact is that it will not go away – the problem will not go away – the problem is here now, and it has to be faced and it has got to be tackled. Let us come back to this disgusting behaviour yesterday. I accept that Mr Sams is upset. I do not dispute that he has possibly got a right to be upset. But we are a little bit upset about one or two things, too. Let me place them on the record, right now. This morning, the branch secretary of the AWU in New South Wales, Mr [Ernie] Ecob, rang Mr Manning of the Livestock and Grain Producers' Association and advised Mr Manning, who is a member of this hearing…that Mr Manning's private property is black banned.[123]

Soon after this exchange between Sams and Houlihan, Commissioner McKenzie also voiced his disapproval of the media demonstration:

I, too, saw Channel 10 last night. I found it greatly misleading. I do not deny your right to invite the press to do what you want. You know my views, and I made them very strongly last time before me, as to this obsession for publicity. But that was wrong, that report last night. In the first instance, it inferred that I was present at that demonstration, and…that was not the demonstration which was done with the approval of the Commission. The second point was that it was said that Mr Manning had made the statement and said it was a pity the union could not be here today. That is totally misleading, because at that stage the union had not been invited to attend, when that [statement] was made. The union attended a properly conducted demonstration at the request of this Commission. Anybody looking at that last night, that had not been in the proceedings, would have got the impression that the Commission approved of that demonstration, and that the union had failed to attend. We all know that is wrong, and I expect that to be corrected.

…I feel this matter has had enough publicity. The sooner it disappears from the TV and from the newspapers and we get down to trying to do what we are trying to do – resolve the dispute – we will make progress. The fact that you did it yesterday, I do not think it was very clever. I will be quite clear about that. That is your right to do what you did. However, I do object strongly to the inaccuracy that was put forward in the report that I saw anyway. I do not think it is good enough. And as for this type of action, as the old story goes, in physics, each force attracts an equal and opposite force. That is what is going on. If we keep this up, we will have the whole country, as far as the pastoral industry goes, in chaos.[124]

The fallout from the media demonstration continued the following day, Friday 4 December, when Ernie Ecob gave an interview on the Macquarie *Rural News* radio program. As well as making public the black bans on the properties of the LGPA officials, Manning and CEO John White, he flagged a meeting in Dubbo to discuss possible strike action. 'Because of the happenings which have occurred over the last couple of days, the New South Wales Branch [of the AWU] has called a meeting of all pastoral workers, which will be held in Dubbo on Sunday, 21 February 1982, to discuss the [possible] national stoppage and particularly a stoppage throughout the whole of New South Wales,' he said. In the heat of the moment, Ecob also said union representatives would not attend any hearings in which Manning was involved, and that they no longer recognised him as being the LGPA's industrial officer. And he also warned that the union would consider organising some sort of action against New Zealand shearers coming into Australia, although it was not clear what he had in mind.

However, the LGPA's president, Harold Balcomb, defended the media demonstration, describing it as 'an historical event which would allow shearers and wool-growers to evaluate the advantages and disadvantages of wide combs'.[125] And years later, while reflecting on the wide combs dispute, Paul Houlihan downplayed the furore the demonstrations caused, saying,

> That morning I was in the Arbitration Commission arguing why the Commission should go and see this (demonstration) and my colleagues were out at the showground demonstrating this to the media. In the end, Commissioner McKenzie ruled the trial would go ahead that afternoon but there would be no press. It was on

every news service. There was a fabulous front-page photo [published in *The Land*] of Robert White shearing there, he was just flying through it. Great photo! Well, the bloody union screamed blue murder, the Commissioner screamed blue murder, we received a very severe dressing down from the Commission amid what I described as the 'manufactured anguish' of the AWU, but I said, 'Look what are we arguing about – the (wide comb) shears can shear any sheep in Australia.'

Although the demonstration had confirmed the merits of wide combs, the argument was far from over.

18

Evidence From the Showground Hearings

When the air had finally cleared in the Arbitration Commission on the morning following the LGPA's 'media stunt', Commissioner McKenzie focused once more on the task at hand – trying to resolve the dispute. Several witnesses were due to give evidence that day (Thursday 3 December 1981) and the next, including some who had been involved in the approved demonstration the previous day. It was now clear to most of those involved in the industrial case that there was still a long road ahead before the umpire would be able to make a ruling. Indeed, the reaction to the media demonstration had highlighted the chasm between the two parties. This did not stop Paul Houlihan, however, from trying to persuade the commissioner that it would be appropriate to immediately make a ruling in favour of wide combs. In what was certainly an audacious if not brash submission, Houlihan tried to short-cut the lengthy process ahead by arguing his side in the dispute had done all it needed to do to demonstrate the suitability of wide shearing combs to be used in Australia.

Decades later, while reflecting on the case, he said,

> We had shown that such combs were able to be used satisfactorily to shear any sheep in Australia and the refusal of the Commission to vary the Award accordingly amounted to a restriction, even a denial, to shearers to maximise their earnings legitimately as pieceworkers under the terms of the [federal] Pastoral Industry Award.

However, Commissioner McKenzie quickly rejected the application, saying any notion that such a complex industrial case would be resolved that day was 'pie in the sky'. Having been slapped down once again, Houlihan began calling witnesses.

Witnesses testify

The first witness for the day was John Rothwell, the manager of the Canowindra district property Canomodine. Rothwell told the commission that he engaged Robert White's team of wide comb shearers in breach of the Award in April that year because of the particular circumstances he was facing – his sheep were in poor condition because of the drought at that time and they needed to be shorn as quickly as possible to minimise losses. White's team promised to slash two weeks off the normal six weeks allocated to shearing – meaning the contract price for the station was much less. However, Rothwell said he understood White was paying his team members above Award rates. He consulted with the LGPA before he engaged White's team and was warned that although the wide gear option made good economic sense, the association could not endorse it because it would amount to a breach of the Award.

Later during his testimony, Rothwell criticised the LGPA for being sluggish to advocate for wide combs on behalf of its members. 'I felt they should have been moving to have a look at wide combs a lot more strongly because of the benefits that farmers and shearers could see,' he said. 'We had black bans placed on the property after shearing in April and [I feel] the LGPA have not done enough to resolve or help resolve this situation… I felt the LGPA did not come out enough to protect their farmers.'[126]

Houlihan then read on to the record a statement from Edgar Ross Charles, a wool grower from Narrandera. Charles attended the shearing demonstration the previous day but had to rush back to his property Rockvale to begin harvesting the summer wheat crop. Charles had an impressive list of credentials in the wool industry. He was a member of the National Wool Producing Industry Training

Committee,[127] which had oversight of shearer training throughout Australia, a member of the LGPA's executive committee, a member of the LGPA's wool committee, and was the LGPA's representative on the Wool Council of Australia. At that time, Charles had 17 years' experience as a shearer and 32 years' experience as a wool grower. In his statement to the commission, Charles said the quality of shearing performed during the approved demonstration was 'faultless' and 'it was evident that second cuts in the wool are caused by the skill of the shearer and not the width of the comb'. Charles's statement concluded,

> I was impressed by the lack of ridges in wool remaining on the sheep after the shearing was completed. It was apparent from the demonstration that by using combs wider than two and a half inches, the shearer was able to increase his productivity without a corresponding increase in energy being expended. If the use of combs wider than two and a half inches was legally permitted, I would have no hesitation in allowing my shearing industry employees to use combs wider than two and a half inches... After having seen the demonstration, I would have no hesitation in recommending that wool-growers permit their employees to use, and that shearing industry employees use, combs wider than two and a half inches, subject only to the provisos that the use of such combs was legally permitted and the width of the comb was not such that it hindered the employee from shearing or crutching in a good and workman-like manner.

Next to give evidence was Geoffrey Charles Still, who had 30 years' experience in the wool industry. He had started as a wool classer, moved into shearing and then into judging. Still had been an accredited shearing judge since 1962 and had on several occasions judged the Diamond Shears Competition in Longreach (Queensland) and the Golden Shears Competition in Euroa (Victoria). These were the two premier shearing competitions in Australia. Houlihan asked Still, 'How impressed were you with the overall shearing that was done...particularly in light of the very mixed bag of sheep that were there?' He replied, 'I can only say, I have seen a lot of shearing and I cannot see very much difference really. I do not think I could see any difference. The sheep were shorn in an average manner.' Garry Johnston, the barrister who represented the union for most of the industrial hearings, did not cross-examine the witness.

Still was to pay a high price for his involvement in the showground demonstration and subsequent testimony. The AWU could be particularly vindictive towards anyone who had the temerity to defy or challenge its authority. It viewed Still's involvement as support for the wide comb cause and a betrayal of the union, and set about having him deregistered as a shearing judge. Shearing competitions in Australia were carefully controlled by the AWU and judges were accredited through an organisation called the Australian Competition Shearing Federation, which operated under the auspices of the AWU. Early the following year, on 22 February, the union's Victorian branch secretary Ian Cuttler wrote to the union's federal Executive Council urging it to 'act to curtail his [Still's] activities [in helping to promote wide-gauge shearing combs]'. It took a while for the Executive Council to respond, but during its meeting on 22 July, it resolved, 'That Mr G Still be informed that he is no longer acceptable as a shearing competition judge by the Shearing Competition Federation of Australia.'[128]

Robert White takes the stand

Houlihan then called Robert White to testify and indicated that Ian Manning would question the witness. White started by outlining his background in the shearing industry and explaining how he first came to be exposed to pulled combs then wide combs while learning to shear in Western Australia during the early 1970s. He gave evidence that he used wide combs in the Oberon district of New South Wales as early as 1975, in sheds where the wool growers and other shearers had no objection to their use. Indeed, upon seeing the relative ease with which he was shearing, the other shearers in these sheds were 'converted' to wide combs. White said that when he returned from Western Australia to New South Wales to shear in early 1980, the wide combs garnered so much interest among colleagues he shore with that he became a quasi-distributor of wide gear, sourcing it from suppliers in New Zealand and Western Australia and organising delivery to customers all over the state. Eventually he could not keep up with demand and had to advise shearers to contact the suppliers directly.

Manning went on to ask White whether he could shear more sheep using wide combs compared to narrow combs. White replied, 'I would shear approximately forty sheep a day more with the wide comb, and easier.' Commissioner McKenzie asked, 'What percentage would that be?' White said, 'I used to shear 200 with narrow combs. I still only shear 200 a day with wide combs. I just do it much easier. I would shear 240 with the wide comb if I worked as hard as I have with a narrow comb.' (White's highest tally is believed to be 317. However, he told the commission he deliberately shore within himself to reduce the physical strain on his body and maximise his longevity in the industry.)

Manning then asked a series of questions relating to the commission-sanctioned shearing demonstration. White conceded the quality of his shearing of the 12 demonstration sheep was only average but said it was difficult to concentrate and shear in the competition conditions under which the demonstration was held and the constant change of sheep breed and size made it hard to get into a rhythm. Manning then focused on the intricacies of shearing each type of sheep in the trial, asking White to describe each successive blow required to defleece the various sheep and compare them to the corresponding sequence of blows when using narrow gauge combs. While going through this process, he asked White to outline the advantages and disadvantages of using wide combs for each type of sheep. White then gave the commission a blow by blow description of how he would shear different types of sheep – starting with lambs, then repeating the process for wethers, ewes and rams. He compared each blow used with wide combs to the blows necessary for narrow combs and outlined where there were 'savings' to be had. For example, 'To do the belly on a lamb, the wide comb, you can just about do it in two blows and you virtually cut down on one blow.' Describing the process of shearing along a lamb's back, where the long blow is used, he said, '… About six [blows] on a lamb with the narrow comb, and what I can do in four with the wide comb…you just remove the wool so much quicker.' (Although White was not asked to summarise the savings he could achieve using wide combs, he was to later tell the *Sydney Morning Herald*, 'It takes about sixty blows to shear a sheep with a narrow comb. The wide comb reduces that to about forty-five blows.')[129]

Commissioner McKenzie asked White about the ease of use of wide combs. 'What about the physical effort using the wide gear? Does it require more physical effort?' he asked. White conceded that when he first saw wide combs, he thought, 'How in the hell can you push that?' However, he said the original combs were not designed to shear merino sheep and the design of the combs had greatly improved during the past few years.

> … With the combs I have now, it is far less physical [strain] on me to shear a sheep with a wide comb than it was when it was a narrow comb… The cutting of the wool is virtually the same [as] with the narrow comb, because with the narrow comb you have ten teeth and you have three cutter pieces to go across it. And the wide comb, you have thirteen teeth, but you have got four cutting teeth to do it. And as far as pushing it through the wool, it just seems to glide through the wool. There is no effort to push it. And if you can shear in less blows and not as hard work, it is just less physically and mentally too.

White's evidence covered several other aspects of wide comb usage. He told the commission he had never come across shearers who started using wide combs only to voluntarily return to using narrow gear. 'Lots of times when they shear with other shearers, or farmers even, where they will not let them use wide combs, but of their own accord they would just not use anything else but wide combs,' he said. Manning asked White if wide combs currently on the market required further improvements to the design. White said the most recent iteration of

Sunbeam's Hustler and Fine Wool combs, which had been commercially available since August that year, could be used 'out of the box'. These long-bevel combs were designed specifically to shear merinos. 'I have used them and anyone I got them for, they have used them, and they have no complaints whatsoever,' he said. White was asked if he had made 'any commercial gain' from advocating the use of wide combs. He said if anything he had lost money because he had been bearing the cost of freight to send wide comb orders to shearers all over Australia. However, he conceded he had benefited indirectly through some new wide comb converts joining his contracting team.

Commissioner McKenzie wanted to know if switching to wide gear involved a change in shearing technique and, if so, how long it took to adapt to the change. White said the technique was essentially the same, but it was important to fill up the comb a bit more and to keep it full of fleece. Most new wide comb shearers had to concentrate more and get used to the 'feel' of the comb. He said it was not unusual for a new user to shear as many as seven extra sheep during their first run (an extra 28 sheep per day) with wide combs.

The day's proceedings concluded with submissions by the opposing parties' legal representatives. Paul Houlihan said wool growers, through the LPGA, had genuinely tried to enforce the Award with its members. He said the LGPA had wanted to pursue industry trials of wide combs but the obstinacy of the union had forced it to take drastic action. 'We felt it was necessary that the Commission should see firsthand the fact that a very wide range of types and breeds of sheep in markedly varying condition are able to be handled, able to be shorn, able to be crutched with this gear, before the Commission was put in this position of making what we appreciate is a very major change in the Award. We would stress, sir, that it is more a major change in the Award than it is, in fact, in the industry,' he said. Wide combs were already being used and the scale of their usage was becoming more widespread despite opposition from the union, he said. Houlihan also sought to have any variation in the Award backdated as a way of effectively invalidating the prosecutions against White and his team that the union was pursuing. '… We should like some consideration (to be given) to these people facing prosecution,' he said. 'The people who have been caught are patently the tip of the iceberg, and it is far from any concept of justice or equity that the tip of the iceberg be made to pay for the whole iceberg.' He implored the commissioner to resolve the matter as quickly as possible.

Garry Johnston, for the union, was brief. He said the union was yet to decide whether it would call witnesses in the industrial case or apply for a series of shed inspections to take place to highlight certain facts relevant to the case.

Manning also addressed the commissioner, and again placed on record that wool growers were not attempting to use wide combs to surreptitiously seek reductions in pay rates or break down Award conditions. He also pointed out that key arguments the union had used to justify its stance against wide combs did not stand up to scrutiny. These included arguments that some union officials had used wide combs during the late 1950s and had found them wanting; and union members did not want to use wide combs. He said the evidence before the commission showed that wide combs in the late 1950s were vastly different to those currently on the market; and the growing demand for wide combs showed there were a significant number of shearers who did want to use wide combs. He concluded by saying the LGPA's wool grower members had been placed in a bind – being forced to choose between risking legal sanctions (for engaging wide comb shearers) or losing money through the additional costs incurred by using standard-gauge shearing equipment.

Commissioner McKenzie, once again, urged the union to lift the black bans it had placed on various properties and implored the LGPA to avoid any 'further actions which stir up this emotive issue'. About 12.30 p.m., he adjourned the matter to a date to be fixed.

19

The Sunbeam Ban

As 1981 was drawing to a close, the AWU was becoming increasingly frustrated at the continued and steadily growing use of wide combs, and the escalation of its dispute with the key farmer groups. Despite adopting tactics such as black-banning multiple properties, organising several shearing strikes including a week-long national strike at the end of November, and steadfastly refusing to be involved in commercial-scale trials, the wide combs issue was not going away. And every time the union tried to douse the issue, it seemed to flare up and spread. There had now been roughly 18 months of bickering and tension in the pastoral industry – ostensibly over three steel teeth on a shearing comb. As both sides dug in, the stakes became greater. The prospect of losing somehow became increasingly untenable.

And so, in an effort to swing the balance in favour of the union, many rank and file members began agitating for a black ban to be imposed on shearing equipment manufacturer, Sunbeam Corporation. In the lead-up to the 1982 AWU Annual Convention, scheduled for late January, local pastoral committees from all over Australia were invited to put forward motions for debate. Several committees, including Kingoonya and Port Augusta in South Australia and Penshurst and Beaufort in Victoria, drafted motions calling for a boycott of Sunbeam-made combs and cutters. The most radical motion came from the Penshurst committee, which advocated not just a ban on Sunbeam's shearing equipment, but 'a total ban on the purchase of all Sunbeam products, including all those products not associated with the pastoral industry'. The committee also called for '…a list comprising the various products produced by this unscrupulous company [to] be circulated to all AWU members, including those members not associated with the pastoral industry'. As explained below, Sunbeam made much more than just shearing equipment. A ban on its shearing combs would make it more difficult for rebel shearers to acquire the outlawed gear and potentially limit the spread of wide combs within the industry. Any broader ban would place commercial pressure on Sunbeam to try to exert greater control over its offshore distribution networks, to try to ensure wide combs were not exported back into Australia.

Sunbeam success

At the time of the dispute, Sunbeam was the largest manufacturer of shearing combs and cutters in the world. But it was best known in Australia as the maker of kitchen appliances such as toasters, kettles and Mixmasters, as well as the famed Victa lawnmower. The company operated out of a large factory in Campsie, in Sydney's inner south-west. The site once was host to Mackinders Market Garden, a family run business that grew potatoes, beetroots, carrots, pumpkins and squashes for more than 40 years until 1951, when it was sold to the Sunbeam Corporation. Sunbeam immediately went about establishing electrical goods and shearing equipment factories on the site. At the time of the wide comb dispute, Sunbeam had manufactured more than one million handpieces and hundreds of millions of combs and cutters. It had also been at the forefront of most of the major innovations in shearing technology throughout the world.

The general manager of the company's rural division was John Allan, who was well known in the pastoral industry as a former champion shearer. He went on to become one of the legends of Australia's pastoral industry – in 1988 he received a Medal of the Order of Australia (OAM) for his services to the Australian wool and shearing industries and in 2009 he was inducted into the Australian Shearers'

Hall of Fame, which is based at the Shear Outback museum in Hay in the New South Wales Riverina. As a youngster, Allan bred and sold mice for a shilling each to help support his family. He had a love of horses and became a jockey before he moved into shearing when he was 19. He broke numerous records, won dozens of competitions, and took part in shearing events all over the world. At the time of the dispute, he was the only non-New Zealander to have won the prestigious New Zealand Golden Shears Competition. As well as shearing sheep, he had also had experience shearing alpacas in Chile, Patagonia and Peru. Allan eventually became involved in the product development side of shearing and had stints with the three major combs manufacturers of that time – Lister, Sunbeam and Heiniger. During his time with Sunbeam, in the early 1980s, he helped increase the company's export business by more than 50 per cent. Given his experience and expertise in shearing as well as comb and cutter design, Allan was to become a key witness in the wide combs industrial case.

Ban implemented

When the Sunbeam ban motions came up for debate at the AWU Annual Convention, delegates were undecided and voted to ask the union's Executive Council to make a decision on the matter. During a separate debate, delegates resolved to support a single-day national shearers' strike on 25 February to protest against wide combs. However, less than a month after the convention, on 21 February 1982, 260 shearers meeting in Dubbo were more forthright – they passed their own resolution on the Sunbeam matter, calling for an immediate ban. The resolution read,

> We call on all good unionists employed in the pastoral industry throughout Australia to gradually phase out the use of all Sunbeam products by the following method: (A) Where all combs and cutters are worn out which are presently in use that they purchase combs and cutters which are manufactured by companies other than Sunbeam; (B) When employees can, that

they advise graziers or contractors when purchasing new handpieces that they should insist that Lister handpieces be purchased. That this resolution take effect immediately and that the resolution be forwarded to all Branch Secretaries and published in *The Worker*.[130]

Not surprisingly, Sunbeam was miffed. It seemed it was being singled out for being the dominant producer in the industry, but also because Robert White's testimony in the Arbitration Commission had given prominence to Sunbeam gear. White had made it clear that he used Sunbeam combs exclusively and during his 'showground hearings testimony' he said Sunbeam manufactured wide combs that had greatly improved over the years and since August 1981 they had become perfectly suited to shearing merino sheep 'straight from the factory, out of the box'. He said, 'Now they have produced a comb called a Hustler and Fine Wool, and they are called a long bevel. They are designed to shear merino sheep. I have used them and anyone I have got them for, they have used them and they have no complaints whatsoever.'[131]

An interesting point that few people picked up on at the time was that most of the workers involved in the production of shearing equipment at Sunbeam (as well as Lister and Heiniger) were members of the AWU. In effect, the union was imposing a ban on a company that employed its own members.

Shearing executives give evidence

Meanwhile, as the union's ban on Sunbeam was starting to have an impact, the Arbitration Commission hearings were continuing. John Allan and his counterpart from R.A. Lister Australia Pty Ltd, David Nankervis, were summoned to appear before the commission in late April 1982 to give evidence on behalf of the LGPA and NFF. Unlike Allan, Nankervis did not have a background in shearing. He had been employed as the company's division manager (agriculture) for five years. Depending on seasonal conditions and demand, Lister employed 80 to 100 people at its plant in Marigold Street, Revesby, roughly 10 kilometres west of Sunbeam's factory. Lister's operations differed from Sunbeam's in that the Revesby plant was merely a 'finishing' plant – the company imported 'blank' combs and cutters from its headquarters at Dursley in Gloucestershire, England. The blanks were then ground, polished and packaged at the Revesby plant, ready for distribution in Australia and overseas. Sunbeam's process, on the other hand, included the local manufacture of the blank combs and cutters.

Nankervis, during his testimony, said Lister exported both narrow and wide combs to the United States, South America and some Middle Eastern countries. He said the bulk of the export orders were for wide combs and, as far as he was aware, none of the countries into which Lister exported imposed width restrictions on shearing combs. When asked about the suitability of wide combs for use in Australia, Nankervis replied, 'I would say there are certainly some sheep in Australia that could be shorn with wide equipment.' But when pressed, he conceded that, given his lack of industry experience, 'Crossbred sheep have been shorn in Australia with wide gear. I would not know whether all the merino sheep in Australia could be shorn with wide gear. I do not think anybody can answer that question.'

John Allan tried to answer it when he gave evidence. After outlining his background and explaining details of Sunbeam's export operations, he spoke about the suitability of various Sunbeam wide combs to shear Australian merino sheep. Allan said he believed the company's Topflight comb was unsuitable for merinos but that it could be modified to make it suitable, the Fine Wool combs were of doubtful quality for merinos, but the Hustler combs were satisfactory. He said all the company's wide combs had been developed for the New Zealand, Argentinian and South African markets, as the Award restriction in Australia meant it could not effectively develop and test products specifically for Australian merinos. Later, when handing down his decision in the dispute, Commissioner McKenzie recognised that he could give added weight to Allan's testimony because of his standing in the industry.

On 2 May 1982, just days after testifying before the commission, Allan wrote a memo to all staff in Sunbeam's rural division, updating them on the AWU-imposed ban on the company. He told them the union was convinced Sunbeam was selling wide gear in Australia and reassured them that this was not the case. 'Sunbeam has not and does not sell or distribute wide combs and cutters in Australia. Sunbeam will not sell or distribute wide combs and cutters in Australia while their use contravenes the Federal Pastoral Award,' he said.

> Sunbeam's New Zealand distributor has not and will not re-export wide combs and cutters to Australia, as their distribution agreement with Sunbeam prohibits their selling Sunbeam equipment in Australia. We believe that any wide combs and cutters entering Australia are being supplied from New Zealand by independent resellers, over whom neither ourselves nor our New Zealand distributor have any control. These independent New Zealand resellers are supplying against orders received directly from wool growers and shearers, but mainly from shearers, in Australia, all of whom we believe to be AWU members. The same situation applies to wide combs and cutters available in New Zealand from our major competitor.[132]

Allan said Sunbeam's position had remained unchanged since it had first started manufacturing in Australia more than 50 years previously. He said he was planning to meet with the AWU to try to have the ban overturned.

Dealing with the union

Two days later, Allan wrote to AWU federal secretary Frank Mitchell, demanding that the union lift the ban. He said Sunbeam had previously assured the union that it had not and would not distribute wide comb gear in Australia 'until such time as the use of these combs no longer contravenes the Pastoral Industrial Award'. He told Mitchell that during his testimony before the Arbitration Commission the previous week, he had explained that Sunbeam had recently contacted its New Zealand distributor and some New Zealand resellers. He testified that the distributor had reassured Sunbeam that it would not fill any orders from Australia, however, he said the resellers had refused to provide a similar pledge. There was nothing Sunbeam could do to challenge this position, he said. However, he also explained that other shearing equipment manufacturers in Australia were in the same position as Sunbeam – they could not exercise any commercial control over New Zealand resellers – and both Lister and Heiniger wide gear was also being ordered from resellers in New Zealand. The orders were coming mainly from AWU members in Australia, he said. 'It is the company's view that in these circumstances there is no valid basis for the union's ban or its continuation,' Allan wrote to Mitchell.

> Sunbeam has given the appropriate assurances, that it does not distribute wide combs in Australia and it has taken all steps the union could reasonably expect of it… The company has no control over the importation of wide combs into Australia from New Zealand or elsewhere… In these circumstances the company feels that the union's ban on its equipment is unfounded, unjustified, unfair and discriminatory and should be lifted immediately… The company now calls on your union to take effective steps as a matter of urgency to ensure that the union's ban on Sunbeam equipment is lifted immediately. The company reserves its right to consider its position if the ban is not lifted in the near future.[133]

Upon receiving the letter, Mitchell contacted Ernie Ecob and asked him to handle the matter. Ecob phoned Allan the following day, Wednesday 5 May 1982, and asked him to 'put in writing the relevant facts regarding the union-imposed black ban on Sunbeam shearing gear'. It was obviously a stalling tactic, as Ecob knew very well the full details of the ban – he had been involved in the discussions that resulted in the ban. Nevertheless, Allan wrote to Ecob, on 10 May, outlining all the information requested. Allan also stated that the actions of AWU organisers in visiting sheds and advising shearers, shearing contractors and shed owners not to purchase Sunbeam equipment had already resulted in a significant loss in shearing equipment sales revenue for the company. He said the union had ample evidence that wide combs made by the other manufacturers were freely available and were being used – making the ban on Sunbeam discriminatory. He demanded Sunbeam's case be brought before the union's Executive Council with a recommendation that the ban be discontinued. Allan sent copies of all correspondence relating to the ban to the Arbitration Commission. As such, it became an exhibit and part of the evidence of the industrial case. As it turned out, it took another six months before the ban was lifted. And once again it was union delegates meeting in Dubbo, rather than officials from the Executive Council, who led the way. A report to the meeting of AWU pastoral workers on 31 October 1982 noted that the ban was having an impact on jobs at the Sunbeam plant – meaning the union's own members were being put out of work. To try to make up for this own goal, members quietly passed a motion, 'That bans be lifted on Sunbeam gear in New South Wales.'[134] Having been forced into an embarrassing backdown, the union recorded nothing else in the minutes about the issue.

20

Shed Inspections Begin

In mid-December 1981, just weeks after the showground hearings ended, the Arbitration Commission notified the parties to the dispute that it intended holding a series of shearing shed inspections beginning early in the new year. Commissioner McKenzie wanted to hear what shearers and wool growers from representative properties all over Australia had to say about the relative merits of different gauge shearing combs. Commission staff had to organise and coordinate flights, accommodation, and hire cars for the commissioner and his support staff as each new inspection was confirmed. It was a significant administrative and logistical exercise to transport a small group of city-based office workers to remote venues all over Australia, together with the equipment they needed to do their jobs. The shed inspections were crammed into a hectic 10-week schedule beginning in mid-January 1982. However, associated hearings continued in the commission until early June, when the case was finally adjourned. Proceedings during the first half of 1982 were to place an enormous strain on the commission's resources, the staff involved in the case, and the legal teams representing the parties to the dispute.

Outback evidence

Properties from South Australia (Erudina Station and Commonwealth Hill), Tasmania (Frodsley Station), Victoria (Ennerdale Station) and Western Australia (Waitemata, Fermoy, Snaigow, and Talerno) ended up hosting inspections. As well, supplemental hearings were held in the capital cities of each of these states preceding the local shed inspections. In all, 83 witnesses were called to give evidence during this phase of the industrial case.

The hearings began in Adelaide on Tuesday 12 January 1982 at the Arbitration Commission's offices in Grenfell Street. One of the key AWU witnesses during these sittings was John Hutchinson, a champion shearer who became the first inductee into the Shear Outback Shearers' Hall of Fame in Hay. Hutchinson was a third-generation shearer who at the time was a six-time Australian Open Shearing Champion. He had 24 years' experience as a shearer and had won the prestigious Australia Shearer of the Year titles in 1975 and 1976, as well as numerous state titles, and had represented Australia in several overseas competitions. In 1990, Hutchinson was awarded a Medal of the Order of Australia (OAM) in recognition of his contribution to the Australian wool industry. Hutchinson also ran a grazing property in South Australia and was a member of both the AWU and the United Farmers and Stockowners of South Australia, an industry body representing the interests of the state's farmers and wool growers. He was, by any measure, an impressive witness.

Hutchinson testified that he had shorn most types of sheep from around the world and although he had used wide combs in New Zealand, he believed narrow combs were the most practical combs for shearing merino sheep and that when used correctly they did a much better job than wide combs. Hutchinson said wide combs were harder to push and the small increase in tallies, which he estimated would be only eight to 10 sheep per day, was not sufficient to justify the damage wide combs would do to the fleece. When cross-examined by Paul Houlihan, Hutchinson said that when he used wide combs in New Zealand he could not eliminate second cuts and he believed the average shearer would have the same problem. He said he had carefully assessed the relative merits of both gauge combs and had decided in favour of narrow gear. He believed the introduction of wide combs would also lead to a large influx of New Zealand shearers and a consequent reduction in work for Australian shearers.

Next to give evidence for the union was Stephen Pittaway, another outstanding shearer from South Australia. Pittaway was an extremely successful show shearer – he had won the Victorian Open Championship and South Australian Open Championship multiple times, the Australian Open Championship several times, and had been named Australian Shearer of the Year in 1977. He had represented Australia in several international competitions. In 2009, he was posthumously inducted into the Shear Outback Shearers' Hall of Fame. Pittaway had heard the evidence of Hutchinson and said he agreed with just about everything the earlier witness had said. He said he too had worked in New Zealand using wide combs and he believed them to be unsuitable for shearing Australia's predominantly merino flock. He said wide combs would cause increased problems with ridging and second cuts, as well as employment chaos if New Zealander shearers were to be given a greater incentive to work in Australia.

Allan Begg also testified for the union. Begg, from Henley Beach in Adelaide, was secretary of the South Australian branch of the AWU as well as president of the federal branch of the AWU. He started his working life as a shed hand at Brewarrina in north-west New South Wales in 1937 and went on to become a shearer. During his 20-year shearing career, he gradually became more involved in the union. In 1964, he was employed as a full-time organiser for the AWU's South Australian branch, working in the Whyalla and Port Augusta areas. In 1971, he continued his organising role from Adelaide, before becoming the state branch secretary in 1975. Begg told the commission there were about 1,800 shearers in South Australia, 90 per cent of whom were members of the union. He said in 1980, the emerging issue of wide combs had prompted meetings of shearers in Adelaide, Broken Hill, Hallett, Naracoorte and Port Augusta. Shearers at those meetings had resolved overwhelmingly to continue the wide combs prohibition, he said. Begg had travelled to New Zealand in 1979 to meet officials from the AWU's local counterpart, the New Zealand Workers' Union, which represented shearers across the Tasman. He said he received varying reports on the effectiveness of wide combs and held grave fears for job opportunities, harmony in shearing sheds and the quality of shearing if wide combs were legalised. During cross-examination, he said if the wide gear ban were lifted there would almost certainly be immediate disruption in the industry and given the strength of opposition to wide combs it was unlikely the union would be able to control the reaction of its members.

Several other witnesses gave evidence during the Adelaide sittings. Then, on Thursday 14 January, the commission and its entourage boarded a charter plane and flew one hour and 40 minutes north of Adelaide to Yunta. From there they drove about 120 kilometres further north to Erudina Station, which sprawled across 1,500 square kilometres and bordered the eastern slopes of the Flinders Ranges. Erudina was owned by John and Sue McEntee and had been in their family for 60 years. John McEntee, like many remote-living outback folk, was a colourful character and accomplished landholder. He made his own musical instruments and had a passion for baroque piano music, which he played by ear. He also spoke several Aboriginal dialects and had written extensively about Aboriginal history and culture in the region. The commission heard evidence from the station manager, Frank Guildford, as well as six shearers employed at Erudina through the shearing contractors, L&M Saunders. However, the evidence was unremarkable – the shearers were all narrow comb users and supporters and the contractor favoured retaining narrow gear as a means of ensuring uniformity in the industry.

The Tasmanian and Victorian hearings

In early February, the commission travelled to Tasmania, which at the time was home to 420,000 people and 10 times as many sheep. About 80 per cent of the sheep were merino Polwarths, a fine wool variety bred in Victoria during colonial times. The remainder of the flock comprised mostly Corriedale, Cormo and Dorset varieties. When the shed inspection hearings resumed in Hobart on Wednesday 3 February, the union called Kevin Nye to testify. Nye was a shearer with more than 20 years' experience and a union stalwart who used only narrow gear. He gave evidence that wide combs had been steadily creeping into Tasmania during recent years and were becoming a concern. Following his evidence, the commission travelled to Frodsley Station, a large wool growing property near Fingal in the state's north-east, where it took evidence from three shearers and the property's owner, James Brodribb.

That evening the commission flew to Melbourne, where hearings resumed the following morning. Several witnesses were called, including David James 'Daffy' Ryan, who was arguably the best shearer in Australia at the time. Ryan, who testified for the union, had been shearing since he was 14 and had almost 20 years' experience in sheds all over Australia. He held the world record for the number of merino lambs shorn in one day (501). Few shearers could boast an average daily tally greater than 300, but Ryan was one of them. He said that he had used wide combs while shearing in New Zealand and believed they were totally unsuitable for shearing merino sheep. He said they would be harder to push through the fleece of merino sheep but conceded they could probably be used effectively on some other types of sheep. Ryan also predicted problems with second cuts and ridging using wide combs and suggested there would be friction in the industry between shearers using different gauge combs.

Humorous moments were elusive during the hearings, which were generally dour and often intense. However, Paul Houlihan later recalled one light-hearted moment that occurred during Ryan's testimony in Melbourne. 'The top shearer at the time was David 'Daffy' Ryan,' he said. 'The union put him in the witness box: "Mr Ryan you've shorn 412 sheep in four two-hour runs using narrow combs?" He said, "Yes." The Commissioner was just eating out of his hands. I am not a great cross-examiner, but the best day's work I ever did was that day on Daffy Ryan. Eventually, after about two hours [of testimony], I got up and said: "Now, Mr Ryan you say you've shorn 412 sheep in four two-hour runs. Is that right?" he said, "Yes." I said, "Mr Ryan, to your knowledge, how many other Australian shearers have shorn that many?" He said, "How many?

None." So I said, "You are totally unrepresentative of Australian shearers." I said nothing more and sat down.' Despite this exchange, Houlihan had great admiration for Ryan, who ended up working as an instructor for the large contract shearing business, National Grazing Services, for whom Houlihan was a long-time director. He recalled of Ryan, 'He had the slowest hands as a shearer; it was like watching Greg Chappell bat. He could shear sheep all day and not raise a sweat. The sheep virtually lay there for him. The really good shearers have slow hands.'

Other witnesses to testify for the union included William O'Connor, a shearing contractor who had been involved in the industry for 26 years, and Don MacIntosh, a former shed hand and shearer who had notched up 50 years of membership of the AWU and at one stage was the union's Victorian branch secretary. Both were wary of wide combs, believing their legalisation would be a backward step for the industry. O'Connor, who had also worked as a regional shearing instructor for the Australian Wool Corporation, said shearers would find it difficult to adapt to wide gear and there would be a resultant decrease in the quality of shearing. He said he had witnessed a reduced standard of workmanship in Western Australian sheds where wide combs had been used.

The following day, Friday 5 February, the commission travelled two hours west of Melbourne to inspect Ennerdale Station, near Darlington, a property that had been owned by the Luckock family since the early 1930s. Several shearers gave evidence, with their testimony reflecting the union's general views towards wide combs.

The first three shed inspections and associated hearings had run fairly smoothly. However, the next leg of the inspections, in South Australia and Western Australia, was to be particularly testing. Tensions between the union and farmer groups boiled over, resulting in the union boycotting one inspection and taking legal action against a shearer involved in another inspection. As well, the intense workload for the legal teams involved in the case took its toll on Paul Houlihan, who became extremely ill and was hospitalised. Just about everyone who was closely involved in the dispute was starting to feel the strain.

21

Commonwealth Hill and Snaigow Stations

Commonwealth Hill Station in the remote north-west of South Australia was earmarked for the fourth of the eight shed inspections that the commission was organising. At the time, it was the largest sheep station in Australia, spanning more than a million hectares of flat, sandy plain country (that's 10,000 square kilometres – about one-seventh the size of Tasmania). It had a flock of 75,000 merinos. Because of its proximity to the Woomera rocket range, the station had a blast-proof concrete shelter installed, courtesy of the Commonwealth government, to help protect the owners, their staff and families from flying debris from the odd, wayward blast during the rocket-testing program. The government installed 48 such shelters on properties adjacent to Woomera during the late 1950s. The protocol was that Woomera staff would telephone each station three times in the lead-up to a test to give residents time to take shelter, with the final call 15 minutes before launch. While many residents initially complied, eventually most ignored the warnings and went about their business. Indeed, rather than congregate inside the sandbag-lined shelters, some residents climbed on top of them to watch the rocket and missile pyrotechnics.

Union boycott and other dramas

A prominent South Australian family, the MacLachlans, had owned Commonwealth Hill Station since 1888. The family ran several other sheep stations through the Jumbuck Pastoral Company and were among the largest private landholders in Australia. At the time of the wide comb dispute, Hugh MacLachlan was the third-generation manager of the company. The commission had been scheduled to visit Commonwealth Hill during the week after the Victorian inspection. However, the schedule was inconvenient for some of the AWU officials who were to be involved, so the inspection was postponed until Wednesday 17 February. In the meantime, the union discovered that one of the inspections being organised in Western Australia involved a wide comb shed. This sparked outrage and the union announced it was boycotting the Commonwealth Hill inspection in protest.

This was not the only glitch relating to the inspection at Commonwealth Hill. The station had two shearing sheds about 35 kilometres apart, with the main shed 70 kilometres from the homestead. In 1982, separate contractors were engaged in mid-January to operate at the two sheds. Laurie Polomka, a 31-year-old shearer from Lucindale in South Australia, ran a team in the main shed, and Neil Ellery, a 35-year-old former provincial wrestling champion from New Zealand, had a team shearing in the other shed. Ellery had worked extensively in Western Australia, was vehemently anti-union and was to become more prominent later on in the dispute (see chapter 29). Polomka's team started work on 10 January and for the next two weeks the temperature barely dropped below 40 degrees. This was the first significant contract for Polomka's shearing business. His shearers, who had an average age of 23, were using a combination of narrow combs, pulled (standard) combs and wide combs, while Ellery's team was using wide combs exclusively.

With the Arbitration Commission inspection imminent, the union's South Australian branch became aware that wide combs were being used at the station and complained to Marcus Moore, the station manager. Moore was not overly concerned – he simply warned both contractors to make sure they were not caught using wide gear. However, during a union inspection a few days later, Ellery's team was caught using wide combs and was sacked, leaving Polomka's team to shear roughly 70,000 sheep and to front the commission's inspection.

Polomka recalled Ellery and his team being 'fairly flippant' when it came to wide combs because they had been used to using them with impunity in Western Australia. 'He was the sort of bloke too who would have simply told the [union] organiser to piss off,' he said.

The inspection party, minus union representatives, flew from Adelaide to Commonwealth Hill as planned on 17 February. Like many large outback stations, Commonwealth Hill had a landing strip. Included in the party was Ian McLachlan, who had been subpoenaed to give evidence on behalf of the Wool Council of Australia. Marcus Moore testified that a combination of narrow gear, pulled standard gear and wide gear was being used to shear the station's flock and that the quality of the shearing, for each of the different types of combs, was good. Laurie Polomka told the commission that most of the 40 shearers he employed through his contracting business wanted to use wide gear because they believed it was easier to work with than narrow gear. He believed shearers should be able to use whatever type of gear they wanted to, as long as it was approved by the employer. Each of Polomka's eight team members gave evidence. Most of the shearers said they preferred to use wide combs. However, one member, Peter Hollenberg, said he favoured standard gauge combs. Hollenberg, a former wool classer who had been shearing for three years, said he was concerned about a potential increase in second cuts with wide gear. He also worried there would be too many New Zealand shearers working in Australia if wide combs were legalised.

Ian McLachlan, who was the Wool Council's chairman, said he had observed the shearing that had been performed earlier that day as part of the inspection. He said the quality of the work, which had been carried out mostly with wide combs, had been perfectly adequate. McLachlan said it was apparent that the use of wide combs was growing and he believed wide gear would not in any way compromise fleece quality.

Mid-flight medical emergency

Although the day's formal proceedings had been completed, the dramas that beset this inspection were not over yet. Late that afternoon, members of the inspection party boarded their aircraft, a twin-engine Beechcraft King Air, and departed for Adelaide. The flight went smoothly until the aircraft was approaching Whyalla on the western side of the Spencer Gulf, about 120 kilometres north-west of Adelaide. Paul Houlihan, who was sitting next to Ian McLachlan, had been feeling progressively unwell during the flight. Suddenly he realised he could not talk and knew there was something terribly wrong. He found himself desperately pointing out the window at Whyalla below, in a futile bid to indicate he wanted the plane to land so he could get to a hospital. McLachlan, understandably, did not catch on. He casually looked down to where his friend was pointing and said, 'Yeah, that's Whyalla.' As the aircraft crossed the Spencer Gulf, Houlihan's condition deteriorated. Frustratingly, he could not alert his fellow passengers.

Eventually, Commissioner McKenzie's associate, who had once been a registered nurse, realised Houlihan was seriously ill and there was a medical emergency underway. The pilot radioed the control tower at Adelaide airport and organised for an ambulance to be on hand when the aircraft landed. Houlihan was taken directly to the Royal Adelaide Hospital, where he was diagnosed with pneumothorax – a collapsed lung, a condition caused by air leaking into the area between the lungs and the chest wall. His wife, Mary, flew from Sydney to join him as he recuperated. He spent the next five days in hospital, followed by three or four days convalescing at Ian McLachlan's Adelaide house, before returning to Sydney for more rest. It was five to six weeks before he was able to return to work.

Houlihan said he had no doubt this health scare was the result of months of stress related to the wide combs case. 'I was a heavy smoker back then and I went out to Commonwealth Hill with what I thought was just a cold,' he said. 'However, I was run down. I had been for weeks. I was on the verge of exhaustion.' The case had become all-consuming; he had been regularly working into the early hours of the morning and then getting up before dawn to start again.

Western Australian hearings

The final four shed inspections were scheduled for Western Australia. They were to be bookended by hearings at the Arbitration Commission in Perth, beginning during the week following the Commonwealth Hill inspection.

One of the first people to testify during the Perth hearings was Peter John Lee, who gave evidence on behalf of the Farmers' Union of Western Australia. (The Farmers' Union changed its name during 1982 to the Primary Industry Association, in part to distance itself from the trade union movement.) The Farmers' Union was opposing the AWU's bid to have the shearing comb width restriction extended to the west. Lee ran a small flock of 2,000 sheep on 1,800 hectares at Kulin, in the state's eastern wheat belt, about 400 kilometres from Perth. He was also involved in agri-politics, serving on the executive of the Wool Council of the Farmers' Union, for whom he was also a vice-president. He said the shearers employed by the contractor he engaged to shear his flock were using wide combs, while in the past he had had shearers using pulled standard combs. Lee said he as the owner did not dictate to his contractor what combs had to be used but rather it was a process of negotiation. He said second cuts were associated with the skill of the shearer rather than the tools used by the shearer. Ridging was more related to pulled narrow combs than wide combs, he said. Lee said he had not encountered any industrial issues relating to wide combs. However, this was most likely because wide combs were not a contentious issue in the west. During cross-examination. Lee conceded that some farmers in the state did not allow wide combs to be used to shear their flock.

Arthur Crane also testified for the Farmers' Union. Crane operated a wool growing enterprise at Jerdacuttup, 600 kilometres south-east of Perth, in the Esperance region. Crane ran 4,500 merino sheep and a cropping enterprise and employed his shearers directly, rather than through a contractor. He had some 20 years of experience shearing before focusing on his farm business. He gave evidence that during the past three or four years, the shearers he engaged used a variety of shearing equipment, including narrow gauge, pulled standard combs and wide combs obtained from New Zealand. He said there had been no disharmony in the shed because of the mix of gear. Crane said that if the width restriction clause applied to Western Australia, shearers would simply ignore it. (Members of the Pastoralist and Graziers' Association had to observe Clause 32 of the Award, but members of the Farmers' Union did not.) He said the issue of combs use was a matter between employer and employees and he could see no advantage in using narrow gear over wide gear. Crane also attributed fleece damage during shearing to the skill of the shearer rather than the equipment being used.

Several other witnesses appeared on behalf of the Farmers' Union, including Colin James Barnett, who went on to become Western Australia's 29th premier from 2008 to 2016. At the time, Barnett was a lecturer in economics at the then Western Australian Institute of Technology (now Curtin University of Technology). The most significant aspect of his evidence related to a survey that assessed the standard of the shearing in the state, based on the incidence of skin cuts. Barnett said the results showed the percentage of skin cuts in Western Australia was below the Australian average – this was significant because most of the state's flock was shorn with wide combs.

The commission went back on the road during the last week of February, carrying out its fifth inspection at Waitemata, an 11,000-hectare property near Wandering, about 100 kilometres south-east of Perth. Evidence was heard from wide comb and pulled standard comb shearers.

In the following days, the inspection party visited three more properties, beginning with Fermoy, a station at Broomehill in the state's south, where the shearers were using narrow gear. A key witness here was John Edge, who had been a shearing contractor for 29 years. He told the commission that although he thought wide combs were suitable for shearing some types of sheep, he did not believe they were appropriate for merinos. He said they tended to leave trimmings on the legs of merinos and were 'hopeless' when it came to smaller merinos. Edge said he believed there had been a significant decrease in the quality of shearing in Western Australia during recent years, something he attributed to the influx of New Zealand shearers and the prevalence of wide combs in the industry.

Snaigow Station

Next, on 25 February, the commission travelled north to Williams, a two-hour drive south-east of Perth, to inspect the shearing shed at Snaigow Station. Snaigow was owned by Charles Gerald John Cadogan, better known as Earl Cadogan, a British peer and landowner. The earl, whose family married into wealth in the 18th century, owned a sizeable chunk of Chelsea, a swish part of London. At the time of the inspection he was chairman of the Chelsea Football Club. His 5,000-hectare Western Australian property, which he bought in 1969, was named after his estate in Perthshire, Scotland. During the early 1980s, Snaigow ran a merino flock of 13,500 (half ewes, half wethers), with shearing normally starting during the second week of February.

The station's manager, David Lawrie, told the commission there was a mix of wide and narrow comb shearers working at Snaigow, although most were wide comb users. He said there had been no tensions or blues in the shed because of shearers using different gauge combs. Several members of the contracted shearing team also gave evidence. William Spencer, who had been a shearer for 18 years, said he had been using wide combs for the last two years and found them to be superior to narrow combs. Rod Balgrove said he had learnt to shear 12 years ago in New Zealand and although he had used all types of combs, he found wide combs the easiest to use. Peter Challenor, who had been wool classing for five years, said he found there was no difference in the quality of the fleece cut by wide and narrow combs.

Prosecution backfires

One of the most interesting aspects of the Snaigow inspection, however, went largely unnoticed. Upon the inspection party arriving at a shed, Commissioner McKenzie's usual practice was to begin proceedings by suspending Clause 32 of the Award (the width restriction clause). From the participants' perspective, this was like being given an insurance policy protecting them against any potential prosecutions for breaching the Award while taking part in the inspection. The need for such an order was debatable – at the time, the AWU was still fighting to have the reach of Clause 32 extended to Western Australia, where not all farmer organisations were respondents to the Award. However, irrespective of the relevance of the suspension order, there was a question mark over whether one was actually issued that day. The significance of this only became apparent much later.

While Paul Houlihan was recuperating, Patrick Gethin, the industrial director of the Farmers' Union, represented the NFF and LGPA during the Western Australian proceedings. Gil Barr, the AWU's Western Australian branch secretary, represented the union. Barr later said no suspension order was issued in his presence. When he entered the Snaigow shearing shed that morning, he quickly became incensed. The union only had about 250 pastoral industry members in the whole state in the early 1980s, and three of them were there, and they were shearing with wide combs. Barr was so miffed, he consulted with the state branch executive and later issued a notice to each of the three shearers charging them with breaching AWU Rule 123, which stated, 'No member shall use a broad-gauge comb and cutter. Members violating this rule shall be fined forty dollars ($40). The meaning of broad-gauge comb shall be any comb exceeding 2½ inches from the outside of the top tooth to the outside of the bottom tooth.' One of the trio charged was Ray Lawrence, who had been a member of the AWU for some 40 years. Lawrence, like his two colleagues, was normally a narrow comb user. However, he had been asked by his employer, the shearing contractor, to use wide combs for that day so the commission could witness them being used during the inspection. Lawrence was assured by the contractor that there would be no repercussions for him for using wide combs that day. However, on 30 July 1982, Barr wrote to Lawrence notifying him he had been charged with breaching Rule 123 for using wide combs during the Snaigow inspection. He was invited to appear before the state branch executive on 21 September 'to show cause…why you should not be fined'. Lawrence sought an adjournment. However, members of the executive dealt with the matter in his absence – he was found guilty and fined $40. Although the fine was meagre, Lawrence was not impressed. He had supported the union for four decades and had only used wide gear at Snaigow at the request of his employer and on the understanding that there would be no backlash. Lawrence refused to pay the fine and, with the support of the farmers' groups involved in the wide comb dispute, appealed against the decision. The matter was decided in the Federal Court of Australia's Industrial Division (Western Australia), with His Honour Mr Justice Toohey handing down his ruling on 18 February 1983.

Justice Toohey criticised the union for pursuing the prosecution in the first place. He said,

> …however laudable the union's desire to enforce its rules in general and the operation of Rule 123 in particular, to seize upon the use of the wide comb on an isolated occasion as part of an inspection by a Commissioner of the Conciliation and Arbitration Commission was a particularly unhappy choice.

He also criticised the process the union followed in prosecuting Lawrence, saying that the union's own rules required it to bring a charge via a statutory declaration setting out the facts, and this had not been done. However, the ruling did not turn on either of these two points. Rather, the issue came down to a legal technicality – essentially Justice Toohey found Rule 123 was contrary to the public interest and to the provisions of the pastoral award covering Western Australia. Although the union rule prohibited the use of wide combs, the award binding the Primary Industry Association of Western Australia had no such restriction. At the time, the extension of the restriction clause to Western Australia was still being considered as part of the union's roping-in application in the wide comb case. Lawrence won the appeal and the court voided Rule 123, meaning that the union could not prosecute and fine wide comb users in Western Australia. However, the application of the ruling did not extend beyond Western Australia – it was still illegal to use wide combs in other states. This situation did not last for long, however, as the issues involved in this case were soon to be superseded by a final ruling in the wide comb dispute.

The late shearing contractor Robert White, from Mandurama, takes a break while shearing in the Blayney district in March 1983 during the national shearers' strike. Robert was the key advocate for wide combs during the early 1980s. Former National Farmers' Federation industrial director Paul Houlihan said Robert's determination and courage in the face of hostile opposition from the Australian Workers' Union led to wide combs being introduced into the industry as much as a decade sooner than they otherwise might have been. (Photo: Peter Solness, used with permission.)

Former New South Wales Livestock and Grain Producers' Association industrial director Ian Manning, pictured in 1985. Ian was a key player in the dispute, even though he kept a relatively low profile. He helped prepare the industrial case supporting the introduction of wide combs and his meticulous approach to his work earned him widespread respect. (Photo: New South Wales Farmers' Association, used with permission.)

Shearing contractor Bruce Turton helped establish the Yass Shearing Committee during the national shearing strike in 1983. The committee aimed to ensure that the local pastoral industry could operate as smoothly as possible during the strike. (Photo: Mark Filmer.)

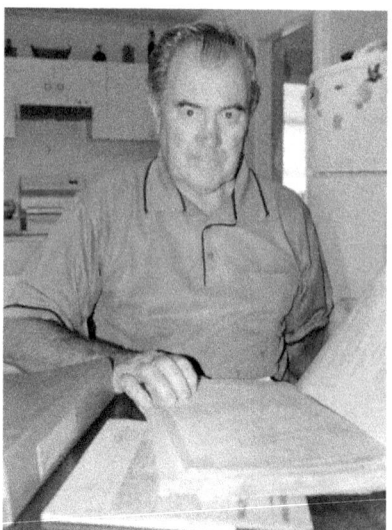

Former AWU organiser Peter White looks through union papers from the early 1980s. Peter fell out with his brother Robert, a shearing contractor from Mandurama, when Robert started advocating for the legalisation of wide combs. (Photo: Mark Filmer.)

Frank Myers first encountered wide shearing combs during a holiday in New Zealand with his wife Libby in 1978. While watching a shearing demonstration near Rotorua, he noticed the shearers were going unusually fast. He spoke to them after the show and discovered they were using wide combs. Intrigued, he brought some back to Australia and started using them. Without any extra effort, he increased his daily tallies by up to 40 sheep. (Photo: Mark Filmer.)

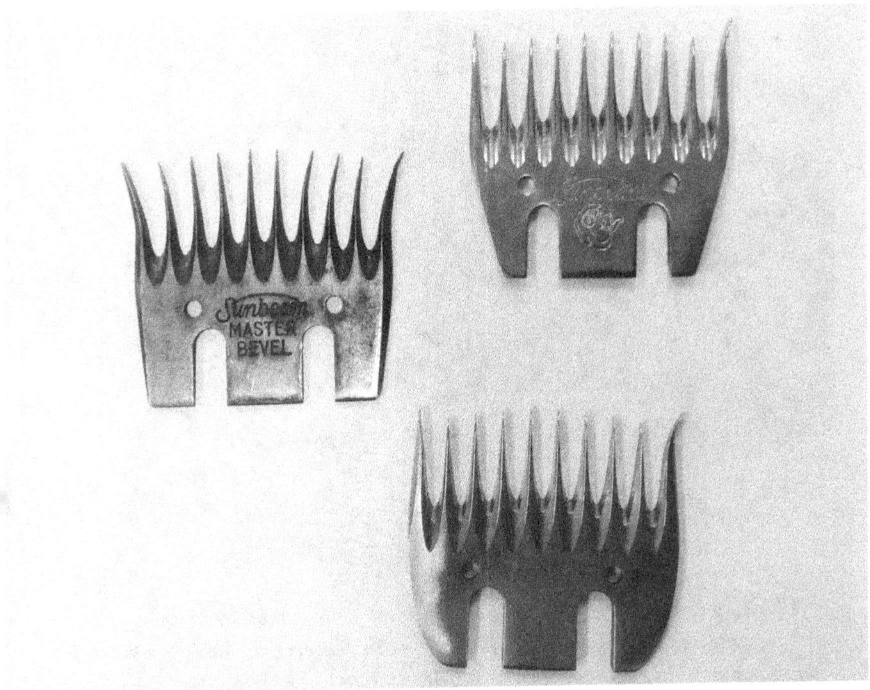

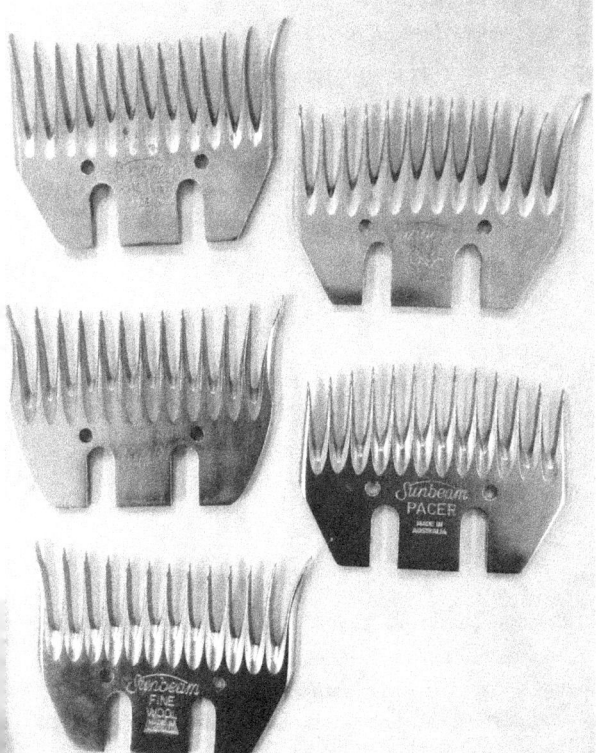

Above: These three narrow gauge combs (10 teeth) were used as exhibits in the Arbitration Commission industrial case.

Left: These five wide combs (13 teeth) were also used as exhibits in the industrial proceedings before the Arbitration Commission. Robert White told the commission in December 1981 that the latest iterations of Sunbeam's Hustler comb (top left) and Fine Wool comb (bottom left), which had been commercially available since August that year, were sufficiently well designed that they could be used 'out of the box', without any modifications. (Photos: Mark Filmer.)

Champion shearer Mel Johnston looks over some memorabilia. Mel was a strong unionist and strict narrow comb user. He did, however, use wide combs while competing in New Zealand. During the Arbitration Commission hearings, he testified that wide combs produced ridging on sheep, as well as more second cuts and skin cuts. (Photo: Mark Filmer.)

New Zealand born shearer Paul Woollaston used wide combs during the dispute and suffered for it. For me, he summed things up better than anyone: 'My argument was if they [wide combs] were no good, they would die a natural death. Who is going to use them?' (Photo: Mark Filmer.)

Allan and Betty Watt, Tenanbung, Cumnock. The wide comb dispute escalated dramatically following the alleged assault of AWU organiser 'Bluey' Rodwell during an inspection at Tenanbung in October 1980. Allan was adamant that there was nothing to the incident and no charges were laid. However, one shearer was caught using wide gear. (Photo: Mark Filmer.)

Shearing contractor Brian Clarke of Eaglehawk, Victoria. Brian played a key role in getting a motion supporting the implementation of wide comb trials passed during an AWU meeting in Bendigo in November 1981. The union was caught by surprise and embarrassed by the resolution. The decision was reversed a week later, and Brian subsequently became the target of a union smear campaign. (Photo: Mark Filmer.)

Shearers gather outside the Dubbo Civic Centre in Darling Street for an Australian Workers Union meeting on 1 June 1981. Two hundred and ninety shearers from all over New South Wales and interstate attended this meeting. The shearers passed a resolution pledging 'implacable hostile opposition' to wide combs. (Photo: Oliver Strewe, used with permission.)

Australian Workers' Union officials, from left, Charlie Oliver (NSW Branch President), Ernie Ecob (NSW Branch Secretary) and Laurie 'Bluey' Rodwell (NSW Branch Organiser) walk to the Dubbo Civic Centre for the 1 June 1981 meeting. Shearers passed several resolutions at this meeting reinforcing the union's fierce opposition to wide combs. (Photo: Oliver Strewe, used with permission.)

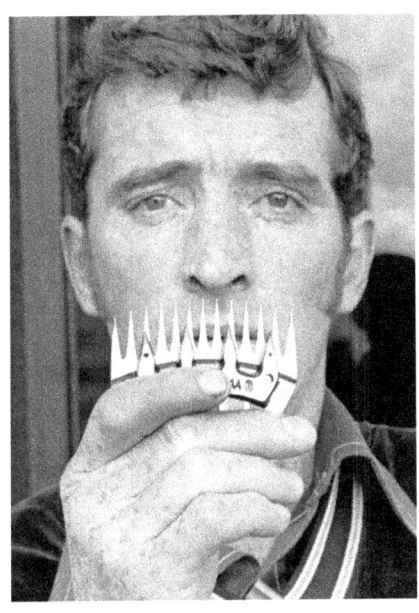

Young district shearer Peter Sheehan shows off a Sunbeam Pacer wide comb and four-pronged cutter outside the AWU's Dubbo meeting on 1 June 1981. Organiser Mick O'Shea asked Peter to purchase some wide gear and bring it to the meeting to demonstrate to members how readily available it was becoming. Peter purchased the comb and cutter through the post office store at Monteagle, between Young and Greenethorpe. (Photo: Oliver Strewe, used with permission.)

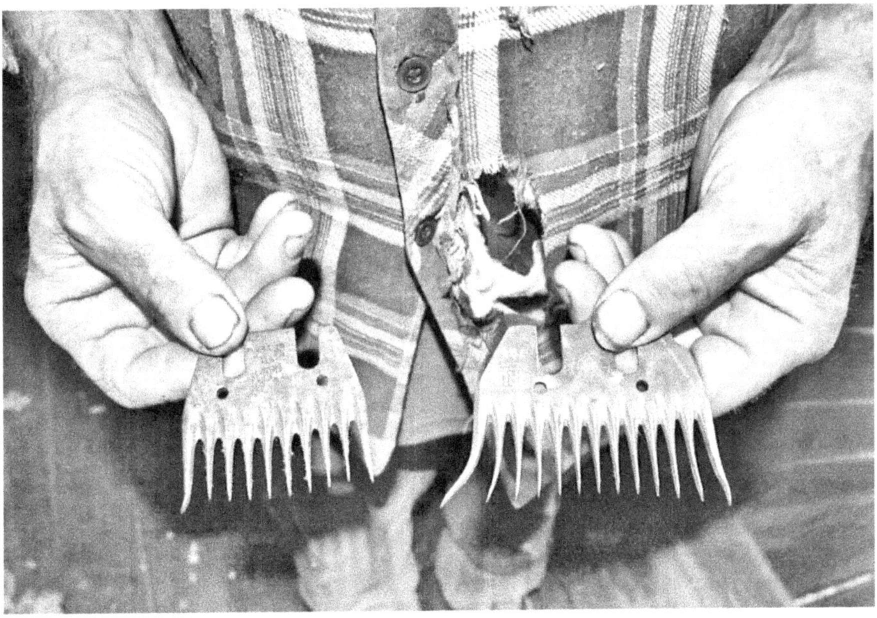

A shearer holds a narrow 10-tooth comb and a wide 13-tooth comb. Essentially the wide comb dispute was over three steel teeth on a shearing comb. Many union shearers condemned wide combs without ever having used them. Indeed, Commissioner Ian McKenzie, who presided over the wide comb industrial case, said a significant weakness in the AWU's industrial case was that many of the union's witnesses, who testified that wide combs were unsuitable for shearing merino sheep, had no experience in using wide combs. (Photo: Mark Filmer.)

Paul Houlihan, pictured in 1988, was the National Farmers' Federation industrial director during the dispute. In the Arbitration Commission proceedings, Paul was the key advocate for wide combs. (Photo: Noel Butlin Archives Centre, ANU, used with permission.)

Laurie 'Bluey' Rodwell addresses shearers at the union's 1 June 1981 meeting in Dubbo. Bluey was a long-time organiser who went on to become vice-president of the New South Wales branch of the union. (Photo: Oliver Strewe, used with permission.)

AWU New South Wales Branch President Charlie Oliver. The Welsh-born Oliver, pictured here in 1981, aged 80, dominated Labor Party politics in New South Wales for decades. Charlie, together with AWU New South Wales Branch Secretary Ernie Ecob, heavily influenced the union's approach to the wide comb shearing industrial dispute. (Photo: Oliver Strewe, used with permission.)

Former Prime Minister Bob Hawke, pictured here in the late 1970s, when he was President of the Australian Council of Trade Unions. Mr Hawke headed the ACTU for 10 years before being elected to Federal Parliament in 1980. He led the Labor Party to a landslide election victory in March 1983. Two weeks later, the AWU called a national shearers' strike when its appeal against the Arbitration Commission's decision to allow wide combs was rejected. Mr Hawke's government was to come under increasing pressure to solve the impasse in the nation's pastoral industry. (Photo [identifier http:// digitalcollections.anu.edu.au/handle/ 1885/48468]: part of the ACTU collection housed in the Noel Butlin Archives Centre at the Australian National University in Canberra, used with permission.)

Former Canberra Times cartoonist Geoff Pryor's take on the violence that plagued the shearing industry in the early 1980s. Geoff donated his entire Canberra Times cartoon collection (more than 5,000 drawings) to the National Library of Australia. (Cartoon [NLA identifier http:// nla.gov.au/nla.obj-156492424] published in 1984, used with permission of both Geoff Pryor and the National Library of Australia.)

As head of the Wool Council of Australia and a member of the National Farmers' Federation Industrial Committee, Ian McLachlan was a key player in the wide comb shearing dispute. Ian's savvy handling of the live sheep export dispute in 1978 and his leadership during the wide comb dispute catapulted him into a stellar career in agribusiness and politics. Ian has a framed set of wide shearing combs in his Adelaide office as a reminder of the significance of the wide comb dispute.

New Zealand born shearing contractor Neil Ellery, pictured here at the Dubbo saleyards in 1984. Neil ran shearing teams mostly in Western Australia during th[e] early 1980s, but as the wide comb dispute intensified, he started moving teams into the eastern states too. It was the availability of shearing teams from 'rebel' contractor[s] like Neil and Robert White, together with teams employe[d] indirectly by Grazcos during the national shearers' strike, that helped force an end to the strike in May 1983. The AWU claimed Neil was regularly breaching the Pastoral Industry Award through 'illegal' work practices such as weekend work. In response, Neil challenged the union to prosecute him. Strangely, it never did. Neil died in a car accident near Collarenebri i[n] northern New South Wales in 1988. (Photo: Peter Barnes, Brisbane, used with permission.)

Joe Nobes, of Cowra, grew up in fine wool country near Crookwell and started shearing as a 16-year-old after the 1956 strike. He shore extensively in Queensland and throughout the New South Wales Southern Tablelands and Central West regions. Joe regularly notched 300+ tallies, won numerous competitions and represented Australia in 1974. He preferred narrow combs but eventually switched to wide gear – 'no good bumping your head against the wall forever'. (Photo: Mark Filmer.)

Robert Foster runs a small farm near Wagga Wagga. He worked on and off as a shearer over many years. When he first tried wide combs during the early 1980s, he could not believe how much more efficient they were. 'Everyone who got to use the wide combs said they would never use a narrow one again… I could not believe it, I could not believe we could give ourselves such a big pay rise so quick because it was quite easy to shear 10 to 15 sheep a run more.' (Photo: Mark Filmer.)

Champion shearer John Conlan shore throughout the Riverina and central Victoria during the wide comb dispute. He used narrow gear up until wide gear was legalised in 1983, when '…we just went straight onto wide gear: you are going to make more money and make the job easier'. Even after wide combs were legalised, the AWU pressured John to stay on narrow gear because he was such a high-profile shearer, but he refused to do so. (Photo: Mark Filmer.)

Former shearer Garry Doyle from the Wentworth district near Mildura. His father and grandfather were also shearers. Garry used narrow combs up until the national strike in early 1983, when he decided to try wide combs. He said wide gear 'was a little bit hard to get used to when you started…but it was just easier, quicker'. Garry shore during the strike because he was so upset with the AWU. 'How could they go against something that had to be better?' He went on to work for Grazcos, where he became a regional manager. (Photo: Mark Filmer.)

Geoff 'Andy' Anderson of Beaufort, Victoria, was a long-time shearer and early wide comb supporter – he started using wide combs in the late 1970s. Andy shore mostly by himself in small sheds but eventually other shearers got to know he was using wide gear. 'Curious blokes used to say, "Well, give me a go." … You would give them a handpiece with wide gear and you could not get it off them,' he said. 'All it boils down to, in my opinion, is that the union backed the wrong horse.' (Photo: Mark Filmer.)

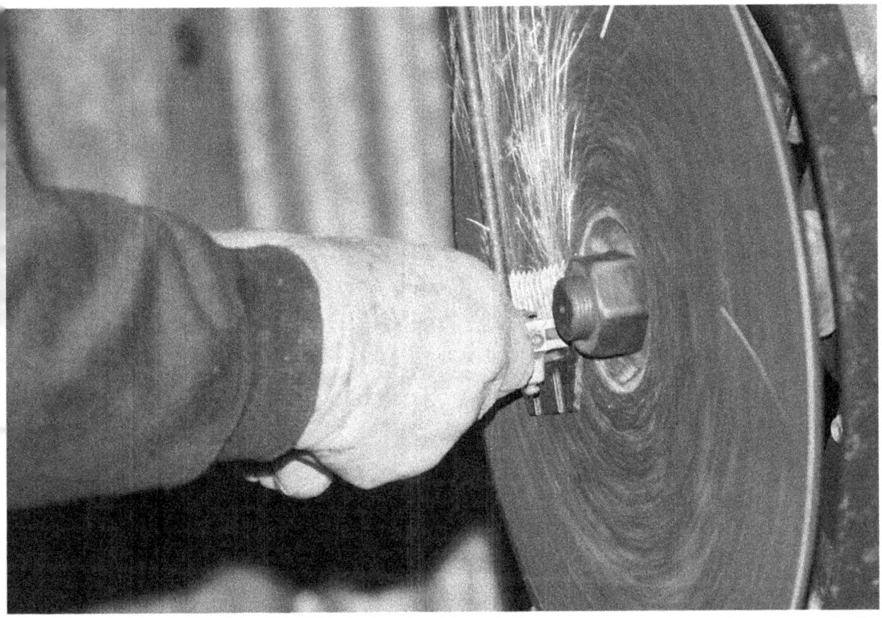

An old-time shearer grinds a comb to suit his requirements. Shearers have always 'tweaked' their combs by applying slight modifications to improve overall performance. Such modifications commonly include thinning the width of the comb and adjusting the arc of the bevel on the tips of the teeth. (Photo: Mark Filmer.)

Paul McGaw, a third-generation shearer from Lucindale, South Australia, checks some of his gear. Paul grew up in Tibooburra, New South Wales. As a 17-year-old, he secured a learner's pen at a shed at Kerrs Creek, near Wellington. From there, he moved to Broken Hill, where he shore for Grazcos at numerous sheds in remote north-west New South Wales and north-east South Australia. He viewed wide combs as an 'advancement' for the industry: '[It's like] you have a kettle that you put on the stove, then you have one that you plug into the electricity.' Although he had a union ticket, Paul had an ambivalent relationship with the union over the years. He believed the union was necessary in the industry but he strongly disagreed with the way it managed the wide comb dispute. He shore during the national shearers' strike in 1983 largely as a protest against the union's handling of the dispute.
(Photo: Mark Filmer.)

Shearers at Kentucky Station in the New England district of New South Wales in the mid-1980s take a break after the second of four two-hour runs for the day. Studies have shown that shearing is, if not the hardest, certainly one of the hardest physical jobs to perform. (Photo: Oliver Strewe, used with permission.)

Shearers hard at work at Kentucky Station in the New South Wales New England district during the mid-1980s. A typical day consists of four two-hour runs, from 7.30 to 9.30 a.m., 10 a.m. to 12 noon, one to three p.m. and 3.30 to 5.30 p.m. Shearers incur workplace injuries at a much greater rate than almost every other occupation. Nearly every aspect of the job raises workplace health and safety warning flags. (Photo: Oliver Strewe, used with permission.)

22

The Long Wait

By the end of February 1982, the commission's shed inspections were over. The eighth and final inspection had taken place at Talerno Station near Northam, about an hour's drive north-east of Perth. The station's four-member shearing team favoured narrow gear and testified that there was a noticeable difference in quality between narrow and wide gear. One team member, Brian O'Neil, who had been a shearer for 11 years, said wide combs produced more second cuts, and if made legal would lead to a two-tiered payment system for shearers, which would cause division and disharmony in the industry.

The commission convened again in Melbourne and Sydney in early March, before returning to Perth to gather more evidence in mid-March. There were additional proceedings in Sydney during April and May before the case was adjourned on 1 June, after 50 days of hearings. At one stage, Commissioner McKenzie considered extending the hearings to conduct a series of shed inspections on the South Island of New Zealand, however, he decided against this option. The inspections were summed up by Paul Houlihan as follows:

> The union said you could not shear merinos with wide combs and we spent a couple of months visiting shearing sheds where we demonstrated you could shear merinos with wide combs.

Houlihan could be brilliantly blunt. But while his summation was accurate, it was also an oversimplification. The union had also presented evidence during the inspections that raised questions about the quality of shearing carried out with wide combs. Commissioner

McKenzie wanted to hear more from the union on this and other issues, so in early April, in the lead-up to the resumption in proceedings, he made it known he would welcome hearing evidence from the New South Wales branch of the AWU. He also wanted representatives of the major shearing comb manufacturers to participate in the inquiry.

Ecob rejects invitation

Under normal circumstances, in such a contentious industrial matter, a union would have seized upon an invitation such as this as an opportunity to reinforce its case. However, Ernie Ecob was not someone who kept to a script – his public utterances often seemed more ad-lib than measured. Within a week or so of Commissioner McKenzie saying he wanted more evidence from certain parties, including the union's state branch, Ecob came out publicly and berated the commission's inquiry. He said the New South Wales branch of the union would not be giving any evidence when the hearings resumed in Sydney on 27 April. He was quoted in *The Land* as saying,

> We have not given any evidence, and we will not be putting any evidence – our only evidence is that no wide combs will be used in this state. We will not be a party to the hearings – we will not lower ourselves to be associated with such a scabby turnout.[135]

It was an extraordinary response, even for Ecob. It was one thing to be forthright and say the union would not testify; it was another entirely to publicly challenge the credibility of the inquiry. But Ecob had not stopped there – he'd added a pinch of intimidation for good measure, insisting 'that no wide combs will be used in this state'. That was actually the commissioner's decision to make! Ecob's RSVP to Commissioner McKenzie's invitation was, basically, 'Piss off.' The union's hierarchy must have been scratching their heads. This highly inflammatory approach was certainly at odds with the more measured strategy that had been outlined a couple of months earlier, at the

AWU's 96th Annual Convention in Sydney. Federal secretary Frank Mitchell told delegates the union would be mounting the strongest possible defence in the wide comb case. He said,

> Over the last few months the union's dispute with the employers has reached a highly volatile and difficult stage. We now have found ourselves in the position of mounting a full-scale case against the employers in their aim of introducing wide gear in the pastoral industry to the detriment of the membership. The next stage of the case would be the union's reply to the employers. It is proposed to inspect shearing in four states and present to the Arbitration Commission detailed evidence and documentary material. These proceedings will occur in the first three months of the new year. I am confident that the quality of the case being prepared by the union will be sufficient to convince the Commission of the wisdom of retaining the wide gear prohibition.[136]

All indications were that all branches of the union would not only cooperate with the commission, but that they would be presenting a thorough and rigorous defence of their objections to wide gear. The union had mounted a defence in the hearings in South Australia, Tasmania, Victoria and Western Australia. But when it came to New South Wales, Ecob had his way, and rather than presenting 'detailed evidence and documentary material' as was foreshadowed, the union boycotted the Sydney hearings. It was another odd stance that would come back to bite the AWU.

Union seeks to pressure the commission

Although it snubbed the commission's New South Wales hearings, the AWU had nevertheless been working behind the scenes to try to pressure the commission to reject the LGPA's application to legalise wide combs. On Sunday 21 February, during a meeting at the Dubbo Golf Club, 260 AWU rank and file members made several significant resolutions. This meeting had been called in response to an AWU

Executive Council decision on 17 November 1981 to organise a stoppage to protest against the LGPA and NFF application to amend the federal Pastoral Industry Award's shearing comb width restriction clause.

One resolution called on all AWU pastoral committees in the state to send telegrams to Commissioner McKenzie later that week, on Friday 26 February, as a protest against wide combs. Most committees complied and protest telegrams were received from Ivanhoe, Mudgee, Walgett, Orange, Goulburn, Grenfell, Coolah, Coonamble, Griffith, Dunedoo, Bourke, Tamworth, Cootamundra and Dubbo. Although the wording of the telegrams was different, they all contained the same sentiment – condemning wide gear. For example, the Walgett committee's telegram read, 'We members of Walgett AWU Committee are incensed and reject the actions of the LGPA to change Rule (Clause) 32 to allow wide combs. If granted this will result in industrial revolution.' Another key resolution mandated the same day, 26 February, as a national strike day to protest against the growing 'threat' of wide combs. The day after the strike, the *Sydney Morning Herald* reported that an estimated 16,000 shearers had taken part in the protest.[137] Interestingly, another discussion that took place at the Dubbo meeting focused on efforts to win a shorter working week for shearers. Both Ernie Ecob and Charlie Oliver spoke on this issue, which had loosely been on the union's agenda for a couple of years. The irony, once again, was that had the union been willing to negotiate over the peaceful introduction of wide combs, reduced hours could have been one of the trade-offs used in the bargaining process. The Dubbo meeting also instructed Ernie Ecob to organise an immediate and indefinite strike should the Arbitration Commission give wide shearing gear the green light.

And finally, in taking an altogether different tack, shearers at the meeting initiated a push that was to later snowball into a major campaign to limit work opportunities for New Zealand shearers visiting Australia. They instructed Ernie Ecob to put a motion before the next meeting of the AWU federal Executive Council directing the council to pressure the Australian Council of Trade Unions (ACTU), which was the peak union body at that time, to push for legislative reforms. In particular, they wanted the AWU to have a role in the visa approval process for every shearer entering Australia from New Zealand, and for all work visas to be limited to three months. Although these proposals fell flat, the union eventually succeeded, after a relentless campaign, in having the federal government hold a parliamentary inquiry into the 'Employment of Visitors to Australia in the Shearing Industry'. The inquiry was initiated in 1992 and the final report was presented to parliament in February 1994. (For more details, see chapter 37.)

Petition falls flat

It did not take long for the AWU to have second thoughts about its boycott of the Sydney hearings. Within weeks of Commissioner McKenzie adjourning the case, the union's New South Wales branch sought leave to have it reopened. Despite the union having only recently flipped it the bird, the commission responded graciously – it granted the application and the matter was relisted for hearing in Sydney on 21 July. So, in late June and early July, the AWU was madly scrambling to prepare material to present to the commission. The focus of its proposed submission quickly settled on a petition it planned to distribute to wool growers throughout the state, asking them to support the union's opposition to wide combs. This was certainly a long shot, given that most wool growers were members of the LGPA, which was leading the charge to have wide gear legalised. In a sense, it was also an attempt to show there was division among wool growers on the issue. If the union could demonstrate that enmity towards wide gear extended beyond its membership, it would certainly bolster its case.

But on Friday 16 July, just days before the matter was due to be reopened, the union's plan started to unravel. Counsel for the union throughout the dispute, Garry Johnston, forwarded legal advice to the AWU suggesting that reopening the case could ultimately work against the union. Johnston, from Selborne Chambers in Phillip Street, Sydney, said the petition would carry little weight, as it had been signed by only about 50 graziers from the Bourke area. He said if the petition was submitted, it would give the LGPA and NFF an opportunity to seek another adjournment and call more evidence. He said some graziers in other states had already testified against wide combs or called for trials to be implemented to assess their suitability. Without detailed evidence being heard from a wide range of graziers in New South Wales, the petition was effectively worthless, he said. The union was in a bind – it had failed to provide evidence when urged to do so; now its hurried efforts to reopen the case would most likely work against it. Really it had no other choice than to follow Johnston's advice – it decided against reopening the matter. It was now a matter of waiting for the umpire's decision. However, the AWU was also fighting another battle in the pastoral industry.

Wage claim frustrates the AWU

The wide comb dispute was not the only dispute shearers were engaged in during 1982. They were also pursuing a wage claim and by the middle of the year the AWU was becoming increasingly frustrated at the slow progress of the claim before the Arbitration Commission. Interestingly, Commissioner McKenzie was also handling this matter.

At the time, shearers were paid according to a complex formula that generated a base rate per 100 sheep shorn. In 1975, that rate was $45 per 100 sheep. It rose steadily each year and in March 1979, Justice Mary Gaudron, a deputy president of the Arbitration Commission, approved an increase of $4.90 per 100 sheep shorn – equivalent to about $25 per week, taking the rate to $66.38 per 100 sheep, effective from the following month. From September 1980, shearers were paid $75.22 per 100 sheep, and in 1982 they were earning $82.88 per 100. Also, in June that year, shearers ramped up their push for an additional increase as a flow-on from a general wage rise of $25 per week and a metalworking industry increase of $14 per week that came into effect in October 1981. At the time, Australia's complex industrial relations system, which was overseen by the Arbitration Commission, used the metalworking wage as a benchmark for many other industries. Invariably, these industries would seek increases to their award rates to match any increases granted to metalworkers. Pay rates in the Pastoral Industry Award had been tied to metalworkers' pay rates since 1974.

In January 1982, the AWU had lodged a claim with the Arbitration Commission seeking the $25 per week general increase as well as the $14 per week metalworkers' increase. Any pay rise granted would be built into the pay formula to produce an equivalent weekly rise for shearers. The LGPA was opposing the claim on the basis of 'capacity to pay' – it was arguing worsening seasonal and economic conditions, as well as a downturn in the wool industry at that time, meant approving the full amount would result in a poorly timed and disproportionate cost burden for wool growers. (The Commonwealth Bureau of Agricultural Economics had forecast a 30 per cent drop in real net farm incomes for 1982.) However, by the middle of the year there was still no word on the pay claim and the union was getting impatient. Shearers met in Dubbo on 27 July and warned that unless the claim was settled by Friday 13 August, they would strike for a week from 16 August, before meeting back in Dubbo again on Monday 23 August to decide how to proceed. The resolutions were sent via telex to the Arbitration Commission to ensure Commissioner McKenzie remained fully informed of the union's position. However, not surprisingly, the commissioner did not fulfil the union-imposed deadline, and shearers went on strike.

The subsequent meeting in Dubbo resulted in a return to work on Wednesday 25 August and an extension of the deadline for the pay claim to be settled by 10 September, with another day-long strike planned for that day if the matter remained unresolved. By early

September there was speculation that a decision was imminent. The LGPA issued several press releases about the matter, including one on 7 September in which it stated that the Arbitration Commission had warned shearers that any strike action would only delay its deliberation of the wage claim. Ernie Ecob weighed in, warning that shearers would strike indefinitely if the claim was not finalised.

As it turned out, the union's threats again had no effect on the Commission and the revised deadline came and went minus any decision. Shearers immediately went on strike. Two days later, on Sunday 12 September, shearer representatives from throughout the state travelled once more to Dubbo to chart the union's next course of action. At this meeting, Ernie Ecob revealed that Commissioner McKenzie had sent the union a telex stating that he would hand down his decision later that week, on Thursday 16 September, and that he intended awarding shearers a $22 per week general pay rise. (There was no mention of the $14 per week they were also seeking.) Delegates were furious and condemned the commissioner for failing to formally hand down his decision, saying his 'pettiness and lack of knowledge of one of Australian's most important industries and how it operates' had placed them in a position where they were now disadvantaged compared to other Australian workers.[138] They resolved to write to the president of the Arbitration Commission, Sir John Moore, to ask that Commissioner McKenzie be barred from handling any matters relating to the federal Pastoral Industry Award, and that he be 'replaced with a person who is sincere and willing to help in industrial disputes, and who is willing to give assistance not hindrance in the future'.[139]

Commissioner McKenzie did deliver his decision that Thursday, as he had foreshadowed, making the $22 per week rise effective immediately. However, he made no ruling on the $14 per week claim, announcing it would be relisted for mention again early the following year, on 16 February. The union was not happy. Shearers met again at the Dubbo Golf Club on 19 September to consider their options. They voted to have the union pressure the Arbitration Commission to bring forward the proposed hearing. The commission relented to an extent, agreeing to hold a preliminary hearing to hear arguments about the proposal for the relisting to be brought forward. However, at this hearing, on 29 October, Commissioner McKenzie refused the union's request and maintained the February relisting date. When the case resumed in February, the LGPA and NFF maintained their opposition to the increase and applied for the matter to be heard by the full bench of the Arbitration Commission.

Commissioner McKenzie granted the application and the matter was adjourned to 20 June 1983. At the June hearing, the full bench, comprising commission President Sir John Moore, Deputy President Keith McKenzie and Commissioner Ian McKenzie, accepted the employers' argument and deferred any further consideration of the application for another six months. In February 1984, the matter was again delayed before the Arbitration Commission eventually awarded shearers an $11 per week pay rise in July that year. By this time, however, the matter had been dwarfed by other events relating to the wide comb dispute.

23

The Eromanga Ambush

Mount Margaret is a large sheep station located about 100 kilometres west of Quilpie in south-west Queensland. During the early 1980s, the station had a footprint of almost 600,000 hectares, making it one of the largest sheep stations in Australia. Most importantly, in such a remote location, it boasted a reliable water supply, courtesy of roughly 80 kilometres of frontage to the Wilson River and Bellalie Creek. It featured a varied landscape, including open and shaded plains, Mitchell grass floodplains, mulga, coolibah and red rolling pebbly country, and Flinders, buffel and bluebush grasslands. At times the property ran more than 70,000 sheep, but during the early 1980s it stocked 50,000. The nearest town to the station is Eromanga, which, during the wide comb dispute, had a pub, police station, petrol bowser, public phone box, general store and two-digit population. On Friday and Saturday nights, however, the population often reached three digits as people from surrounding stations converged on the Royal Hotel for a night out.

In late 1979, about the time wide combs began popping up in the eastern states, there was a change in ownership of Mount Margaret Station. Alexander Thyne (Sandy) Reid and his wife Georgina added the property to their already extensive pastoral holdings in Australia and Vanuatu. The Reids were based at Narrangullen, a renowned cattle farm between Yass and Wee Jasper in the New South Wales southern tablelands. At one stage, the 8,000-hectare Narrangullen boasted Australia's largest imported Aberdeen Angus cattle stud. Their neighbours included media tycoon Rupert Murdoch, who owned

Cavan Station, known for its magnificent gardens as well as its high-quality sheep, wool and beef production, and Princess Diana's mother, the late Frances Shand Kydd, who divided her time between London, a home on the Scottish island of Seil, and her Yass district property. The Reids were highly regarded in their local community and indeed in the broader Australian pastoral industry and were known for their generosity and philanthropy. Tragically, Sandy and Georgina died in a light plane accident in 1990 as they were landing on the airstrip at Mount Margaret Station. Adding to the tragedy, one of the couple's adult children had landed at the airstrip in another plane only minutes earlier and witnessed the crash. Mount Margaret stayed in the Reid family until 2005, when it was sold to the Bydand Pastoral Company.

In early October 1982, two shearing contractors were engaged to shear the Mount Margaret flock, beginning later that month. The station had two 10-stand shearing sheds – the main Mount Margaret shed, which was about 10 kilometres from the homestead, and Ulloomunta, which was about 40 kilometres to the north-west of the main shed. Each team was to shear about 25,000 sheep. One of the contractors was Robert White, who by this time had become a target for the union. White and his team, and indeed his family, were increasingly subject to threats and intimidation from some of the more militant-minded AWU members. It had reached the point where White was keeping his movements secret to try to protect himself, his shearers and his family. The shearers in the second team were strictly narrow gear union members, mainly from the Longreach area, almost a seven-hour drive to the north. Somehow word had got out that White would be shearing at Ulloomunta, and even though the two teams were well away from each other, it seemed inevitable that there would be some sort of clash.

White's team attacked

Arthur Watson, a New Zealand-born shearer from Cargo, west of Orange, did a lot of work for Robert White. Watson came to Australia in the late 1970s intending to stay for a two-week holiday. However, while here he met his future wife. He ended up coming back to get married and live in Australia. Known as 'Kiwi', Watson was one of eight shearers in a 13-member team that White took to Ulloomunta. He had a clear recollection of the drama that unfolded. 'We went up there to shear 50,000 – 25,000 in each shed – the unionists had Mount Margaret…and we had Ulloomunta,' he said. 'We were wide [gear] and they were narrow…we travelled three days to get there and shore for four days and three days to get home again because that's all we could get in…they were coming after us,' Watson said.

The team arrived on Monday 18 October 1982 and started shearing the following day. On the Saturday, Robert White went into Eromanga with his wife Gayle and three of the shearers. 'The pub was full of blue singlets [union shearers]…and they were attacked, they actually bashed Gayle,' Watson said. 'The police stood by and did nothing. They bashed Gayle, they bashed Bob and they bashed Clarky [Allan Clark, one of the other three shearers], until the police [finally] stopped them and told them [the union shearers] to get back inside.' He said when they returned they were 'visibly shaken'. Some of the shearers involved in this ambush were from the other team at Mount Margaret.

Robert White spoke about this incident months later during an interview for a feature report *Wild and Woolly* for Channel 9's flagship current affairs program *60 Minutes*. White told reporter Ian Leslie, 'As we pulled up, there were about nine or 10 blokes came out [of the pub]…never said nothing to us, and they were straight into us and bashed us, plus my wife as well, no warning, not a word spoken, just straight into us.' Leslie reported that the town's sole police officer had witnessed the assault, in which Robert White was punched in the head. The police officer said on camera, 'One of the narrow comb fellas, he took an almighty, round-house swing at White…if it was me, it would have lifted my head off my shoulders, it was pretty hard.' Referring to Gayle White, he said, '…she copped a smack in the mouth for her trouble too.' Gayle White confirmed that the attack on her was no accident. She told Leslie her attacker had '…lined me up and looked me in the eye and said, "I'll give you one for good measure". I was hit well and truly.' Incredibly, no charges were laid.

Watson said the team had intended finishing the shed, but the day after the attack, the station manager drove out to Ulloomunta and warned them that he had heard a group of unionists was 'coming out from Charleville to get you' first thing the following day, Monday 25 October. Charleville is about a four-hour drive to the east of Mount Margaret Station. He advised them to pack up and leave, in the interests of their own safety. The team would normally have departed via Charleville, but they took a back road to Thargomindah to avoid any over-eager union shearers. From there they drove to Cunnamulla, before heading south over the border to Bourke, which they reached on the Sunday evening. 'It was supposed to be on the quiet, but word got around,' Watson said. 'Once we were over the border we felt safe.'

Brief strike

The revelation that White's team had been shearing at Mount Margaret triggered an immediate but very brief strike by about 500 Queensland shearers. Alec Walton, an organiser for the Queensland branch of the AWU, inspected the Ulloomunta shed on Friday 22 October and found White and his seven shearers were using wide gear. He notified the Queensland branch secretary, Errol Hodder, of the breach of the state award. Hodder immediately issued a notification of dispute and organised an urgent conference in the Queensland Industrial Commission between union officials and the United Graziers' Association of Queensland for the following Monday, 25 October. Word of the dispute spread quickly and Hodder began receiving telegrams and telex messages notifying him that various state branch committees of the AWU were going on strike. By the end of that weekend, up to 500 shearers had gone out on strike. Under the Queensland award, White, as the contractor for the shed, could have been liable for a $2,000 fine and each of his shearers could have been fined $200 for shearing with wide combs. As it turned out, the team's hasty retreat back to New South Wales on the weekend rendered the Monday conference unnecessary and the strike was soon called off. However, Hodder was later quoted in *The Worker* as saying,

> I might add that members within the industry in Queensland have made it known to officials of the union that they are prepared not only to take industrial action to ensure that wide gear is stamped out in its usage in Queensland, but that if it is used in Queensland, they will also take action against people which would result in them finding it very difficult to shear sheep for a good length of time.

The threat of violence was hardly subtle.

Hodder attended a meeting of AWU pastoral workers at the Dubbo Golf Club the following weekend, on Sunday 31 October, in which he gave members an update on the Mount Margaret incident. He said a strike had been called off following the departure of White's team and that 'The response of AWU members to this threat to their conditions of work was immediate and overwhelming.'

Ernie Ecob was invited to speak on ABC Radio 2CR in Orange the following day, to provide listeners with an update on the union's pay dispute and the wide comb dispute following the weekend meeting in Dubbo. He warned that union members were getting sick of Robert White and said, 'There has been a report…this morning that Mr White will be coming in the next day or so into the Dubbo area to commence shearing. We have made the necessary arrangements. There are people who have been put on the alert and Mr White will receive the same treatment as he received when he left Mount Margaret.'

Interviewer: And what was that?

Ecob: Well, I think Mr White and his team would be feeling sorer than what the Australian football team are feeling this morning.

(The Australian rugby league team, the Kangaroos, had defeated England 40-4 in a bruising first Test at Boothferry Park in Hull overnight on their tour of Great Britain and France.)

Throughout the dispute, union officials were normally quick to publicly condemn violence. But here was the union's state leader condoning it. He made it very clear that members would not hesitate to use violence, at least against Robert White. The nature of the dispute was now changing.

Houlihan writes to the commissioner

The attack on five members of White's team at Eromanga and the continued threat of violence against Robert White was a game changer. Up until this point, the dispute had featured very little physical violence, even though there had been plenty of intimidation and threats and the odd scuffle in a country pub between union shearers and rebel wide comb users. But the Eromanga incident could not be ignored – it had effectively notched up the intensity of the dispute and created a new baseline for confrontations between rival shearers. Paul Houlihan was concerned about where things could go from here. He wrote to Commissioner McKenzie on 16 November 1982 to brief him on the latest developments. In his letter, Houlihan explained what had happened at Eromanga, then wrote the following about the second team of shearers at Mount Margaret:

> The other contractor had picked up a team of shearers from Longreach, Queensland. After the sheds had been going for two days the Longreach team, who outnumbered the New South Wales team very handsomely simply 'beat up' members of the New South Wales team in the local town, including several women members of the team. They were driven off the property. Two days later the Longreach team left their shed and surrendered their employment leaving over 20,000 sheep still to be shorn. The only conclusion we can draw is that that team went to that station for one purpose. Not to shear but to physically stop Robert White's team from shearing.

Houlihan also included information about the ongoing threat to White and his team, noting Ecob's warning on ABC radio that they would 'receive the same treatment' as they had at Eromanga. He told the commissioner that extraordinary steps were being taken by the LGPA to try to ensure the safety of White and his family.

In early November, the association notified the superintendent of the Bathurst area police command of the Eromanga incident and provided him with a transcript of Ecob's recent interview. The police stations in Blayney and Millthorpe were subsequently put on notice to watch out for White and his family. Soon after, one incident sparked a security scare when White and his team were shearing at a shed near Orange. Houlihan described the events as follows:

> The shearing team had gone to considerable trouble to prevent anyone from knowing where they were shearing and felt fairly secure until a local TV station rang the wool-grower for permission to come out on to his property and take film of White's team. At much the same time, the police in Blayney, close to where White lives, came to his home and urged Mrs White (who still had the bruises and cuts from where she was knocked down and kicked in Queensland) to come to the Blayney Police Station for her own protection. The policeman advised her that there were five or seven union organisers in the district and that they had with them four or five 'professionals' i.e. thugs from Sydney, and they were letting it be known that White, his family and team were not going to stay in business. One member of White's team overheard one of these thugs stating quite matter-of-factly that they were in town to 'break the arms and legs of White's team members but White himself will be blown off the face of the earth'. When White realised that the media knew where he was shearing he stopped his team and headed home. He was interrupted by police who directed him to go to the Blayney Police Station because that was the only place he could be guaranteed protection. While at the police station, White made arrangements for his children to be taken from the local school and looked after. The police advised him that organisers and their helpers were keeping a close watch on the school. That night the whole team stayed at White's home, under armed police guard. Up to eleven policemen were at his house that night. The next morning, acting

on police advice, the team dispersed and left town. White and his wife returned on the Sunday, determined to finish the shed that they had started on the previous Thursday. However, other members of his team were so alarmed that they refused to return without guarantees of police protection at the shed. This the police said they could not do.

Allen Murphy is a former policeman who was stationed at Millthorpe, near Blayney, during the early 1980s. He met Robert White and actually shore with him on several occasions – before joining the police force he had been a shearer. Murphy grew up on a farm at Temora in the north-east of the Riverina district of New South Wales. The oldest of 13 children, he left school at 13 and worked on the farm before starting shearing when he was 16. He had stints with the national shearing contractor, Farmers Grazcos, in sheds around the state and grew to love the mateship of the shearing life. He travelled roughly 65,000 kilometres and shore more than 250,000 sheep before an uncle of his, who was a detective sergeant, persuaded him to join the police force. Murphy signed up when he was 29 and was initially stationed in Clarence Street, Sydney. But he hated city life and nagged his senior officers for a country posting. Eventually he was sent to Hay, where he was stationed for 11 years, before being transferred to Millthorpe in 1973. Then in 1984 he was posted to Orange, where he finished his career and retired.

Murphy and his wife had 11 children, so he would often supplement his income with contract shearing work. Towards the end of 1981, he got a call from a local wool grower. 'I had gone out to a place at Forest Reefs [just south of Orange] one day; the bloke that owned it rang up and said, "Look, Bob White is shearing lambs out here, and he is not going to finish today, and he wants to go somewhere else. Could you come out and help him?" I went out and I shore about 30 to 40 lambs with him and that was the first time I struck Bob White,' Murphy said. He worked with him on several other occasions in the local area. 'He was very good; he was a very good shearer, a very clean shearer and fast. With most sheep he would do his 200 a day, and he was a great little bloke to work with,' Murphy said.

His other dealings with White were through his main job as a policeman. There were several occasions when the local police had to step in to protect White and his family. He said there were times when 'we were guarding his place for two or three nights' and on some occasions they got White to sleep in local police lock-ups at Blayney and Millthorpe. 'We had to put him somewhere otherwise they would have murdered him. Bob was hard to control because he had been told not to go away shooting – he used to go and shoot rabbits for dinner and that – and if somebody knew he was there, he would have got shot,' Murphy said. 'He was only there [in the lock-up] overnight…he was quite happy, it meant he could have a sleep. We would let him out the next morning and he went out shearing.' On these occasions, when there was an increased threat to White's safety, White's wife and children would have a police guard on the family property Robayle. However, there was almost always a layer of protection for the family, in that several New Zealand shearers who worked for the Whites would camp on the property at Mandurama. Murphy recalled telling Robert White he would have to watch out for his safety. He responded, 'They [the union] can get stuffed as far as I am concerned… I'm only doing my job; I am going to keep shearing with the wide combs.'

It was about this time, in late 1982 when White was subject to increased threats, that the LGPA and NFF became increasingly concerned for his safety. Ian McLachlan, then chairman of the Wool Council of Australia and an NFF industrial committee member, remembers discussing the situation with his father. 'I was telling him about the problem we had and Bob White…now Bob White, he said he was very worried about his family and he worried about himself,' McLachlan said.

> And my old man said, 'Well, why don't you go and get him a dog?' I said, 'Well, what do you mean?' He said, 'People train up Alsatians [for protection].' So that's what we did. We had one for

his wife and one for him. And nobody touched Bob, even though the dog was only half trained, nobody knew that…the fellow we rang said it's amazing what they do but he didn't have a fully trained dog.

White's dog went with him just about everywhere from then on. AWU organiser Fred McInerney, who was based in Coonamble, recalls bumping into White and his dog at a service station in Walgett sometime in 1983. McInerney had called in to get a new car windscreen fitted. White had pulled in for petrol. 'I didn't see him at first; he was there and I just wandered into the service station to get a bottle of drink,' McInerney recalled. When he came out, the two men exchanged unpleasantries. McInerney said White threatened to sool his dog onto him, to which he replied: 'Well, let him out, I'll pull a leg off him and f— belt you with it.' White just put the car into gear and drove away.

As well as putting on the record these latest worrying developments for Commissioner McKenzie, Houlihan's letter was a subtle attempt to speed up the decision on the wide comb dispute. All parties to the matter were growing impatient. The recent violence and the threat of more violence had everyone in the industry on edge. A decision was needed soon.

24

Judgement Day

The 52-storey Nauru House, which had a brief reign as Melbourne's tallest building during the late 1970s, was the venue for the decision in the wide combs industrial dispute. The octagonal-shaped building, on the corner of Collins and Exhibition Streets in the city's CBD, was owned at the time by the government of the Republic of Nauru, which had embarked on a program of international real estate investment using the proceeds of its phosphate sales. The Arbitration Commission rented space on the building's 34th floor. It was there on the morning of Friday 10 December 1982 that Commissioner McKenzie delivered his decision. It had been more than two years now since wide combs had emerged as an issue in the pastoral industry, and 18 months since the issue had been formalised with the lodging in May 1980 of the LGPA application for 'field research trials' of wide gear. The dispute had been simmering ever since but with the events and rhetoric of recent months, it was threatening to boil over. There was a discernible air of anticipation as most of the people who had been closely involved in the case, including Robert White, gathered to hear the umpire's decision. South Australian wide comb supporter and shearing contractor Laurie Polomka was among several other shearers who attended that day.

The AWU was expecting Commissioner McKenzie to give the green light to a trial of wide combs. At a meeting of the union's pastoral members in Dubbo just weeks before, on 31 October, Ernie Ecob told the 220 attendees,

Indications are that Commissioner McKenzie may bring down a decision legalising wide combs on a trial basis. Members must fight this action because contrary to the NFF and the LGPA statements, the price of shearing will be forced down and Award conditions will be shattered with varying prices for different sheep, etc. We have the evidence of what has happened in Western Australia to show us what will happen.[140]

Ecob recommended the old, let's bombard the commissioner with telexes saying we oppose the legalising of wide combs trick. Given that he had refused the commissioner's invitation for the union to present more evidence, it was a desperate, last-ditch attempt to sway the case in the union's favour. The AWU's pastoral committees across the state duly complied and throughout November, as well as receiving Houlihan's letter concerning the Eromanga ambush, the commissioner received reams of telex messages from various AWU committees expressing their hostility to wide combs.

The ruling

Commissioner McKenzie's written ruling stretched over 36 pages. It included an extensive background to the history of the case and a summary of the key evidence that he had relied on in reaching his decision, which was summarised on the final page:

> ... Based on the evidence placed before me and my own observations at shed inspections, I am satisfied that there is a place in the Australian shearing industry for the manufactured wide comb, although not to the extent of the loose provision sought by the employers. To this end I propose to vary Clause 32 of the Pastoral Industry Award 1965... The new clause will permit subject to the shearer...electing to do so, the use of combs wider than the standard (64 mm) comb in accordance with the following:
> • The owner or his representative must agree to the use of such combs.
> • All combs used by a shearer or crutcher...subject to fair wear and

tear to thickness, must comply to the manufacturer's specification for that particular comb.

As it will be obvious from (ii) above the use of 'pulled' combs will be prohibited, I propose to grant an amnesty of three months to assist the current users to phase them out without experiencing financial hardship… The date of operation will be from today and it is my intention to review this decision in approximately 12 months.

In his decision, Commissioner McKenzie gave great weight to the evidence of John Allan, the general manager of Sunbeam, describing it as 'strong and compelling'. Allan's evidence could be summarised as follows:

- Australian merino sheep were similar to other merino types throughout the world.
- Shearing in other wool producing countries was done predominantly with wide combs.
- Wide combs made up the bulk of export orders received by his company.
- No other country prohibited the use of wide combs.
- The wide merino comb was developed in response to requests from shearers in other countries with merino type sheep who had used the narrow merino comb.
- All types of wide combs would not be suitable for use on merino sheep and in general the wrong type of wide comb was being used in Australia.
- There was no need for further trials on wide combs that Sunbeam made for the world market.

The commissioner also made the following observations about the case:

- The union had not answered an important question – if narrow combs were superior in all respects to wide combs, why were so few shearers in Western Australia using narrow gear?
- The union's contention that the quality of the wool clip from Western Australia had deteriorated in recent years, corresponding to the increased use of wide combs, was not supported by the

evidence. Indeed, several expert witnesses had testified the opposite – that the state's wool clip was of a higher quality than clips from the eastern states.
- Counsel for the wool growers, David Bleby, had pointed out that most of the shearers who had testified against wide combs, had little or no experience in their use and their opposition was 'conceived in prejudice and born out of ignorance'.
- Formal wide combs trials would be pointless because of the union's ongoing opposition to wide gear and because an informal trial had already taken place in Western Australia during the past five years – and it had demonstrated that wide combs could be used effectively.
- Evidence before the commission pointed to the fact that standard pulled combs, not manufactured wide combs, were responsible for the majority of skin cuts on sheep.
- The union's 'intransigent attitude' toward the use or even trials of wide combs was hard to fathom.

Reaction to the decision

The effect of the Arbitration Commission's decision was that wide combs were in, pulled combs were out – with shearers able to use wide or narrow combs, as long as the wool grower approved of their choice. Robert White was naturally chuffed at the decision. He was quoted in the *Sydney Morning Herald* the following day as saying the judgement was 'A great breakthrough for the wool industry and the right decision.'[141] But the AWU was peeved. In the same article, Ernie Ecob slammed the decision, saying, 'There is no way the men will cop the wide comb and they will strike until the year 2000 if it's necessary to stop it.'

Indeed, within hours of Commissioner McKenzie handing down his decision, shearers had gone on strike. The AWU had anticipated the result and had a press release prepared in advance. Moments after word filtered through about the decision, Canberra-based AWU organiser Bill Preece distributed the release to most major media outlets –

announcing that union shearers were immediately going on strike and would remain on strike until Sunday 19 December, when they would meet in Dubbo to decide what to do next. The release warned that the Arbitration Commission's decision 'could lead to the most serious confrontations seen within the pastoral industry for decades'. The AWU said about 5,000 New South Wales shearers supported the strike, but the LGPA later said this was a gross exaggeration, as many shearers had continued working. Shearers in Victoria, South Australia and Tasmania also walked off the job the following day.

AWU launches appeal

Commissioner McKenzie's decision triggered a frantic series of meetings, as the AWU scrambled to work out how it should proceed. The union's federal Pastoral Committee met on the Monday after the decision (13 December), its federal Executive Council met the following day, the Victorian and South Australian state branch executives met on the Wednesday, and the New South Wales branch executive met on the Thursday. Following the federal Pastoral Committee meeting, a statement was prepared in which the committee expressed 'strong resentment at the decision in that the order handed down by the Conciliation and Arbitration Commission gives strong favourable support to the desires of mainly non-unionists working in the pastoral industry and completely ignores the express wish of unionists, which is to maintain the standard 64 mm comb'. It described the decision as being 'repugnant to any loyal union member' and said the union would launch an appeal. The statement was sent to the other union bodies meeting that week. They endorsed the committee's statement and were similarly critical of the ruling.

In between these meetings, senior union officials were meeting with the union's solicitors, Commins and Company, whose main offices were on the 27th floor of the AMP building in Bridge Street, Sydney. Together they drafted a notice of appeal. Federal secretary Frank Mitchell signed it and solicitor Rodney Commins lodged it with the Arbitration Commission on Thursday 16 December. The grounds for the appeal were wide-ranging – it was something of a scattergun approach, identifying multiple 'deficiencies' in the ruling in the hope that at least one would have merit. The union claimed the commissioner's decision was flawed because it went against the weight of evidence; it used information that was not the subject of evidence; it had not paid sufficient attention to the history of the use of shearing combs and the nature of the pastoral industry; wide combs would be detrimental to the industry and its employees and would harm shearing conditions and the quality of shearing throughout Australia; and the decision would cause more industrial disputes and friction between workers in the pastoral industry.

The Arbitration Commission granted the AWU application and set the appeal down for a hearing in February 1983. The union had also sought a stay order, which would delay the implementation of Commissioner McKenzie's decision until the appeal was finalised. This application was set down for hearing on 21 December.

Shearers meet in Dubbo

The union's 19 December meeting was held at the Dubbo Civic Centre. More than 820 shearers from South Australia, Victoria, Queensland and New South Wales jammed into the building to hear the latest on the dispute. It was one of the largest shearers' meetings Dubbo had hosted. Ernie Ecob was suitably fired up and rose to the occasion – describing Commissioner McKenzie's decision as 'the most disrespectful decision ever handed down by any industrial commissioner'. However, he admitted that the union's appeal would more than likely fail because of 'the cunning way the decision was worded'. Indeed, Ecob had been quoted in *The Land* newspaper a few days earlier as saying, 'The wording of the final decision is such that any attempts to appeal against it would be futile.' He told the newspaper the union would nevertheless fight to have the decision overturned. 'We will apply pressure through strike action, and when graziers start screaming because they can't get their sheep shorn, they will push Commissioner McKenzie to reverse his decision.'[142] At the Dubbo meeting, Ecob blasted Commissioner McKenzie who, he claimed, 'had been selective in the use of evidence in summing up and gave his decision using all the weaker points in the union's evidence'. He said the union had received reports 'that 75 per cent of graziers do not want any variation to Clause 32 of the Award and oppose the use of wide combs'. No details were provided about these reports. He then attacked the media, saying, 'Coverage of this dispute has been biased as in all other disputes' and '...much damage has been done to this industry by bad and unjust media coverage'.

Until this point, several media representatives had been present, covering the meeting – the dispute was big news, particularly in rural communities. But immediately following Ecob's criticisms of the media, the Queensland pair of Errol Hodder and Bill Ludwig moved and seconded a motion calling for the media to be removed – the motion was carried, and members of the media were ejected. The shearers resolved to endorse the continuation of the strike 'until a complete settlement is achieved' and 'only 64 mm combs with suitable cutters are used'. They also voted to ask the ACTU and its union members to support the strike by preventing New Zealand shearers from entering Australia as long as the strike continued. However, this resolution was more bluster than a ban – the union movement had no power or capacity to stop people entering Australia!

Stay order hearing

A full bench panel consisting of Justice Judith Cohen, Deputy President Michael Keogh, and Commissioner James Sheather heard the AWU's stay order application. The hearing took place in Sydney, beginning at 4.10 p.m. on Tuesday 21 December. It lasted two hours, most of which was dominated by legal argument by the respective counsel – Garry Johnston for the AWU and David Bleby for the LGPA and NFF. Johnston said there was a strong public interest argument to granting a stay, as the original decision would be a recipe for industrial chaos, given the strong feelings and extreme views within the industry about wide combs. He also argued that rejecting the stay order application would almost certainly lead to the widespread distribution of wide combs in Australia, as the key manufacturers would be free to sell wide gear in the domestic market. This would make it almost impossible to control and rid the industry of wide combs should the appeal subsequently succeed, he said. Johnston effectively argued there was less harm in staying the order than in not staying it. He foreshadowed that during the appeal case the AWU would challenge aspects of the evidence of John Allan (Sunbeam Corporation) and David Nankervis (R.A. Lister Australia Pty Ltd) – the union believed their testimony was given too much weight. It also believed that, based on the evidence before him, the commissioner was not entitled to conclude that the available manufactured wide combs were suitable for Australian shearing conditions.

Bleby said his clients opposed the stay application and argued there needed to be exceptional circumstances for the order to be granted. However, Justice Cohen said the reverse emphasis generally prevailed: 'The commission's usual practice is to grant a stay unless good cause is shown why it should not be granted.' Bleby cited case precedents to show that a stay order did not have to automatically follow the granting of an appeal. He also argued that the commission, in granting a stay order, had to be reasonably satisfied that the associated appeal had some prospect of success – and there were strong grounds to say Commissioner McKenzie had given due weight to all the evidence and made the correct decision. Bleby said the proposed 12-month review of the original decision would give the commission some confidence that the decision could, if necessary, be modified to offset any outcomes that proved harmful to the pastoral industry. Having this built-in backstop effectively reduced the need for the stay order, he said.

At this point in the hearing, someone in the public gallery stood up and demanded to be heard. It was Ernie Ecob, who was attending as an observer on behalf of the New South Wales branch of the AWU. It was quite a shock to those present and a rude interruption to the normally ordered and staid proceedings of the Arbitration Commission. Ecob sought to intervene, telling the commissioners he would like to make a submission and that he was 'the only person in this room who understands the industry'. However, Justice Cohen said the union was already legally represented and as such Ecob's application to be heard was refused.

The full bench adjourned briefly for the commissioners to consider their decision, before returning to grant the union's application for a stay pending the outcome of the appeal – meaning the ban on wide combs was reinstated for now. The commission also ordered the union to immediately end its strike action.

Two days later and two days before Christmas, shearers met again in Dubbo, where they agreed to return to work on 29 December. They also asked Ernie Ecob to pressure the union's federal Executive Council to replace Garry Johnston, who had been the union's main legal representative in the wide comb industrial case, as 'the majority of the rank and file were dissatisfied with his handling of the case'. Ecob said the state branch secretaries would discuss this matter and raise it at the next Executive Council meeting in the New Year.

Most of the 312 shearers attending this meeting would have left feeling somewhat ambivalent – they had won a stay order and, for the immediate future at least, wide combs were outlawed. Christmas was imminent and the New Year might just bring about some better fortunes in the wide comb case. However, their own leader had just conceded that the prospects of the union appeal succeeding were negligible. And, as they would soon find out, Ernie Ecob's prediction concerning the appeal was prophetic.

25

The Appeal Hearings

The union's appeal against the decision of Commissioner McKenzie was heard in Sydney beginning on Tuesday 8 February 1983. Following rank and file dissatisfaction with the way the main arbitration hearings played out, the union engaged the services of Charles (Joe) Bannon QC to run the appeal. A prominent Sydney barrister from the highly reputed Selborne Chambers in Phillip Street, Bannon was appointed a silk in 1969 and went on to become a judge in the New South Wales Land and Environment Court. Garry Johnston, who was also from the Selborne Chambers, continued to play a key role – given his extensive knowledge of the case he was retained to assist Bannon. The LGPA legal team consisted of the pipe-smoking campanologist David Bleby, who had been appointed a QC since his previous appearance in this matter, with Luigi Lamparti as his junior. Presiding over the appeal was a full bench panel – two deputy presidents, Justice Peter Coldham (who had been awarded a Distinguished Flying Cross as an RAAF pilot with the English Bomber Command during World War II) and Justice Stephen Alley, and Commissioner Bevan Johnson.

The first day of proceedings did not start smoothly. Almost immediately there was confusion over the schedule. Both Bannon and Bleby had been notified by the commission's registry office that only one day had been initially set aside for submissions. The commissioners, however, were anticipating sitting for at least the remainder of the week. The QCs had other commitments in the following days but the commissioners made it clear they would have to prioritise this matter and reschedule all others. Another glitch occurred when Bannon foreshadowed that he wanted to call fresh evidence – something that was not normally allowed during an appeal hearing. This took the commissioners by surprise but they agreed to at least consider his application at an appropriate time.

An appeal in a protracted industrial case such as this essentially involved drudging through reams of transcript evidence (in this instance more than 1,400 pages), arguing over legal technicalities, pointing out different ways of interpreting evidence and 'weaknesses' in the original ruling, and highlighting any evidence that could support an alternative finding. It was a painstaking and dreary process. Bannon relied on several key arguments. Essentially he said that Commissioner McKenzie had relied too heavily on the evidence of John Allan, the head of Sunbeam Corporation; he placed too much emphasis on the economic advantages of wide combs to wool growers and too little on the industrial matters the union presented; he failed to take into account the importance of standardisation and harmony in the shearing industry; and he should have made specific reference to the type of wide combs that could be used because there was evidence before the commission that not all such combs were suitable for Australian conditions.

Incredibly, Bannon also raised the issue of trials, arguing that Commissioner McKenzie should have made provision for an extended trial of wide combs to take place across Australia before approving them for general use. This submission was particularly galling to the wool growers' representatives as the union had for the past 18 months steadfastly refused to cooperate with formal wide comb trials. This point was not lost on the commissioners, who noted the union's bloody-mindedness. At one point, Commissioner Johnson asked Bannon, '… What is the position of your clients now in connection with participating in or cooperating with such trials?' Bannon, however, could not say with any certainty that they would agree to participate.

Mr Commissioner, I do not have the advantage of having them

sitting in court with me. I would imagine that a federal union of this nature, if this bench decided that that should happen and expressed that view, the union executive would pay great respect to the views of the Commission. I cannot answer for them but I have no doubt that any such order could be made on a basis that said that this order [of Commissioner McKenzie] would be varied subject to the union agreeing to the trials.[143]

Bannon later tweaked or refined this submission to suggest another trial option would be to limit the use of wide combs to Western Australia. This option, however, appeared at odds with his previous submission stressing the importance of standardisation in the shearing industry.

There were several 'lesser' grievances at the ruling from the union's perspective, including,

- The requirement to carry additional sets of combs would place a severe economic burden on shearers (most already carried more than $1,000 worth of combs and cutters);
- Wide combs would place an increased strain on shearers and shed hands (who had to cope with an increased throughput of fleeces);
- The additional force required to push wider combs and use a bigger, heavier handpiece would lead to more industrial accidents and claims for workers' compensation.

Commissioners seek shearing demonstration

On day two of the appeal, Wednesday 9 February, it became apparent that the commissioners were struggling with some technical details about the design and operation of shearing combs. At one point, Justice Coldham asked if a wide comb had more teeth than a narrow comb – even though one of the exhibits tendered during the main hearing and available to the commissioners was a selection of shearing combs. However, seeing and handling the combs did not automatically instil an understanding of how they worked. The commissioners soon realised that they were at a distinct disadvantage to Commissioner

McKenzie, who had spent several months presiding over hearings at shearing sheds around the country, observing shearing taking place with both standard and wide gauge shearing combs. However, they were having to deliberate on an important industrial matter relating to equipment they had never seen being used. So the commissioners proposed a shearing demonstration be organised for their benefit. Bannon opposed the suggestion but the commissioners were insistent. Luigi Lamparti therefore contacted the LGPA, who arranged for a demonstration to take place the following morning. It was to be a repeat of the demonstration that had been organised for Commissioner McKenzie at the start of the original hearings – same venue, same format, same shearer.

Also on day two, Bleby indicated he would object to the union presenting fresh evidence. He said,

> … As a general proposition judgements or decisions regularly obtained ought not to be disturbed by the admission of further evidence without some compelling demand that justice requires it… It must be pointed out I think at the outset when considering an application in this case what the commissioner himself said, as he did say on several occasions, about a plea for evidence to be put before him on the nature and effect of this proposal… The importance of that passage in my submission is this: that the commissioner was saying to the parties and more particularly to the AWU, if you have got a case and you want to put material before me as to what the effect of this decision is going to be, then I want to hear some evidence about it. There was the invitation, perfectly clear, perfectly open, and now what is being sought to have put before this commission in the form of four affidavits is evidence on just that point; evidence which they chose deliberately not to bring before the commissioner.[144]

The affidavits Bleby referred to were from four union officials, but the key affidavit was from Allan Begg, the AWU's South Australian branch secretary and federal branch president. The other three sworn statements relied heavily on information used by Begg.

Justice Coldham noted that some of the evidence in Begg's affidavit covered points that the union had already raised before Commissioner McKenzie. Bleby said much of the affidavit was more 'opinion' than evidence. For example, at one point, Begg stated, 'Narrow gear advocates will not work with wide gear advocates and vice versa.' Bleby said there was evidence before the commission that this was simply not the case. He said the material the union was now seeking to introduce could have been presented during the main hearings – it was not material that had become available subsequent to the hearings. Bannon cited case law to argue it was appropriate to allow the material. However, the commissioners ruled against him and refused his application. Ernie Ecob's snubbing of the commission again came back to haunt the union!

Days three and four

Robert White's second shearing demonstration for the Arbitration Commission took place at the Sydney Showground Agrodome at nine a.m. on day three of the appeal, Thursday 10 February. He again shore two small pens of sheep, one using a standard gauge comb and the other with a wide comb. Proceedings then resumed back at the commission's premises in the Queen's Square law courts building in Macquarie Street, where Bleby began his case for the LGPA and NFF. He said the evidence had demonstrated wide combs could be used effectively in Australia; there were wide combs available that suited Australian conditions; the quality of the wool clip harvested with wide combs was not compromised in any way; and much of the evidence presented by unionists opposing wide combs (and on which Bannon was now relying) was opinion not fact, as most of these witnesses had never used wide combs. He dismissed Bannon's argument that the commissioner should have specified certain types of combs as being eligible for use, saying that sort of decision should be left to the shearer, who would only use combs that suited the particular type of sheep he was shearing. Just as Bannon had done, Bleby went through the transcript in detail, with his submissions spilling over to day four, Friday 11 February. Bleby argued that Commissioner McKenzie giving significant weight to John Allan's evidence did not mean that he had disregarded all other evidence. He said too there was no evidence before the commission to support the union case that wide combs would cause severe economic hardship for shearers, increase industrial unrest and disharmony in sheds, and increase injury rates.

Two more sitting days were added to the schedule, Wednesday and Thursday 9 and 10 March, when both counsel finalised their submissions. The Thursday sitting lasted just over an hour before the case was adjourned for a decision on a date to be fixed.

The appeal decision

The decision in the appeal was handed down in Melbourne two weeks later on Wednesday 23 March. It ran over nine pages. The full bench found the evidence supporting the conclusion of Commissioner McKenzie was 'clear and compelling and had the additional force of having been given by witnesses with practical experience of the matters to which they deposed'.[145] The commissioners made the following six points about the original decision:

> 1. The evidence at the academic or scientific level was undisputed that wide shearing combs offer the prospect of an immediate benefit to the industry. Combs of differing widths were supported as a practical scheme and it was deposed that the prohibition of combs exceeding two and a half inches in width, if allowed to stand, would have the effect of restricting productivity. This evidence rejected the view that wide combs are unsuitable for shearing merinos, or sandy or dirty sheep.
> 2. Practising shearers expressed their view that wide combs are not only suitable but superior to standard combs in most instances. It is apposite to add that some of these witnesses gave their evidence in the shearing shed whilst engaged on a wool clip.
> 3. According to practising shearers, the use of wide combs occasions no additional effort by comparison with narrow combs.

Indeed, their evidence indicated that wide comb shearing is less fatiguing.

4. Shearers who had worked with non-standard combs amongst shearers operating with standard combs deposed to the absence of any industrial disharmony on such occasions.

5. It appeared that the introduction of wide combs has had no detrimental effect, and will in the future have no such effect, on the quality of the Australian wool clip. This view was deposed to by shearers, by wool growers, by manufacturers of shearing combs and by an academic specialist. Indeed, the use of such combs was expressly supported by the chairman of the Wool Council of Australia.

6. It was clear that wide combs, now available and in use, are suited to the Australian industry without any requirement for modification by the shearer.[146]

The commissioners accepted that in the main the evidence of AWU witnesses was given by people who had little or no practical experience of wide comb shearing. They said the union's vigorous opposition to wide combs and its pursuit of the matter through the appeal appeared to any objective observer 'to be hedged in by conservatism and tinged with hysteria'.[147]

Of Commissioner McKenzie's decision, they said,

> Not only do we consider that his decision and the orders he made are acceptable as being within the exercise of a valid discretion, we are of the view that no other course was sensibly open to him in the circumstances.

The union's argument that the commissioner should have specified the type of combs that could be used was rejected, with the commissioners saying such a restriction would have smothered the development and manufacture of more efficient combs within the Australian industry. The decision of which comb to use was 'better left to the good sense of the shearer, in conjunction with his employer' they said.

In rejecting the appeal, the commissioners made a minor

amendment to the wording of Commissioner McKenzie's original decision – they changed the phrase 'grower or his representative' to read 'employer' – the original wording had created some difficulties in circumstances where the grower was not the employer of the shearer. So the key part of Clause 32 now read,

> *Unless he elects to do so with the express approval of his employer, no shearer or crutcher shall use or be required to use any comb wider than 64 mm between the points of the outside teeth.*

Dismissal of the substance of the appeal effectively lifted the stay order on Commissioner McKenzie's ruling. Shearers could now use wide combs legally. Ernie Ecob had been right when he said it would be very hard for the union to win an appeal.

26

The Strike – Events Speed Up

While the AWU's appeal was being heard, an event took place that was to have a significant impact on the political and economic backdrop against which the dispute was to continue to unfold. That event was a federal election. For the past seven years, since 1975, Australia had been governed by a Liberal National Party coalition led by Malcolm Fraser (prime minister) and Doug Anthony (deputy prime minister). But the national economy had not been performing well, and by the time the 1980s popped up, it was well and truly in recession. High unemployment and high inflation were stifling economic growth. Industrial disputes were crippling productivity and disrupting national economic output. To top it off, in the early 1980s much of eastern Australia was hit by widespread drought, which devastated many rural industries and communities.

Coinciding with this national economic decline in the early 1980s, there was a growing mood of discontent within the opposition Labor Party, as various factions and senior figures became disheartened with the performance of its leader, Bill Hayden. By February 1983, the party had reached a tipping point. Two days before caucus was due to meet in Brisbane on 3 February, several senior Labor figures attended the funeral of Frank Forde, a leading Queensland Labor politician who had served as Australia's caretaker prime minister for one week following the death of John Curtin in 1945. After the formalities, Hayden's close friend Senator John Button, the then Shadow Minister for Communications, advised him he needed to step aside as leader to make way for the party's rising star, Bob Hawke. At that stage Hawke, the member for Wills (Melbourne), had only been in parliament for two years and had not even held a shadow portfolio. He had, however, already had a crack at toppling Hayden – he narrowly lost a caucus leadership ballot to Hayden during the party's federal conference at Canberra's Lakeside Hotel the previous July. This time Hawke had the numbers to win a leadership vote. So, when the caucus meeting started, Hayden resigned to avoid a messy and damaging showdown and Hawke was elevated to opposition leader. Later that day, still upset at being usurped, Hayden famously said, 'A drover's dog could lead the Labor Party to victory the way the country is.'

As it turned out, Fraser had picked that same day to call an early election. The full parliamentary term still had seven months to run, but he was aiming to take advantage of the infighting and uncertainty over the Labor Party leadership, which had intensified since the Christmas–New Year holiday period. The Senate had twice rejected several pieces of legislation, so he was planning a double dissolution of the parliament. Well before the caucus meeting was due to start in Brisbane, Fraser jumped in his Comcar at Parliament House in Canberra and was driven to Government House in Yarralumla, the official digs of the governor-general. At the time, the occupant of Government House was the British-born Sir Ninian Stephen (1923–2017), a distinguished former justice of the High Court of Australia and Australia's only immigrant governor-general. However, things did not go as smoothly as Fraser had anticipated. For starters, he did not have an appointment and, even though he was the prime minister of Australia, Sir Ninian made him wait. Indeed, it was a three-hour wait while Sir Ninian fulfilled a previous appointment. When Fraser eventually got to see Sir Ninian, the governor-general asked many questions and it took another hour for the pair to complete the paperwork that goes with dissolving both houses of parliament and approving the issuing of election writs. Meanwhile, the Labor caucus meeting had wrapped up in Brisbane. There were no smartphones or instant messaging in those days – Fraser only learned that Hawke was the new opposition leader when he returned to Parliament House. Fraser had intended to catch Labor off guard, but it was he who had been caught out.

The election was held on Saturday 5 March and Labor won in a landslide, taking 24 seats from the Liberals. Hawke was sworn in as prime minister on Friday 11 March, the day after submissions in the union's appeal hearing were finalised. Hayden went on to serve as Foreign Minister in the Hawke government, which extended over four terms and into the early 1990s. Before entering parliament, Hawke had been president of the ACTU for 10 years and it was his close ties with the union movement that allowed the Labor Party to form one of its key economic reform policies – a prices and incomes accord. This was a treaty between the ACTU and the Labor Party in which the ACTU agreed to restrain wage claims and minimise industrial disruption, and the government committed to reducing inflation and improving the 'social wage' – this included education, health and welfare spending. This consensus approach to government effectively gave the union movement a small role in the economic management of the nation while Labor was in power.

The significance of the change in government for the wide comb dispute was that the AWU now had a more sympathetic ear to speak to and greater access to key political leaders. This meant that when the union's appeal was rejected, less than two weeks after the new Hawke government was sworn in, the dispute would steadily become more politicised than it had been to date. The AWU would pull out all stops in its quest to have wide combs banned, including appealing to government ministers and, indeed, the prime minister, to intervene and help.

The dispute gathers pace

Developments in the dispute sped up following the full bench's rejection of the union's appeal. Anticipating that the appeal would fail, the LGPA had prepared a media release welcoming the commission's decision. It was distributed on the afternoon of Wednesday 23 March. In the release, LGPA president Harold Balcomb said wool growers were relieved and heartened by the Arbitration Commission's decision, which had acknowledged that '...many shearers had found wide combs preferable to standard combs, and easier to use'. Balcomb ended by saying, 'Because the Arbitration Commission has rejected outright all grounds of union opposition to wide comb use, it is wool-growers' sincere hope that the union will adopt a more open-minded approach to the whole issue of shearing combs.'[148] The union, however, had no such intention.

Shearers call national strike

Indeed, even as the LGPA's media release was being distributed, shearers and shed hands in South Australia, Victoria, Tasmania and New South Wales were walking off the job. This was no surprise, as officials had foreshadowed a widespread strike. A meeting of New South Wales shearers had been organised for Dubbo on Thursday 24 March, the day after the appeal decision was handed down, with similar meetings to take place in other states. In the lead-up to the Dubbo meeting, Ernie Ecob told *The Land* that there would be an indefinite stoppage by up to 20,000 shearers and shed hands throughout Australia. 'There will be no union shearing – there will be a few scabs, but we will handle them,' he said.[149] This information was published on the morning of the meeting, before any deliberations by rank and file members.

According to the minutes, 532 shearers from 60 districts attended the meeting, which was held at the Dubbo Golf Club and lasted two hours. Predictably, Ernie Ecob slammed the decisions of both Commissioner McKenzie and the full bench, suggesting much of the union's key evidence had been unfairly ignored. However, while lamenting the failure of the union case and subsequent appeal, he revealed that earlier that year he had written to the premiers in the key pastoral states (Neville Wran, New South Wales; John Cain, Victoria;

John Bannon, South Australia; and Robin Gray, Tasmania), as well as the then federal opposition leader Bill Hayden, and Shadow Minister for Immigration Mick Young, urging them to enact or support legislation outlawing wide combs on safety grounds. Young, the member for Port Adelaide, was a former shearer who entered politics on the back of his experience as an organiser for the South Australian branch of the AWU. He had been included in the correspondence because of the union's ongoing concern about New Zealand shearers working in Australia. Ecob's plea to these Labor politicians was like a desperate trick shot to get out of the snooker he was in after snubbing the Arbitration Commission during its New South Wales hearings. Unfortunately for the union, the shot did not come off.

Given that the union had no fallback position from its *implacable hostile opposition* to wide combs, it had little choice other than to pursue a strike – shearers voted overwhelmingly (531–1) to strike indefinitely but to meet again on 12 April to review developments in the dispute. One immediate casualty of the strike was Sydney's annual Royal Easter Show, which was due to begin the following day. All shearing events had to be cancelled. The day after the Dubbo meeting, Victorian shearers voted 299–3 to strike indefinitely, and in South Australia the aggregated vote from four of five regional meetings on the Friday was 196–13 in favour of striking. The fifth meeting, in the state's north the following day, added about 60 yes votes to the overall count.

Legal advice sought

Still convinced their objections to wide combs were justified, the New South Wales shearers asked the AWU Executive Council to pursue a High Court challenge to the Arbitration Commission's decision. They had just been clean bowled and were asking the umpire for a review. However, it took just four days for the huff and puff of another legal challenge to deflate. On Monday 28 March, AWU federal secretary Frank Mitchell received legal advice from the union's long-time solicitors, Commins and Company. Stripped of the jargon, the single-page letter said there were no legitimate grounds for an appeal – not what the union wanted to hear.

Dispute becomes politicised

Conscious of the recent change in government, the shearers at Dubbo also voted to have the union's Executive Council ask the ACTU to help organise a deputation to the new federal Minister for Employment and Industrial Relations, Ralph Willis. They wanted to implore him '… to have a full investigation into the Award and the unsatisfactory decision of Commissioner McKenzie, as it will only bring industrial turmoil into the shearing industry and take away the equality of workers'.[150] The next quarterly meeting of the national executive of the ACTU was scheduled for Melbourne the following week (Tuesday and Wednesday 29 and 30 March). But like Harold Balcomb's recently expressed desire for industrial harmony, any proposed investigation was little more than wishful thinking. Willis was, however, closely watching developments in the dispute and was willing to meet with both parties to play some sort of mediation role. His private secretary, Peter Medlock, was quoted in Dubbo's *Daily Liberal* on Friday 25 March as saying, 'Mr Willis has asked the Department [of Industry and Employment] for background information to be used during talks with the parties involved.'[151]

The Dubbo meeting also featured a lively discussion about expanding the strike to involve other unions. A fired-up Bluey Rodwell told the gathering that if shearers had to starve because of the dispute, then wool growers would also be made to starve. His proclamation led to a resolution that sought to enlist the ACTU's help to ban the transport and loading of wool harvested by strike-breakers and the movement of grain to black-banned properties. This would require the cooperation of the Transport Workers' Union, the Australian Railways Union, the Storemen and Packers' Union, the Waterside Workers' Federation, and the State Grain Handling Authority.

This plan sparked outrage from the LGPA, with Harold Balcomb warning of potential industrial anarchy if unions were going to stop the movement of wool and wheat en masse. He was quoted in the *Daily Liberal* as saying, 'If the union goes ahead with threats to halt shipments of wool and wheat, the LGPA will go straight to the ACTU and [Federal] Government. We cannot have a union holding a country to ransom.'[152]

Shearers in Queensland, where wide combs were still banned under a separate state award, met on Sunday 27 March and passed a 12-point resolution supporting their southern colleagues. However, they stopped short of joining the strike. One point called on the AWU Executive Council to appeal to Prime Minister Bob Hawke and his relevant ministers to ensure that all New Zealand shearers working in Australia had some sort of identity card and were subject to a tax check before they left Australia, and also to prevent any more New Zealand shearers from entering the country until the dispute was settled.

It did not take long for the federal Shadow Minister for Primary Industry, Tom McVeigh, to enter the debate. On 28 March he called on the AWU to accept the umpire's decision, which he said had brought the eastern states into line with Western Australia and the rest of the world. 'The present Prime Minister preached much about reconciliation during the election and now, in his first test of reconciliation, he is strangely silent,' McVeigh said.

> It is ridiculous to reject the Arbitration Commission's ruling to allow the use of wide combs when an individual shearer elects to do so and an employer approves. Western Australian shearers have shown the AWU wide combs are effective in clipping their merinos, which make up most of the flock in that state.[153]

AWU Executive Council meeting

Members of the powerful AWU Executive Council met in Sydney on Tuesday and Wednesday 29–30 March. They endorsed the resolutions calling on the prime minister to implement an identity card system for foreign shearers working in Australia and for these shearers to be 'Subjected to a thorough examination by Taxation Department officers before being given a clearance to leave Australia'. They also called on federal Immigration Minister Stewart West to ensure that New Zealand shearers could not enter Australia while the wide comb dispute continued. There was also a discussion about trying to force domestic shearing comb manufacturers to stop making wide combs, with a threat that, if they refused, the union would investigate establishing its own manufacturing company to supply standard gauge combs directly to its members.[154] In the same report, the Executive Council condemned graziers for 'their attempts to deregulate the terms and conditions of the Federal Pastoral Industry Award', describing their actions as 'un-Australian'.

A paragraph in *The Land* editorial on 31 March is worth noting. It summed up the union's intransigence, to date, in the following way:

> The union's reasons for yet another wide comb stoppage were that neither New South Wales Commissioner McKenzie in the first place, nor the Full Bench in the second hearing, took proper account of the union's evidence against wide combs. With the best will in the world, and after reading transcripts of the hearing, it is difficult to see that that 'evidence' amounted to more than a head-in-the-sand attitude that wide combs were different and, therefore, must be bad.[155]

Waiting game

By the end of March, one week into the strike, both parties had major concerns about how things would play out. The union was worried about strike-breakers or 'scabs' – wide comb shearers who would defy the strike, and union shearers who might join them out of economic necessity. AWU organiser Mick O'Shea issued a clear warning when he was quoted in the *Daily Liberal* on 28 March. He said most wool growers could not do their own shearing, estimating only one in 200 could shear proficiently. He said, 'If anyone tries to use scab labour to get their sheep shorn we will act accordingly.'[156] Ernie Ecob clarified this statement the following day by saying that any shearing during the strike would result in both the shearers and wool growers being black banned.[157]

Wool growers were also worried. Depending on their location, they needed to get their flocks shorn before the end of April or by mid-May, in time for the autumn lambing season – some ewes would have difficulty lambing if they had not been shorn and crutched. However, as it happened, the timing of the strike favoured wool growers more than the union. When the shearers went on strike, the Australian Wool Corporation estimated between 85 and 90 per cent of the New South Wales flock had already been shorn. The other states had comparable completion rates. According to Ian Manning, this meant there were only about seven million sheep to be shorn by the end of April in New South Wales. 'With the shearers we have they could be knocked over by smoko,' he said at the time.[158] Manning's statement oozed confidence. However, there was still a major problem to overcome – the union would be going all out to prevent any sheep from being shorn in any of the eastern states.

Brian Clarke, the Dubbo-based New South Wales shearing manager for Farmers Grazcos, was urging wool growers to be patient. Grazcos, as it was known, was at the time Australia's largest shearing contracting business. It would play a key role in developments from this point. Clarke believed that a relatively short stoppage, of up to three weeks, would not have a major impact on shearing. However, a more drawn-out strike, beyond a month, could hurt wool growers. He said at the time, 'We are not negotiating any work until we find out the union's intentions. If they decide to stay out for a long while, we will try to supply personnel to get shearing done.'[159] For now, at least, it was a waiting game.

27

The Strike – Riverina Rebellion

April 1983 was a busy month for Brian Clarke. Leading up to the strike, during the early 1980s in New South Wales, Grazcos had about 200 shearers or roughly 30 teams on its books – nearly all of them were ticket-holding union members. It had about 450 sheds under contract and was shearing more than 1.7 million sheep each year. When the strike started, Grazcos lost just over half of its workforce overnight. It was expecting to lose more, but surprisingly, almost half its shearers stayed on in defiance of the union. So, while Clarke was publicly urging wool growers to be patient, behind the scenes he began a frantic and secret campaign to recruit more shearers to be available to help break the strike. He was, however, in a tricky position – although Grazcos wanted shearing to proceed as normal, it could not be seen publicly at least to be taking sides or openly working during the strike – otherwise the AWU would almost certainly black ban its clients. It was imperative that its recruitment campaign be clandestine and its contracts be indirect, with the paperwork identifying its wool grower clients as the official contractors.

Clarke was an ideal candidate for this campaign – years of experience as a shearer, wool classer and contractor meant he knew the pastoral industry better than most, and in rural circles he was almost as well connected as Telecom in those days. Clarke had grown up on a farm near Gilgandra, north of Dubbo, and was educated at St Stanislaus' College in Bathurst. As a youngster he was dyslexic and struggled to learn but excelled in mathematics. In 1953, aged 15, he left school to help out on the family farm – many male students of that era did likewise. His family ran 700 sheep and contracted an old-time shearer to denude them. This old-timer operated a two-stand, portable shearing plant. Sometimes he had an offsider but when he arrived at the Clarkes' patch that year he was by himself, so Brian Clarke jumped on the second stand to help him out. He went on to spend the next two years helping out this shearer, while studying wool classing via correspondence. Then for a few years he was either classing or shearing at sheds throughout the state and by age 21 he was operating a small rural contracting business, which focused on supplying shearing teams and general farm labour services. During slow times he did some contract wool classing and shearing for Grazcos and eventually they offered him full-time work as an overseer – organising shearing teams. In 1975 he became the company's Broken Hill branch manager, overseeing the merchandise and shearing businesses in the west Darling and northern South Australia areas. Five years later, having generated a tenfold increase in the branch's shearing business, Clarke, his wife Betsy and their 11 children moved to Dubbo, where Clarke took on the role of state shearing manager for Grazcos.

Smuggling shearers into New South Wales

The NFF and LGPA were determined that shearing would proceed as normal, despite the strike. This meant their members had to have access to a large pool of shearers who were willing to defy the union. The best source of such shearers was Western Australia, where there was an abundance of the non-union variety – there were more than 700 New Zealander shearers in the state's southern wool growing areas, as well as plenty of non-union Australian shearers. In early April, Clarke had meetings with LGPA officials in Warren and Coonamble. A key figure in those meetings was George Mack, who was on the LGPA Executive Council and was highly regarded in the state's pastoral industry. He had wool growing properties at Trangie and Bourke at the time. At the start of April, the LGPA had appointed Mack as one of seven regional strike-breaking coordinators (they were called 'back-to-work coordinators'), with the job of helping to organise shearing teams for wool growers in the central part of the state. Clarke assured Mack that he could get LGPA members the labour they needed. 'I told them that anyone who wanted to shear, I would supply them with people,' he recalled. 'I'd form the teams, I'd put overseers in to run them as if we [Grazcos] were doing them, but they [the wool growers] had to take the responsibility as the employer – so if you like we were behind the scenes.'

Clarke travelled to Western Australia, where he met with representatives of the Western Australian Primary Industry Association. He was put in touch with a member who agreed to help recruit shearers and shed hands for work in the eastern states. Clarke booked advertisements in key rural publications and on rural radio stations offering work for shearers and shed hands, with the association member as the contact. Lists of available workers were forwarded to Clarke, who would then contact the workers to provide them with the details they needed. Most workers entered New South Wales via Broken Hill or Mildura. Those earmarked for work in the central region were put up on farms throughout the region – in many cases they even stayed in the main homesteads. Wool growers would ring Mack to request a shearing team and he would organise a team from the list of available workers being billeted in the region. Mack kept a detailed log of all the calls he received and the movement of workers to and from various properties.

He and Clarke worked very closely during the strike – even in late April when Clarke had to be admitted to Dubbo Base Hospital to have his gallbladder removed. His recovery took a week longer than anticipated after he developed a serious infection following the surgery. Mack was a regular visitor, keeping him up to date with local developments and discussing tactics to help thwart the strike.

The Riverina rebellion

Robert White and his shearing teams continued working throughout the strike. Grazcos was also working behind the scenes to supply teams as discreetly as possible. And it was during the strike that two other 'rebel' shearers gained some prominence; first Frank Cox, a 31-year-old contractor based at Wagga Wagga in the New South Wales Riverina, and then in May, New Zealander Neil Ellery joined the fight. Like Robert White, Cox was a physically small but very accomplished shearer. And as White had done during the 1970s, Cox shore in Western Australia where he was exposed to wide combs. He worked in one shed where two Kiwi wide combers seemed to be effortlessly flying through their pens – both notched up tallies of more than 270 while at the end of the day he had shorn 192. He got talking to them about their combs and later that night ordered $600 worth of wide gear. He found it significantly easier to shear with wide combs and never looked back.

When the wide comb strike started, Cox was back in New South Wales contracting in the Riverina. Two weeks into the strike, he became a union target when he organised a meeting of disgruntled shearers and wool growers at the Wagga Wagga RSL Club on Wednesday 6 April. More than 500 people attended from throughout the Central Tablelands, Southern Tablelands, and Riverina districts. Most were wool growers. There were 170 to 180 shearers at the meeting, which attracted widespread publicity because of its outcome – the shearers voted overwhelmingly to defy the union and return to work from the following Monday (11 April), and to endorse the right of all shearers to use wide or narrow combs. The mood of the meeting was one of frustration and dissatisfaction with the AWU and its handling of the dispute – the shearers simply wanted to get on with their work and the wool growers wanted their sheep shorn. In the lead-up to the meeting, Frank Cox told *The Land*, 'We want to show that we must have freedom of choice on shearing combs and the right to work.'[160]

The day after the meeting, Wagga Wagga's *Daily Advertiser* newspaper carried a comprehensive report of the proceedings on its front page. In it, Frank Cox was quoted as saying, 'Why should Ernie

Ecob and the other union organisers say they represent Australia's 15,000 shearers when half the shearers disagree? Shearers here have won the fight – we outnumber the "red-raggers".'[161] Another report in the *Sydney Morning Herald* that day quoted several shearers who attended the meeting as saying they were sick of being stood over by union officials and told what to do.[162]

Needless to say, Ernie Ecob and other senior AWU officials were seething with rage at the Riverina rebels. Ecob scheduled an urgent meeting of AWU pastoral industry delegates at the Royal Hotel in Dubbo for later that day (Thursday 7 April) for the union to plan its response. The 60 delegates who gathered at short notice devised a two-pronged attack. The first was to publicly discredit the Riverina meeting. Organiser Mick O'Shea went straight to work on this one, issuing a statement to the *Daily Liberal* that day condemning the Wagga Wagga meeting as not being properly organised and not truly representative of the views of most shearers. The second aspect of the response was to organise a 'show of strength' meeting in Wagga Wagga for that Sunday, 10 April, 'to clarify the vote'.[163] This would be followed by the previously scheduled state meeting of shearers in Dubbo on Tuesday 12 April.

Robert White had travelled to Dubbo on Thursday 7 April, intending to try to get into the delegates' meeting to again argue his case for wide combs. He was accompanied by a crew from *60 Minutes*, who had started research and filming for a story on the dispute when the strike started the previous month. White told the *Daily Liberal* he contacted officials and asked if he could be heard. However, he was warned he would be attacked and bashed if he came to the meeting. So instead he spent the day holed up in a motel room where the *60 Minutes* team was staying and later had to be escorted out of town by police to ensure his safety. However, White told the local newspaper there was a good chance the meeting planned for Wagga Wagga that Sunday would turn violent if the union tried to force its position onto local rebel shearers intent on returning to work. 'Shearers at Wagga are determined to return to work,' he said. 'If they do that the union will try to stop them. I think it will all blow up this weekend.'[164] Interestingly, during the same interview, he told the paper, 'I may have to leave New South Wales because of the violence. But I, and other wide comb supporters, will win the fight eventually.'[165] White got it right, on both counts.

Violence erupts in Wagga Wagga

The 'show of strength' meeting was scheduled to start at 11 a.m. in the Ladies Lounge of the Wagga Wagga Leagues Club, but there was nothing ladylike about it. The meeting was always going to be controversial because it was never going to be truly democratic. The AWU could not afford to allow a large group of rebel shearers to openly express their views in the meeting and vote against continuing the strike – it had to try to maintain a united front. To ensure that this happened, it stacked the meeting. It brought in busloads of shearers from outside the Riverina, with some reports suggesting there were shearers present from Broken Hill and South Australia; and it denied entry to anyone who was recognised as having attended the rebel meeting a few days previously or who was a known wide comb supporter. So even before the meeting started, there were violent scenes at the entry to the venue.

Frank Cox, a ticket-holding union member, was denied entry. The *Daily Advertiser* reported that Cox 'feared for his safety after being threatened, insulted and abused outside the meeting'. He told journalist Guy Freeman, 'I tried to get into the meeting but was told I was nothing but a scab. A couple of minutes later a couple of men with union tickets tried to get in and a brawl broke out.' He claimed that when the meeting started, union officials called for anyone who was intending to oppose the union's position on the strike to leave the meeting or risk being thrown out. Cox said the meeting was 'a truly appalling demonstration of what the union represents'.[166] A union spokesman later told the newspaper that there had been 503 shearers present and they voted 480–20 to continue the strike. He would not say anything more about the meeting.

The crew from *60 Minutes* had also tagged along. It turned out to be a good decision. The cameraman captured some compelling and disturbing pre-meeting footage. One clip showed Frank Cox being denied entry. He insisted he was a paid-up ticket holder, but union officials told him he was not going to be allowed into the meeting because he was a scab. Another union member, Paul Woollaston, who worked for Robert White, was also filmed trying to get into the meeting. He too was denied entry with one union official telling him he was 'unfinancial and a scab'. That official then proceeded to physically attack Woollaston, pushing him backwards and eventually onto the floor. Although the view of the camera was then obscured by all the men surrounding him, it was pretty clear the men were bashing him. Soon after this incident, the cameraman and reporter Ian Leslie caught up with Woollaston as he was washing blood from his face in a bathroom. There was a brief exchange.

Leslie: Did you expect that this might happen?

Woollaston: Oh, I didn't think it would be that bad, no.

Leslie: How many people punched you?

Woollaston: Oh, I don't know, I just went down and they were putting the boot in, and I tried to cover my head over as best I could.

Leslie: Did they say why they did this?

Woollaston: Because I'm a scab.

Leslie later interviewed organiser Mick O'Shea and asked him about the union's stand on violence.

Leslie: Do you as a union leader condone those sorts of attacks?

O'Shea: I never condone any sort of attacks, any sort of violent attacks.

Leslie: Would you stop your men from attacking Bob White?

O'Shea: Would I? I'd sool them onto him.[167]

Right of entry application

The events at Wagga Wagga that Sunday were very concerning for both sides of the dispute. For the AWU, it was a public relations disaster –

or at least it would have been if it had cared more about its public image. The union certainly resented what it perceived to be the overwhelmingly biased and negative reporting it had received during the dispute. But it also seemed to adopt something of a victim or siege mentality – this view that it and the conditions it had fought so hard to achieve were under attack from all sides, including from a small number of its own members. In such circumstances, negative media coverage was unwelcome, but it was also to be expected.

Nevertheless, when Leslie's *60 Minutes* report *Wild and Woolly* beamed into living rooms across Australia the following weekend, the union would not have won any friends. The 15-minute report showed footage of a heavy-handed union official attacking Paul Woollaston; other officials intimidating Frank Cox; Mick O'Shea denouncing violence then seconds later saying he would readily 'sool' AWU members onto Robert White; and a veteran union shearer proudly boasting about how he had taken part in the bashing of Robert White and his team at Eromanga, and justifying the assault on Gayle White during the same incident. It was outrageous stuff – the union was made to look like a bunch of thugs.

When they next met in Dubbo, nine days after the program was broadcast, union officials were still sufficiently riled to demand Ernie Ecob obtain legal advice about a possible defamation suit against Channel 9. No legal action was ever taken.

For the wool growers, the Wagga Wagga confrontation was the trigger to lodge an urgent application with the Arbitration Commission. Paul Houlihan wrote to Commissioner McKenzie first thing the following day (Monday 11 April), saying the actions of the union were placing the continued functioning of 'Australia's greatest industry' at risk. 'NFF believes, as a first step, this Commission must remove the right of entry from the Pastoral Award for the duration of this stoppage to enable those shearers who wish to shear in accordance with the Award to do so,' he wrote.[168] This was a radical step – a union's right of entry to a workplace was seen at that time as being almost sacrosanct. It recognised that union officials, under certain circumstances, should be allowed to enter workplaces to speak to their members without fear of being prosecuted for trespass. Commissioner McKenzie agreed to at least entertain the application and the matter was listed for hearing that afternoon in Sydney.

Houlihan represented the wool growers, and Michael Forshaw, the then senior industrial officer of the federal branch of the AWU, represented the union. Houlihan argued the union was effectively in contempt of the commission, which had a responsibility to ensure its orders were followed. 'We are now in the situation where the union have lost the action before the Commission, they have lost the appeal before the Full Bench, and they are seeking and insisting they are going to win it outside the Commission,' he said.[169] He outlined in detail two instances of the union having abused the Award's right of entry provisions during the strike and said there were now legitimate grounds for the commission to withdraw that right: 'We say there is enough intimidation and harassment on people now post Wagga for this Commission to act in the way we have sought… We do not want to have the [union] heavies coming on to properties telling people that they are never going to get another job, or telling people that they cannot receive their wool, or get stockfeed, and all the rest of this nonsense; we will simply lock the gates. That is our position,' he said.[170]

Forshaw, who went on to become a long-serving Labor senator, rose to the challenge. He calmly pointed out that all of Houlihan's arguments were, in effect, hypothetical, as there was no proper application before the commission to hear the matter; nor was there a proper notification of dispute. The only documentation the union had received was a telexed message about the urgent listing. 'This application that has been foreshadowed to remove Clause 78 [the right of entry clause] is one more attempt by the employers to break down the union's role and rights in this industry to represent its members,' he said.

> I do not want to debate the merits of the application at this time because there is no formal application before this Commission.

There is, in my opinion, no proper notification of dispute. Indeed, the applications relating to matters 3105 and 3221 [the Commonwealth Reporting Service reference numbers for the wide comb dispute] have nothing to do with the right of entry clause in this Award. We protest strongly at being ambushed at the eleventh hour this morning with an application that we have not seen and with a hearing that we believe is a waste of time at this time, but we have attended the hearing because we did receive a notification. Our view is that this Commission should not proceed any further with these proceedings and that the matter should be stood over generally.

Commissioner McKenzie noted that Houlihan had been instructed to file the relevant paperwork with the commission registry the following morning and sought an assurance from Forshaw that the union would agree not to abuse the Award's right of entry provisions. However, Forshaw argued that making any such commitment was akin to admitting that the union had previously abused the clause, and he was not prepared to do that. This prompted some terse exchanges between the commissioner and Forshaw, but Forshaw stood his ground and the result was a stalemate. Commissioner McKenzie adjourned the matter overnight to ensure the required paperwork was completed; he then reserved his decision.

However, further submissions were heard when Paul Houlihan sought an urgent relisting of the matter in Adelaide on Thursday 21 April. Houlihan called as a witness a farmer from western Victoria whose identity was suppressed for fear of possible reprisals. The farmer gave evidence about an attack that occurred the previous afternoon on his property, where shearing had been taking place. He said five or six cars drove onto his property and up to 30 men jumped out; most ran towards the shearing shed. At least 10 of the men were wielding sticks. The farmer ran toward the group and confronted the men, telling them to leave. However, he said the men threatened to kill him (via 'a bullet in the head'), pull down and cut his fences, and burn down his shearing shed. The four shearers fled, and one was hurt while trying to jump a fence to escape his attackers. No one was badly injured, but the incident had spooked the farmer and the shearing team. The farmer said as the men gathered to leave, two of the group told the others to go, then approached him and identified themselves as union organisers. Houlihan reportedly told the commission, 'We have not got an industrial dispute; we have terrorism in the industry at the moment. Men are working in accord with the Awards of the Commission, and the only way they feel confident is with a gun beside them... If someone is not killed before this week is out, it is going to be a miracle.'[171]

According to the *Adelaide Advertiser*, Commissioner McKenzie described the attack as 'absolutely disgraceful'. He said, 'When people have to resort to those tactics, it means there is no logic, reasoning or merit left in their argument.'[172] He also reportedly said, 'We are conscious that something must be done to stop what is nothing short of industrial anarchy.'[173]

The hearing was adjourned, as the AWU had been unable to organise representation at short notice; all its senior officials had been involved in an Executive Council meeting in Sydney. The matter was adjourned to Sydney the following Tuesday, 26 April, to allow the AWU to cross-examine the farmer and finalise its submissions.

Despite compelling evidence about attacks on shearing sheds and his own observation that the pastoral industry had spiralled into 'industrial anarchy', Commissioner McKenzie eventually rejected the NFF's application. These violent incidents were not linked to the right of entry provisions of the Award and withdrawing the right would not prevent a group of men intent on violence from entering properties and causing more violence. This ruling was a small victory for the AWU. Ian Manning later described the wool growers' application as 'Not one of our moments of glory'. Paul Houlihan agreed, but also gave credit to Forshaw for his dogged determination at the bar table, particularly during the initial submissions. 'He really stood his ground and almost bullied McKenzie into not taking the right of entry from them,' he said. 'It was a great bit of advocacy.'

Back to Dubbo

Almost three weeks after the strike had started, on 12 April as scheduled, AWU shearers converged on the Dubbo Golf Club for an update on developments. The meeting was chaired by Mick O'Shea and lasted just over four hours. Proceedings began with a lengthy report summarising the resolve of members in different parts of the state. And while most areas continued to back the strike, cracks were starting to appear in the union's united front. Work was proceeding in the areas around Bathurst, Oberon, Temora, Deniliquin and Broken Hill; and in Wellington local shearers had voted to return to work. As for Wagga Wagga, where there was clearly a strong contingent of shearers who wanted to return to work, the only reference minuted was 'Reported on meeting arranged by scabs and graziers. Meeting to be ignored by members. Also report on meeting held by members Sunday 10th April, where support was solid.'[174] Delegates from South Australia and Victoria also attended and reported there was strong support to continue the strike in those states.

Ernie Ecob told members that during the previous week a delegation of AWU federal branch officials and ACTU president Cliff Dolan, who took over from Bob Hawke when Hawke entered politics, had met with government ministers at Parliament House in Canberra, including Primary Industry Minister John Kerin, Immigration Minister Stewart West, Industrial Relations Minister Ralph Willis, and Special Minister of State Mick Young, as well as an official from the Australian Tax Office, to discuss the dispute. He said the delegation had received 'a sympathetic hearing' and the ministers had promised to 'explore all avenues of support'. Not much more is known about this meeting, which is significant in the context of what took place during the next few weeks. It is known, however, that Ralph Willis asked the Parliament's Legislative Research Service to prepare a briefing paper about the wide comb dispute. He received this four-page report on 7 April, before the meeting with the AWU and ACTU delegation.

Three weeks into the strike, there had been ugly scenes in Wagga

Wagga, a fresh action in the Arbitration Commission and lobbying for political intervention. Still there was no sign either side would back down. Wool growers were determined that freedom of choice should be maintained; and most union shearers were equally as determined that wide combs had to be outlawed. As both sides dug in, the spiteful nature of the dispute was about to intensify yet again.

28

The Strike – Things Turn Nasty

Mutooroo Station is a large sheep run in the remote north-east of South Australia, near the small border town of Cockburn and about 100 kilometres south-west of Broken Hill. It was the early childhood home of pioneering aviators Ross and Keith Smith, whose father Andrew was station manager during the late 1880s and 1890s. In November and December 1919, brothers Ross and Keith became the first pilots to fly from England to Australia. In doing so, they won a £10,000 Australian government reward and kick-started Australia's international aviation industry. During the early 1980s, the station was owned by the Mutooroo Pastoral Company. It had a footprint of 2,180 square kilometres and ran roughly 27,000 sheep.

About two weeks into the strike, the station began shearing. James Morgan, who was the Adelaide-based managing director of the Mutooroo Pastoral Company, told the *Barrier Daily Truth* newspaper the decision to start shearing was not an act of defiance against the union. Rather, it was an act of necessity – the flock had gone through two years of drought and was in poor condition, and had been mustered over vast distances ready to shear in the hope that the strike would soon end. When it dragged on, the sheep simply had to be shorn for their own well-being.[175]

Word got out that shearing was taking place at the station and the AWU twice sent organisers to inspect the shed during the first few days – these visits resulted in two shearers leaving. Seven shearers remained. They were all using narrow gear and were determined to finish the shed. There were another six members of the team. However, about 8.30 a.m. on Thursday 14 April, four vehicles carrying 15 men entered the property and headed toward the shearing shed. The manager, 28-year-old John Manning, and his wife were in the homestead at the time. Mrs Manning spotted the vehicles and alerted her husband, who immediately headed for the shed. She then radioed the shearing shed to warn the team of the approaching vehicles. According to various accounts of the incident published within the following week, John Manning arrived just before the vehicles pulled up. When he asked the men what they were doing, one of them grabbed a nearby shed broom and struck him over the head with it. The force of the blow broke the broom handle and caused a large gash and splintering in Manning's head. Several men then kicked him before the group entered the shed.

The overseer, 50-year-old Bill Allen, later told *The Land*, 'They came into the shed and I tried to delay them by asking "What do you want?" One bloke hit me and called me a…a scabby… I retreated and was in the catching pen and they were hitting me from all sides. I went down and they started putting the boot in.'[176] Allen was badly injured – the article included a photo of his battered and bruised face, which was quite confronting. One report suggested he was struck in the face and on the body with a shearing handpiece.[177] Two shearers were also attacked – one was held by several men while being bashed and he too was struck with a handpiece. Although extremely vicious, the attack did not last long and the men soon left. Manning managed to get the registration details of one vehicle. He called the police, who began an investigation. Allen and one of the shearers had to be flown to Broken Hill for treatment at the local hospital.

James Morgan was distraught at what happened. He told the *Barrier Daily Truth*, 'We never anticipated it coming to this extent. If we had, we obviously would be reluctant to expose any of the shearing team or our employees to any violence. When that happened we immediately declared a cut-out.'[178]

Several union officials were quick to come out publicly to try to distance the union from the attack, saying the union did not condone violence. However, the following month three men were arrested and charged over the attack – all three were union shearers from Broken Hill.

Paul McGaw, a third-generation shearer from Lucindale in South Australia, was shearing at neighbouring Pine Creek Station when Mutooroo was raided. McGaw had had an ambivalent relationship with the union over the years. He had mostly been a strong supporter, but he disagreed with the way the union was handling the wide comb issue – hence he was shearing, with narrow gear, as part of a Grazcos team during the strike. McGaw had been planning to have a break and let the dust settle on the wide comb issue after finishing at Pine Creek Station. But the violence enacted at Mutooroo reinforced his current discontent with the union and changed his mind. 'That's what made me stay on [working during the strike]; when those gutless arseholes picked on that old man. And [another Mutooroo shearer] Dale McAlister got a scar down his face from the corner of a narrow comb,' he said. 'Once they [unionists] did that, it got my back up, and not only me, it got a lot of other blokes' backs up too. You just don't flog an old man like that.'

Graeme Pora, who had taken over from Brian Clarke as manager of the Broken Hill branch of Grazcos, said the union wrongly blamed him for organising the shearing team at Mutooroo – the contract had in fact been organised by Brian Clarke from Dubbo. Pora was an accomplished shearer who grew up in Avoca in central Victoria. He mixed shearing with a variety of other rural jobs over the years but always seemed to come back to shearing. 'I always copped the blame for organising the Mutooroo team…that hung with me for 20 years,' he said. His falling out with the union was compounded when he and his wife Carmel had a holiday in New Zealand that overlapped with the start of the strike. The trip had been organised several months in advance for the couple to catch up with some close friends. 'Because we went to New Zealand, I got blamed for going over there to recruit shearers and I never spoke to one shearer over there…we had had the trip booked for months…that was their small-minded attitude.' Pora said the couple became a target of the union during the strike – Carmel's car tyres were slashed and a couple of small fires were lit against the side of their house. 'It would never have burnt the house, it was cement rendered,' he said. 'They just set a little fire up against the wall and lit it but it was just scare tactics; they were pretty radical people.'

LGPA offers growers support

As the shearing strike entered its fourth week, the LGPA had been number crunching. It estimated the stoppage was costing the state's pastoral industry about $10 million per week. Many wool growers were in a bind – they had been delaying shearing as long as possible hoping the strike would end. They now had to get their sheep shorn. Pregnant ewes need to be shorn at least a month before lambing – shearing is stressful for sheep and any shorter period can result in increased lamb losses. And for ewes not shorn before lambing, a long fleece can make it difficult for their lambs to suckle, leading to losses. The earliest these ewes can then be shorn is two months after lambing and if they are exposed to heavy rain during this period the weight of a saturated fleece can also cause serious health problems. In many areas, that one-month window before lambing was starting to close. But the Mutooroo incident was a reminder of the very real possibility of being targeted by militant unionists and the potential for violent altercations to occur.

Mindful of the dilemma facing its members, the LGPA committed to doing everything it could to provide them with 'moral and physical support'. It issued a media release in which it reassured the AWU that it had 'no intention of seeking a breakdown in the Pastoral Award as a result of the introduction of wide combs'.[179] It also took the rather unusual step of forming a team of on-call bodyguards who would be made available to any wool growers who felt the need for physical protection for their shearing teams. Ian Manning told the *Daily Liberal*, 'Bodyguards will not be standing around looking for trouble. But if any trouble develops, protection will be only a phone call away.'[180]

Meanwhile, the LGPA was ramping up a public relations campaign to 'set the record straight on the wide comb dispute'.[181] The association organised public meetings for wool growers and shearers at Narrandera, Coonamble and Armidale to clarify its position. The meetings, scheduled for Monday 18 April, were to have independent chairs – in Coonamble local AWU members had nominated Frank Fish to chair the meeting; Fish was a former shearer and Labor Party candidate for the federal seat of Gwydir during the 1970s. The Narrandera meeting was to be chaired by a local Uniting Church minister and in Armidale, the local mayor, Claude Canerio, had agreed to be moderator. Light aircraft had been organised to shuttle participants and the media from town to town throughout the day, starting in Narrandera at 11 a.m. and ending in Armidale at six p.m. The LGPA invited Ernie Ecob or an AWU representative in his place to attend and have equal time to explain the union's position. Even though the association offered to cover all the costs associated with the tour, Ecob declined the offer. In each town, however, there were local union officials who attended the meetings under instructions that they were not to vote on any motions.

The *Daily Liberal* described the Coonamble meeting as 'a theatre of conciliation between shearer and grazier…aimed at trying to resolve the wide comb dispute'. However, it went on to say, '…the chances of reconciliation already appear doomed because of a decision by union officials to reject an invitation to attend'.[182]

In excess of 2,350 people attended the three meetings – more than 1,000 in Narrandera; 750 in Coonamble; and 600 in Armidale. A couple of interesting points emerged from the tour: it seemed clear that from the perspective of many graziers the dispute had morphed from a purely industrial argument over the merits of wide combs to the bigger picture issue of freedom of choice; and a new voice was joining the debate – the Shearing Contractors' Association of Australia. The association was formed in 1927 to represent the interests of businesses involved in contract shearing. Its vice president, Kevin Humphries, who himself ran a contract shearing business based at Wellington in the New South Wales central west, attended the Coonamble meeting and explained that the association was pushing for a return to work on the basis that its 260 members would only field teams who used narrow gear. The union was resisting this push and it was not clear how the plan would or could be enforced.

Developments in South Australia and Victoria

Meanwhile, following the violence at Mutooroo and the LGPA's offer of bodyguards to protect shearing teams in New South Wales, graziers and rebel shearing teams in other states were also taking extra precautions. In South Australia and Victoria, guns, axe handles, iron bars and even hockey sticks began appearing in shearing sheds. At Didicoolum, a station about 20 kilometres west of Willalooka in the south-east of South Australia, a cache of rifles and shotguns was stacked inside the shearing shed when work started on Monday 18 April. Two of the seven shearers in the team had been at Mutooroo the previous week, so they knew firsthand what could be expected if unionists raided the property. The team was taking no chances.

Didicoolum was owned by Thomas and Patricia Brinkworth, who were prominent and large-scale wool growers – they had many rural holdings in the region, as well as other parts of the state and interstate. The station supported a flock of 10,000 medium wool merino wethers and each year the clip was sent to the Elders Wool Store in Adelaide. Peter O'Brien, who was one of four shed hands at Didicoolum that year, recalled it being 'a tense two weeks' of shearing. O'Brien had worked as a wool classer for Grazcos since the mid-1970s. He was recruited into the Didicoolum team from his role in Grazcos' head office in Collins Street, Melbourne, where he was charged with auditing the shearing books from the company's operations in South Australia, Victoria, Tasmania and the New South Wales Riverina.

When shearing started, Thomas Brinkworth took the unusual step of notifying the AWU's South Australian branch south-east organiser, Neville Thompson, that he had a rebel team on his property. He told Adelaide's *Advertiser* newspaper, 'We did not want them to think we were scared of them. We feel that if we hide what we are doing they will take it as a sign of weakness.'[183] It was, in effect, a subtle way of warning Thompson that the team was well prepared should unionists decide to raid the property. They didn't raid the property, but organisers inspected the shed. 'Shearing was held up many times with the local union representative visiting the shed,' O'Brien recalled. 'On the first visit by a union official, he was escorted to the shed by two police cars.'

The *Advertiser* sent a journalist and photographer to report on the wide comb dispute (on Tuesday 19 April). Next day the shed was on the front page, showing a picture of one of the shearers with a pick handle next to the down tube of his shearing machine and a story of what was happening at Didicoolum. The article quoted a member of the shearing team as saying, 'I have a family to feed and a house and a car to pay for. I don't see why I should go on strike for such a stupid issue and let my family suffer.'

O'Brien said on the first Friday (22 April) shearing finished early to allow the team to return home in daylight. 'Mr Brinkworth got a neighbour who had a light plane to take off and check the nearby roads (to make sure no unionists were waiting to ambush the team),' he said. 'The shearing was completed [on Friday 29 April] after many interruptions. Mr Brinkworth presented all the shed staff with an inscribed cup for doing a good job of shearing the sheep during a difficult period.'

It seemed the 'stupid issue' sentiment was shared by many other shearers in South Australia. Although accurate figures were hard to come by, the United Farmers and Stockowners of South Australia, which represented the state's farmers, estimated that 60 per cent of

South Australian wool growers who were wanting to shear were going ahead. Only Western Australia had a higher rate of shearing – the strike in the west went mostly unnoticed as shearing proceeded as normal.

AWU executive recommends return to work

With no end to the dispute in sight, and still no plan B to its *implacable hostile opposition* to wide combs, the AWU was again canvassing its legal options. Less than a month after its solicitors had torpedoed challenging the full bench decision, saying, '…any appeal would not be a viable proposition', the union wanted fresh eyes to look for any chink in the ruling that could make it susceptible to an appeal. In mid-April, it asked its barristers, Joe Bannon and Garry Johnston, to re-examine two options in particular – a Section 59 application to the Arbitration Commission; and a Writ of Mandamus application in the High Court. Section 59 of the Conciliation and Arbitration Act gave the commission the power to set aside an award or any terms of an award if it considered it desirable to do so, or to remove an element of ambiguity or uncertainty. Lodging a Section 59 application was treated as being notification of an industrial dispute.

A Writ of Mandamus was an order compelling a public authority to perform a duty it had neglected. The AWU still believed its appeal should have been treated as a fresh hearing – it had put this argument to the full bench panel. However, the full bench rejected the argument, saying that if every appeal had to start from scratch to hear new evidence, the arbitration system would very quickly become so clogged it would be unworkable. The union was considering challenging this ruling in the High Court. Bannon and Johnston wrote to the union on 19 April, suggesting both legal options had some merit but the prospects of success would ultimately hinge on the strength of any new evidence it could produce.

This advice was discussed at the AWU's Executive Council meeting in Sydney on Thursday 21 April – a meeting that was to become a turning point in the strike. The minutes show that the executive expressed '…deep concern that members should not be locked into an inflexible position in this dispute'. Almost two years after adopting a stance of *implacable hostile opposition* to wide combs, suddenly the union's leaders were concerned about flexibility. It was, nevertheless, a sign that the executive was starting to think a bit more pragmatically.

It was clear that the strike was not going to reverse the Arbitration Commission's decision. The use of wide combs had been legalised. The longer the strike continued, the greater the financial pressure for shearers and the more likely it was that there would be increased violence. There was, in fact, a possibility that someone would be killed. The union's leaders realised the need for some sort of outside intervention if shearers were going to have any chance of winning the dispute or at least saving face – another legal battle or some sort of political mediation were the only interventions that seemed possible. Given that political mediation was out of its control, the executive was planning to lodge a Section 59 application in the Arbitration Commission to have Commissioner McKenzie's variations to the Pastoral Industry Award set aside. Knowing that any legal action would almost certainly be protracted, it was going to recommend shearers return to work using only narrow gear pending the outcome of the application. The dilemma it faced was how to package this proposal so that it was not interpreted as a complete backdown by the union.

The executive recommended a return to work on the basis that all 'scabs' would continue to be declared black, as would the wool they shore and the properties they worked on. It maintained its complete opposition to wide combs. The following excerpt from the minutes of the meeting shows what members of the executive were thinking:

> We are not prepared to have our members vacate the field so that scabs with wide combs may be permitted to take the work from which our members derive their living honestly and with dignity and to ensure that members are not bankrupted whilst scabs using

wide combs are left with a free hand to shear at will throughout Australia. Our overall strategy has been and will be developed with a number of different tactics designed to maximise the work opportunities of decent members of the Union to ensure that wide combs usage is minimised and eventually becomes non-existent. The Executive Council is aware that if the strike is allowed to continue during this intervening period then we could see violence and bloodshed erupting in many rural centres. In saying this we believe that it would be wrong to have members subjected to an indefinite stoppage while political solutions are being pursued and while our legal options are being examined by our legal counsel, as these matters could take a number of weeks.

Members within each state now had to vote on this proposal. However, it was always going to be difficult to sell to shearers who less than a month ago were talking about striking until the year 2000 if necessary to defeat the scourge of wide combs. The first vote took place on Friday 22 April at Lucindale in South Australia, where more than 250 shearers overwhelmingly rejected the proposal. Reports of the count varied, but it was clear that the vote in favour of the executive's proposal was in single digits. Similar branch level meetings took place over the following days in other parts of South Australia and in Victoria, Tasmania and New South Wales. Every meeting rejected the proposal. The Dubbo meeting was held on Tuesday 26 April, where 136 delegates representing 68 regions of the state were unanimous in their opposition to the proposal. But resolute as the shearers were, their grasp on reality was slipping. The Dubbo meeting passed an eight-point resolution, which included the following two points:

- We call on the Branch Secretary to notify the Executive Council to immediately take the necessary steps to arrange a conference of all parties with the consent or approval of the Minister for Industrial Relations. This conference is to be chaired by someone recommended by the Minister *so that the parties can discuss the dispute and hopefully agree to a settlement of Clause 32 returning to status quo* [emphasis added].

- This meeting decides that under no circumstances shall there be a return to work until the previous paragraph is approved and agreed to by all parties.[184]

The notion that all parties could have a friendly chat and somehow agree to Clause 32 being restored to its pre-McKenzie status amounted to something between denial and delusion. It was never going to happen.

The other thing that became clear at the Dubbo meeting was that shearers were starting to feel the financial strain of being out of work for the past month and not having any work prospects for the immediate future. Many were struggling to meet repayments for cars and whitegoods. A significant chunk of meeting time was taken up focusing on members' rights when dealing with repossessors who were acting on behalf of hire purchase companies. Brian Clarke summed it up perfectly: '…we [the wool growers] were claiming that we were shearing a lot of sheep and we weren't shearing very many…but as we did manage to get sheep shorn that was putting a fair bit of pressure on local shearers because once the sheep had been shorn, you couldn't shear them twice.'

Growing pressure on government

Unemployed shearers were not the only ones feeling the heat. As the dispute dragged on through April, the Hawke government had been coming under growing pressure to intervene and demonstrate its 'conciliation credentials'. The AWU had been calling for support, lobbying various ministers directly and through the ACTU. But other parties were now queuing up to demand action. On Wednesday 20 April, the seven-member executive of the Wool Council of Australia had a telephone conference to discuss the dispute. The Wool Council had applauded the decision to legalise wide combs and was not about to tolerate a return to only narrow gear. President Ian McLachlan wrote via telex to Bob Hawke, imploring his government to support the Arbitration Commission by pressuring the AWU to adhere to the commission's rulings and return to work. He warned the strike had created a 'totally explosive' situation in many rural areas and argued that if unions were going to treat the commission's decisions with disdain, employers would have grounds to ignore the commission's wage decisions.

Tom McVeigh, the Shadow Minister for Primary Industry, was not missing the opportunity for some political point-scoring. The member for Darling Downs, a Queensland seat based around the regional city of Toowoomba, issued a statement on 22 April in which he slammed the government for its '…woeful lack of national leadership in the worsening crisis over the use of wide combs in the shearing industry'.[185] The statement went on,

> …it now seems the Arbitration Commission is being used as a circus that goes round and round at the will and whim of the trade unions, with encouragement from the Government.
>
> Mr McVeigh said the Government had allowed the shearers' dispute to boil up to the extent where sections of the Australian Workers' Union were openly involved in violence, intimidation, destruction of property and general law breaking.
>
> The Government has done absolutely nothing to try and resolve this dispute. All it can now offer is a statement by the Minister for Industrial Relations saying he is pleased the union is to further appeal to the Arbitration Commission, and calling on AWU branches to return to work. Such non-action is simply not good enough.

Ralph Willis was the member for Gellibrand, a safe Labor seat in the western suburbs of Melbourne. He was first elected to parliament in 1972 following a career as a research officer with the ACTU. During most of the seven years before the 1983 federal election, he had held the shadow portfolios of Industrial Relations, Economic Affairs and Treasury. However, in January 1983, just weeks before he himself was dumped, opposition leader Bill Hayden removed Willis from the Treasury portfolio to make way for Paul Keating, who he believed had a bent for economic policy. Mindful of his former ACTU links, Bob

Hawke kept Willis in the Industrial Relations portfolio during his first term in office. Now, less than two months into the job, Willis was in the spotlight. This was the first big test for a government whose campaign slogan was 'Bringing Australia Together' and who boasted of its ability to temper the more radical elements of the trade union movement.

Willis knew the AWU was going to lodge a Section 59 application with the Arbitration Commission. The union's Executive Council had recommended shearers end the strike to allow this process to take place and Willis had publicly welcomed this development. However, shearers were resisting the call to return to work. So, in a bid to speed up the process, Willis pulled out a little known and rarely used power available to the federal government under Section 25 of the Conciliation and Arbitration Act, which allowed the minister to notify a dispute to the commission. This had the effect of forcing the commission to convene a meeting of the two parties to try to settle the dispute. 'The government has taken this initiative in the public interest, in an attempt to get the parties back to the Arbitration Commission, which is the appropriate forum to discuss their differences and resolve this dispute,' Willis said.

> What is required now is for all parties to approach proceedings in the Commission in a cooperative and constructive way, with a determination on both sides to achieve a resolution… Again I would urge AWU members to follow the recommendation of their own Federal Executive and return to work immediately, allowing the dispute to be dealt with in the Commission.[186]

The government's intervention had at least created a mechanism through which shearers and wool growers could come together. But the Arbitration Commission would be reluctant to convene any meeting while the shearers were still on strike.

29

The Strike – an End In Sight

By the start of May 1983, with the strike in its sixth week, the AWU's defiant stance was starting to wobble. Although publicly the union was maintaining a brave face, behind the scenes there were growing signs that wool growers were slowly gaining the upper hand. As *The Land* put it, 'The strike is being settled on the boards.'[187] Shearing was proceeding – even if it was at a much slower rate than normal. *The Land* reported that '…shearing and crutching is underway in the Walgett, Lightning Ridge, Collarenebri, Coonamble, Trangie, Forbes, Dubbo, Nyngan, Warren, Blayney, Oberon, Crookwell and Boorowa districts'.[188] In the same article, the LGPA's Riverina district 'back-to-work' coordinator Mick Charles, of Narrandera, said he and his six fellow coordinators had been 'surprised by the hundreds of shearers already back at work'. He estimated that 70 per cent of the region's wool growers who wanted to shear were shearing.

> Some of the biggest sheds that employ contractors have been slowest to start because their teams are usually staunch AWU men and fear reprisals. The LGPA has uncovered well over 120,000 sheep either shorn, being shorn or about to be shorn [in the Riverina] since the shearing strike started. The crutching tally runs at 17,000. Shearing appears to be proceeding fairly normally despite the strike.[189]

Strike hurts Shearing Contractors' Association

The Shearing Contractors' Association of Australia, whose members shore two-thirds of the nation's wool clip, wrote to the AWU on

Thursday 5 May to outline its concerns about the impacts of the strike. The letter was hand-delivered to the union's Executive Council meeting in Sydney that day. The association's secretary Kevin Crawford questioned the effectiveness of the strike, saying shearing was proceeding in many parts of New South Wales. He said 120 shearers were working in the Hay district alone, including 76 who were working for Robert White. As well, shearing had not stopped in the Deniliquin area, sheds were proceeding in Trangie, 30 shearers were preparing to start work in Walgett the following Monday (9 May) and shearing was taking place in the Mudgee, Yass, Narrandera and Coonamble districts. He said every contractor in South Australia who wanted work was working and many Tasmanian contractors were planning to return to work the following week. 'On information supplied to us by hundreds of members by telephone, they and their shearers are willing to defy union direction and return to work as a mass body. The Shearing Contractors' Association regards this as highly feasible,' Crawford wrote.

Next came the real issue – the association's members were hurting financially. Crawford said the current generation of 'suburban shearers' had little time for nostalgia; they were more concerned with meeting the numerous financial commitments they had via hire purchase agreements, bank cards, housing loans and high interest rates. They could not afford to stay out on strike.

> Our members are losing contracts at an alarming rate to… 'questionable employers' supported by scab labour. [The association's members only employed union shearers.] The situation now is [the] Shearing Contractors' Association [is] losing sheds and runs for AWU members…while the AWU stands idly by and allows the position to worsen day by day. When the dispute is finally settled, large slices of members' and unionists' livelihoods will be lost.[190]

This was a damning indictment of the AWU's handling of the dispute and it reinforced the Executive Council's recent concession that the wide combs dispute would not be won through strike action. The association's solution to the dispute was certainly ambitious – it proposed a return to work in conjunction with a pay claim in the order of 25 per cent for narrow combs users, with the increase to flow on to shed hands and cooks. The logic was that no one would use wide combs if this pay differential existed. But a pay claim of this scale, which indirectly acknowledged the superior productivity of wide combs, was more pie in the sky than a serious solution – wool growers would vehemently oppose such a claim so the chances of it succeeding were, at best, minuscule.

The association's management committee had scheduled a meeting in Dubbo on Monday 9 May to consider its options if the strike was not called off beforehand. Its letter was a major blow to the AWU – many contractors and their teams, it seemed, were on the verge of defying the strike. The union was facing growing pressure to find a solution that would allow its members to return to work.

Neil Ellery moves east

In early May 1983, Peter Prentice, a 50-year-old grazier from Angledool in north-west New South Wales, organised a meeting of local graziers. Angledool, north of Lightning Ridge and just shy of the Queensland border, barely rates a dot on the map. Soon after the strike started, Prentice warned his regular union shearing team he could extend the start of shearing on his property by just three weeks. If the strike went any longer, the shearers would lose the shed. Now, with the strike ongoing and shearing due to start, Prentice decided to act. He rang all the local graziers and persuaded 35 of them to turn up to a meeting in town. Prentice had heard of Neil Ellery, the New Zealand contractor who was running shearing teams in Western Australia, and was keen to lure him east. To do so, he needed to be able to guarantee Ellery a decent run. With most of the other graziers desperate to get their shearing done, Prentice was able to quickly organise a collective run of more than 40,000 sheep. He then contacted Ellery and offered him the run.

Neil Edwin Ellery had no time for the AWU. He was passionately anti-union. He had a stocky, 90-kilogram frame with thick legs and incredible strength – assets that had come in handy in recent years during various pub brawls, mostly with union shearers, and in his younger years as an accomplished wrestler in New Zealand. He was also very ambitious – he told several colleagues he wanted to grow his business into Australia's largest contract shearing operation. Unfortunately, Ellery died in a car accident near Collarenebri in northern New South Wales in 1988.

Col Somerset, a former wool classer who worked extensively with Ellery during the early 1980s, recalls speaking to him in April 1983 when the Kiwi was contemplating bringing contract teams east to help break the strike. Somerset, who lives on a small acreage at Bowan Park west of Orange, became close friends with Ellery. 'He said to me, "What do you think?" And I said, "Well, there would be work, but there would be an awful lot of people who wouldn't be real happy about it." Neil was a bit… "Oh, it shouldn't be a big problem. When the wide gear started being used in Western Australia, it wasn't a big problem. Everyone just sort of went with it." I said, "You might find it a bit different over in the east."'

Ellery, who was 37 at the time, did head east, bringing with him five teams of shearers to start on the Angledool run. However, he also supplied an extra 10 shearers to Robert White and roughly 30 to Grazcos. Ellery's presence in New South Wales soon became known to the AWU – Ernie Ecob warned more than 430 pastoral workers meeting at Victoria Park Oval in Dubbo on Wednesday 11 May that Ellery was working in the state and recruiting still more shearers from the west. It would not be long before Ellery and the union clashed.

Shearers picket, storm Woodside

Like most graziers in the Coonamble district, Russell Smith shore his sheep in autumn. The ewes in his flock of 10,000 sheep were joined to lamb in winter and early spring. Late shearing was risky – it could cause unnecessary stress and pregnancy toxaemia, leading to significant stock losses. Smith, 40, his wife Phillipa and their four young children farmed the 6,000-hectare property Woodside about 20 kilometres north-west of Coonamble on the Carinda Road. It was one of the district's most productive cropping and grazing properties and had been in the family since 1929. Shearing on Woodside usually started in early April but in 1983 the strike intervened. Smith, like many of his neighbours, was desperate to start shearing. He rang George Mack, the LGPA's local back-to-work coordinator, who lived a two-hour drive south on the Trangie district property Weemabah. Mack was able to line up a team to start shearing at Woodside on Thursday 28 April.

It did not take long for the presence of the rebel team at Woodside to become known in Coonamble. On 2 May, the Monday after shearing started, local union shearers began setting up a picket outside Woodside. By the end of the week, 50 to 60 men were camped along the verge near the main entrance. Numerous tents, including a 'kitchen tent' to help with catering, fold-up chairs, eskies, and cars were crammed into the narrow strip of grass. Television news footage of the picket line showed men mingling around campfires. One picketer was practising his golf swing – hitting iron shots along the fence line. It might have appeared mostly peaceful, but the Smiths reported constant intimidation and abuse when they left or entered the property. Police officers from the six-man station at Coonamble were regularly visiting the property to help keep the peace.

That first full week of May was not ideal for camping. It rained from about midweek, halting shearing for a few days. It was not until the following week, beginning Monday 9 May, that the shearers were back in action. By that time, the picketers were tired and agitated. It seemed something was about to give. That morning, several unionists from out of town had travelled to Coonamble to join the picket. They met with local shearers at lunchtime in the Commercial Hotel, a grand country pub wedged between the Castlereagh Highway and Castlereagh River. Barman Allan Small told the Australian Associated Press, 'They had a few beers in the pub here before they went out. I knew there would be trouble.'[191] Smith, too, got wind that trouble was looming. Someone in town had rung to warn him more unionists were heading out to the property. About two p.m., as many as 60 men had gathered outside the main entrance – a number of them emboldened by a few lunchtime beers. Deciding it was time for action, they pushed through the locked gate and stormed the property, heading straight for the shearing shed. Armed with rocks and sticks and various other projectiles, the men bombarded the 20 by 30 metre shed, smashing all the windows and dinting some of the corrugated-iron sheets. Some weaker sections of iron were broken or penetrated. They tried to get inside, but Smith and the shearing team had barricaded the doors and armed themselves with anything they could get their hands on. It's uncertain how many men were inside – some reports said 12, some 14. One said 22! Twelve or 14 was most likely as there were only six men in the shearing team.[192]

With the doors and windows barricaded and guarded, the only way in was via the shearing chutes, which the sheep were pushed through after they were shorn. The chutes led down to a holding pen below. This, however, was a risky option, as any would-be intruder would need to crawl up a narrow race, making them vulnerable to being clobbered as they squeezed out through the chute onto the board.

Smith's wife and parents were inside the main homestead as the attack was occurring and one of them called the police as soon as the men charged through the main gate. They also called some neighbours. But in the meantime, the angry mob of unionists continued to bash on the shed with sticks and axe handles and tried in vain to get inside. They also emptied drums of sheep dip and drench that had been stored adjacent to the shed and broke a small pump. In total, an estimated $1,500-worth of damage was done.

The first police officers and neighbours on the scene arrived mid-afternoon and in the nick of time. According to Lionel Burns, one of the Smiths' neighbours, who was among the first responders, a small number of unionists had broken from the main group and were preparing to set fire to the shed. They were dousing hessian bags in petrol when a policeman noticed them. Burns told the *Daily Liberal* newspaper, 'He [the policeman] put his hand on his revolver and told the shearers he would shoot if they attempted to start the fire.'[193] It took 10 minutes or so for police to establish order – initially there was a standoff with the unionists but eventually, as backup arrived, the intruders decided to leave. By mid-to-late afternoon, about 20 police officers and as many as 70 local graziers were on the scene. The LGPA's policy of lending moral and physical support to graziers who were shearing was certainly working.

Fred McInerney, the Coonamble-based AWU organiser, was one of the unionists who 'went over the fence' that day. He downplayed the incident, saying it was just 'a huff and a bluff' and the unionists in the end 'were outnumbered by the coppers' but it was a different story for those inside the shed. This incident was widely reported in the media throughout Australia and in New Zealand. Smith was quoted as saying,

> It was a terrifying hour or so before police took control... We had to barricade the doors and lock ourselves in. They pelted rocks in through the windows and smashed in the iron panels but we managed to keep them out. The only way in was up the shearing chutes and that would have been pretty dangerous for them. When the police arrived there was a lot of yelling and carrying on. A stand-off developed before the police convinced them (the strikers) to leave… We've been told to expect more trouble. It's real law of the jungle stuff… We're under siege here. My wife, four kids, my mother and father are being intimidated by picketing shearers.[194]

Despite the ordeal, Smith was undeterred. He still had 7,000 sheep to shear and he was determined to finish the job. He told the *Canberra Times*, '…either I shear my sheep or I lose my livelihood and there's no way I'm going to do that. I'm fighting for a principle – the principle of law and order and I won't be dictated to by a few people high up in the AWU.'[195] One of the local graziers who came to the aid of the Smiths said, 'The situation here is explosive. The issue is no longer over the wide combs – we're fighting a battle against thuggery and we have right on our side.'[196]

As shearing continued, both the police and local graziers ramped up security patrols at the property. According to George Mack, Smith also employed two private security guards, both burly South Africans, through notorious Sydney private eye, Tim Bristow. While many of the unionists maintained a picket, there were no more major incidents at the property.

The weekend following the siege, Coonamble marked the centenary of its agricultural show, a major event for any country town. However, celebrations were marred by continuing negative publicity linked to the events that had occurred at Woodside.

A sequel to the siege played out in town a few weeks later, when things had seemingly calmed down. On the evening of Saturday 4 June, 11 members of the Woodside shearing team decided to visit the Coonamble RSL Club. Given their hostile encounter just weeks previously with union shearers, most of whom had been locals, it was a surprising decision. It did not take long for word to spread that the 'rebels' were in town. Fred McInerney was at home in the early evening when he received a phone call alerting him. He helped round up a group of local shearers, who started assembling outside the club. By 8.30 p.m., 30 men had turned up. They stormed in and confronted the rebels, who were playing snooker and table tennis and relaxing. A brawl broke out almost immediately but it did not last long. The police were called and helped break things up. There were no major injuries or damage to the club. McInerney recalled, '…a few punches started flying; it sort of broke up and nobody got hurt really. Oh, there might have been a bit of blood and guts but no serious injuries; nobody had to be hospitalised or anything. They didn't come back to town any more anyway.'

Peace plan

About the same time Coonamble district shearers stormed Woodside, their colleagues in South Australia voted to return to work on

Thursday 12 May. Their decision was in response to a fresh request from the AWU Executive Council for all branches to recommend members return to work – this time on the basis that more legal proceedings were imminent. The union's Section 59 application had been filed with the Arbitration Commission on Wednesday 4 May, the day before the Executive Council met. This application, together with the Commonwealth government's Section 25 notification, had been bundled together for an initial hearing in Sydney on Tuesday 10 May.

The hearing took place before the same full bench panel that determined the AWU's appeal – Justice Peter Coldham, Justice Stephen Alley and Commissioner Bevan Johnson. Proceedings started with the AWU, through Joe Bannon, seeking a stay on the full bench order of 23 March, which upheld Commissioner McKenzie's original decision, pending the outcome of its Section 59 application. However, both the NFF and the Commonwealth government opposed any stay and the application was refused. The commissioners then adjourned for an all-parties conference to see if some sort of agreement could be reached – this was the aim of Commonwealth's Section 25 notification.

The Commonwealth played a key role in brokering a peace deal and after negotiations lasting several hours, a deal was struck. Essentially, the shearers would return to work under the terms of the current Award while the Arbitration Commission conducted an inquiry into the health and safety implications of using wide combs. The Commonwealth pledged to support the inquiry in any way it could, including, for example, contributing to the travel costs of all parties. Proceedings were adjourned until 2.15 p.m. on Thursday 12 May for the agreement to be fine-tuned and to allow shearers to vote on the union's return to work recommendation. On Wednesday 11 May, shearers in Victoria and Tasmania followed the lead of their South Australian colleagues and voted to return to work the next day. However, shearers in New South Wales, who were meeting in Dubbo the same day, took much more convincing.

The Dubbo votes

Two votes took place in Dubbo that day. The first was during a meeting of 134 union delegates, the heads of the local pastoral committees, at the Dubbo Golf Club. The aim of this meeting, which started at 10.30 a.m. and lasted almost three hours, was to decide what motion to take to a meeting of shearers at Victoria Park Oval that afternoon. Ernie Ecob told delegates he was not happy with the proposed health and safety inquiry, but he believed it was the only avenue through which the union would be able to get its case back before the Arbitration Commission. He was confident the union could still win the case against wide combs if it cooperated with the inquiry and was able to present new evidence. However, the delegates were not so sure. A motion was put that the recommendation to shearers would be to return to work under current Award conditions pending the outcome of the proposed health and safety inquiry. It was lost. Instead, delegates voted 97–37 that the recommendation to shearers would be that there would be no return to work unless under the terms of the old Award, which banned wide combs. Delegates travelled back into town for the shearers' meeting at 2.15 p.m. The media were banned from attending. The 431 shearers present endorsed the delegates' motion, voting 275–156 to only return to work under the terms of the old Award.

The union's leaders were in a pickle. For the past two years they had encouraged *implacable hostile opposition* to wide combs, and members had obliged. Now they wanted shearers to work under an Award that permitted wide combs while an investigation was conducted. Even if this was only a temporary measure, until wide combs could once again be banned, it was a big step back.

Ecob, who had to attend the Arbitration Commission in Sydney the following afternoon to explain his branch's decision, must have known the AWU would face some flak. Its Section 59 application was in tatters – it could not progress while shearers were still on strike. And the Arbitration Commission's endorsement of the peace deal and the related inquiry was also contingent on shearers returning to work – the union could hardly be involved in the inquiry if it was not willing to allow wide combs to be used, at least to gather evidence.

When proceedings resumed, Joe Bannon, on behalf of the AWU, sought permission to withdraw the union's Section 59 application. Justice Coldham said it had to be withdrawn because 'it had lost its meaning in light of recent events' and had 'taken on an air of unreality'. He then scolded the union for ditching the agreement it had only two days earlier fully supported. 'I have a strong feeling there is either an inability or an unwillingness to understand what the agreement entails. This bench would not consider a review while there is a strike,' he said.[197]

More pressure on the union

The day had not ended well for the union – it had emerged red-faced from the Arbitration Commission having had to scuttle its own legal case before enduring a barrage of criticism from one of the commissioners. Mind you, the day had not started well either – plain-talking Paul Houlihan was almost taunting the union in the current edition of *The Land*, which had hit news-stands early that morning, claiming that the strike had been ineffective and the scale of the problem facing wool growers in getting their sheep shorn was steadily diminishing. In an article detailing how wool growers were preparing to step up shearing as the strike continued, Houlihan was quoted as saying,

> Producers are left with no option but to slug it out on the grass. We will continue to organise shearing as before. We've already got the runs on the board. Shearing has been going ahead and will continue. The strike has failed to achieve anything after seven weeks. If the union men stay out we will keep organising to get sheep shorn – it's a decreasing problem.[198]

The union's unflinching position could no longer be sustained. Its narrow-minded outlook had only narrowed its options. At this stage, those options were to continue to strike or return to work. If New South Wales shearers continued to hold out and strike, they were destined to lose. The Shearing Contractors' Association had made it clear that many of its members were preparing to defy the strike and return to work. The union had persuaded the association to delay any such decision, but if members did make good with their threat, it would humiliate the union and completely undermine its standing and authority in the pastoral industry. Returning to work would also involve eating humble pie, but a slice or two would be far more palatable than a whole pie.

On Friday 13 May, after learning of the latest developments in the Arbitration Commission, Industrial Relations Minister Ralph Willis sent a telex to the AWU's federal and state branch offices. He urged the union to choose the return to work option. Referring to the agreement his staff had helped broker in the commission earlier that week, he said,

> I am anxious that it be implemented immediately. What is now needed is for shearers to return to work so the agreement can be put into effect. I emphasise again, what my representative advised the Commission on Tuesday 10 May, which was that I would give such assistance and facilities with a view to implementing the terms of the agreement as may be desired by all the parties. With a return to work of all shearers, I will ensure the earliest possible action is taken within the Commission to have the terms of the agreement put into effect. I cannot stress more strongly the necessity for the New South Wales branch of the AWU to resume work immediately.[199]

Ernie Ecob had no choice; he called a meeting in Dubbo for Monday 16 May. The main agenda item: another return to work vote based on the latest developments.

Haddon Rig

The Shearing Contractors' Association, which to date had been restrained in its dealings with the AWU, was now running out of patience. According to George Mack, it was in the days immediately before the 16 May meeting in Dubbo that the association's vice president, Kevin Humphries, contacted Ernie Ecob with an ultimatum. Humphries had 30 years' experience as a shearing contractor and among the sheds he had in his run was the century-old property Haddon Rig at Warren, about 120 kilometres north-west of Dubbo. It had long been regarded as the leading merino stud in Australia. It was a shed he could not afford to lose. Mack had been negotiating with Forbes Murdoch, the property's manager at the time, to get a team in to shear in place of Humphries's regular team. However, Murdoch had been wavering, as Humphries kept committing to starting the shed then postponing. Murdoch wanted to retain Humphries if possible but, as the strike continued, he had to have a backup plan.

It was during the week before the 16 May meeting that Murdoch asked Mack to line up a team for the following week. However, when Humphries heard he was being sidelined, he got back to Murdoch and said his team would definitely start during the following week. Mack said Humphries then rang Ecob and told him he would be defying the strike by starting shearing at Haddon Rig the following week. Apparently Ecob asked him to hold off until after the Monday vote, so he could be seen to be returning to work after the strike had ended (assuming the shearers supported a return to work). If Humphries had gone back while the strike was still on, as he had threatened to do, it would have opened the floodgates for other contractors to follow. Humphries agreed to this request. Mack is convinced that Humphries's ultimatum reinforced Ecob's push for shearers to return to work – he knew the strike was on the verge of collapse.

Back to Dubbo

The 16 May meeting in Dubbo was always going to be big. It attracted 1,151 shearers from all over the state and had to be held at Victoria Park Oval to accommodate the crowd. Media representatives were again excluded, however, many journalists and members of the public stood outside the venue and listened to proceedings, which were broadcast over a loudspeaker. According to various accounts of what happened and details outlined in the minutes, it was a fiery meeting. Ernie Ecob updated members with the latest developments from the Arbitration Commission and talks with the federal government. He couldn't help himself though and digressed, attacking the NFF, LGPA, media and Commissioner McKenzie before summing up by saying, '…with the new evidence available which the union intends to put before the inquiry, the union can win the wide comb issue and once more have combs wider than 64 mm disallowed in Australia.'[200] His reference to 'new evidence' was never explained. The motion, proposing a return to work on Wednesday (18 May) to allow the health and safety inquiry to proceed, was passed 820–266.

After almost seven weeks in South Australia, Tasmania and Victoria, and almost eight weeks in New South Wales, the strike was over. But with the wide combs health and safety inquiry pending, the dispute was certainly not over. Once again, Brian Clarke (Grazcos, Dubbo) summed up the situation perfectly. He said he expected the dispute to slowly dissipate but trouble would continue in the industry for a long time because of the bitterness the dispute had engendered.[201]

30

More Trouble Arrives

Although the dispute was now moving into a new phase, with a fresh inquiry imminent, it did not take long for Brian Clarke's prediction of more trouble to eventuate. Less than a fortnight, in fact. Any hopes of an end to some of the more extreme and ugly incidents of violence that had characterised the dispute to date were dashed on the evening of Saturday 28 May, at the Imperial Hotel in Walgett in the state's north-west. Among the many patrons drinking and socialising there that evening was a large contingent of shearers, including a group of New Zealanders and Western Australians. It was estimated there were seven or eight visiting shearing teams in the Walgett area at that time.

'Wild west' Walgett

The evening started out with all the shearers apparently getting on well; indeed, Australian and Kiwi shearers were playing pool together – something that had rarely been seen in country pubs during the past few years. However, somewhat predictably, things soon turned sour. On Tuesday 31 May, Dubbo's *Daily Liberal* carried a detailed report of the events that had followed. Several witnesses described the ensuing brawl as being like a scene from an old western movie. The barman, Mark Catten, said, 'It was unreal…just like an old cowboy brawl on television. The Kiwis and Aussies were playing pool together early in the night, but then tempers flared and a first punch was thrown.' The fight started about eight p.m. Licensee John Tatters said about a dozen shearers were initially involved. He rang the police and several officers arrived soon after to calm things down. But within about 30 minutes of the peace being restored, two men were fighting again – the blue started inside the pub and quickly moved outside into the street. The police were again called and broke up the fight. But tensions continued to simmer.

Tatters said about 10 p.m. the leader of the New Zealand group asked him to go and get the leader of the Australian shearers. 'They got together and decided to go outside and got into it on the street,' Tatters said. About 20 shearers were involved in the fighting, he said, but other reports suggested as many as 50 men were present – apparently some patrons of the nearby Oasis Hotel couldn't resist a bit of biff and rushed down the street to join in. It was an ugly scene – dozens of men in varying states of sobriety brawling in the street, egged on by dozens of onlookers in varying states of sobriety; glasses and bottles being thrown everywhere. A car windscreen was smashed and tyres on several others were slashed. Once again, Tatters called the police. This time, however, the police could hear the fight from the station, two blocks away, and some officers were already on the way.

In the wash-up of all the fighting, it was clear the Kiwis had come out on top. 'The Kiwis were sober. Most of them were about 22 and built like bulls. Some of the Australians had been in the hotel since the morning,' Tatters said. Catten, the barman, confirmed this: 'They were too good for the locals. They were taking on three blokes and mostly flattening them.' One witness told the *Daily Liberal*, 'One of them [the locals] fancied himself as a karate expert but he was laid out with one round-house punch by a Kiwi.' One of the attending officers, Senior Constable Mike Todd, confirmed that the fighting had been over tensions relating to the wide comb.[202]

Unfortunately, this night of violence was not an isolated incident for Walgett. A week later, on Saturday 4 June, another brawl broke out. Again, the trouble started in the Imperial Hotel and spilled into the street. This time as many as 60 men were involved. Tatters told *The Sun* newspaper, 'The New Zealand and West Australian shearers are not looking for trouble but the local blokes will not be satisfied until they push them out of the district... It has all been blown out of proportion. But the town will weather it until it is all over and done with.'²⁰³ In the same report, Walgett LGPA branch secretary Peter McKenzie said the visiting shearing teams were necessary to help graziers tackle the backlog of unshorn sheep, caused by the shearers' strike and recent flooding in many areas of the state's north-west. Nevertheless, the violence had local citizens worried – especially about the town's image. Wal Coombes, the Walgett Shire Council deputy shire clerk, said, 'Lawlessness of any sort doesn't help the image of any town. No one wants this sort of thing.'²⁰⁴

Collareen Station, Moree

Just hours before the second major brawl in two weeks took place in Walgett, on Saturday 4 June, 11 members of a shearing team were relaxing in their quarters on the Garah district property Collareen, about 50 kilometres north of Moree. Garah is perhaps best known for hosting the Talmoi picnic races – one of the oldest picnic race meetings in Australia, having been founded in 1911. At the time, Collareen was a 6,073-hectare property that was owned by Bill Hunter and his family and managed by Jim Wallace. It ran about 6,000 merino sheep and a large cropping enterprise. Shearing had been delayed because of local floods, meaning the flock was carrying about 14 months worth of wool when shearing eventually started on Thursday 2 June. There were also 4,000 sheep from a neighbouring property to shear in the run. The team, which was one of Robert White's contract teams, comprised seven New Zealanders, three West Australians and a local wool classer. They had got through 1,200 lambs during the first two days and were enjoying some down time before a busy couple of weeks ahead.

The shearers had been cleaning and grinding their wide combs and cutters during the morning. The New Zealanders in the team were looking forward to watching their beloved All Blacks on television later that afternoon when they were due to play the British Lions at

Lancaster Park in Christchurch in the first of a four-test series. (The All Blacks won the test 16–12, and the series 4–0.)

According to the local newspaper, the *Moree Champion*, Jim Wallace was playing bowls at the Moree Bowling Club when he received a phone call a bit before midday alerting him to the fact that local union shearers were planning to raid Collareen that afternoon. The locals were incensed that a non-union, mainly Kiwi team had the shed. Wallace immediately drove back to the property and warned the shearing team, advising them to leave the property, which they did. Shortly after, about 12.45 p.m., 11 vehicles carrying 40 shearers arrived. The men climbed over a locked gate and barged into the shearing shed and nearby shearers' quarters. They broke teeth off 26 wide combs, stole more than 100 cutters as well as tally books and four handpieces, caused some relatively minor damage to the kitchen quarters and poured dirt into the fuel tank of the diesel shearing engine. At least $1,700 worth of damage was done.

This, however, was not the end of the trouble. On Monday morning, the shearing team got back to work. Outside the property, about 10 a.m., as many as 100 union shearers arrived and started picketing the property. The police were called and soon about 30 officers were on hand. A large contingent of neighbours turned up to support Hunter. Word had reached local media outlets and a film crew from the then New England/North West television channel NEN 9/8, an affiliate of Channel 9, also arrived on the scene. A messy confrontation was looking likely. However, one of the police officers, Sergeant Noel Cogan, had specialist negotiator training and organised for the key players to meet and talk. The meeting involved local AWU organiser Bill Sinclair and fellow organiser Cec Newton, Bill Hunter and Jim Wallace, the shearing team's overseer John Schick, and Sergeant Cogan.

The stand-off was resolved after some three hours of negotiations. The parties agreed that the shearing team would leave by nightfall because there were serious concerns for members' safety and the police could not offer them around the clock protection. In their place, a local union team would complete the shed.

It was disappointing for White's team, but it was clear that had they remained, they would have been targeted by the union. Schick conceded that, although the team wanted to finish the shed, the safety of the team was paramount. Things happened fairly quickly from that point. The team packed up and left, with police providing a clear, safe path off the property. Bill Hunter was quoted as saying, 'It could have turned into an ugly incident. We are grateful it ended without violence but it is most displeasing that we were forced to disband a group of very good shearers.'[205]

Although there had been no violence toward the 'rebel' shearing team, the media did not fare as well. NEN 9/8's Ted Hebblewhite, who went on to become a highly regarded country journalist and agricultural reporter, and later a successful chicken farmer, tried several times to interview Bill Sinclair to get a statement on behalf of the AWU. However, a small group of unionists refused to let him speak to Sinclair and the reporter eventually gave up trying. The snubbing of Hebblewhite was retaliation against Channel 9, which had had the 'temerity' to broadcast the *Wild and Woolly* report on *60 Minutes* less than two months previously. As the television crew was starting to drive away, several unionists rushed toward their car and threw stones at it – their actions were captured on film by a quick-thinking cameraman who was sitting in the back seat. The footage was broadcast on news bulletins across all of northern New South Wales as well as in several capital cities via Channel 9 – reinforcing the image many members of the public now had of the union as a bunch of thugs.

Some members of the AWU, it seemed, were becoming increasingly sensitive about being portrayed in this way – so much so that Bill Sinclair told the *Moree Champion* later that week that local shearers were angry at being labelled the 'bad guys' of the dispute. 'The shearer members of our union are disgusted at the way we have been portrayed by the media. We have been cast as the villains and those scab shearers as the heroes. We are not going to tolerate scab labour in our area whatsoever. We won't allow it to break down our conditions.'[206]

Ecob's call to arms

Later that month, on 21 June, Ernie Ecob wrote to all AWU pastoral members in the state. The letter was both a warning and a call to arms. It started, 'Last year members were informed that if wide combs were allowed in the pastoral industry all conditions would be effected (sic). How true those words were.'[207] Ecob cited multiple examples to prove that conditions were being eroded. They included rebel teams working outside normal start and finish times (7.30 a.m. and 5.30 p.m.) and on weekends, doing day and night shifts to work round the clock, living in condemned accommodation, and shearing wet sheep and scabby mouth sheep and so on. There was little evidence to support most of his claims. The idea that rebel teams were living in condemned accommodation was simply not true – they were using the same facilities union shearers had used previously or sometimes staying in local hotels. Two claims did have substance. Many rebel teams were shearing on weekends. However, it was not clear whether this was illegal. Despite repeated assertions by the union that it was, the legality of weekend work in the shearing industry was an untested area. For decades, the AWU had treated weekend work as being a breach of the Award and akin to treachery – under no circumstances were pastoral industry members to work on weekends.

Kiwi contractor Neil Ellery knew weekend work was a grey area. He once told a reporter, 'The fact is that we have never ever been charged [over weekend work], and that's because we work entirely within the law. I don't know what the union is disputing, and I don't think they know themselves. Why don't you ask them why they've never taken us to arbitration and proved that we're breaking the law?'[208] This was a good question – why didn't the AWU prosecute these teams for working on weekends? After all, its members knew when and where weekend work was taking place and it could easily have sent an organiser to these sheds to initiate prosecutions.

Interestingly, later on in the dispute, the South Australian branch of the AWU did prosecute a shearing team for working on a Sunday. The case was heard in Adelaide in the Industrial Court of South Australia on 30 May 1984. And the magistrate, Mr F. Di Fazio, ruled in favour of the shearers. The relevant part of his judgement stated,

> …it [the South Australian State Pastoral Industry Award] does not prohibit work on a Sunday and cannot be construed as doing so merely because the Award does not anywhere prescribe a rate or any other condition for work outside ordinary hours…nor is there evidence of custom or general usage in the industry that no work be done on Sundays… the ordinary and plain meaning of Clause 18(b) [relating to hours of work] does not exclude work on Sunday. Nor is there in the Award, as a whole, any indication that such a prohibition was intended.[209]

Although this judgement related to the South Australian Award, the wording of the relevant sections relating to hours of work was identical to the wording of the corresponding clauses in the federal Pastoral Industry Award.

Weeks after this case was finalised, senior staff in the Commonwealth Department of Employment and Industrial Relations sought clarification from their own technical branch about the legality of weekend work for shearers. The advice came back that the Award did not appear to prohibit it. Perhaps to reinforce its own advice, the technical branch later sought a legal opinion on the issue. It wrote to the Australian Government Solicitor's office in Melbourne in October and received advice on the 19 November 1984. The relevant section of the legal opinion stated, 'On the basis of my instructions it is my opinion that shearers are not prohibited from engaging in weekend work under the Pastoral Industry Award 1965 and consequently they would not be committing a breach of the Award to do so.'[210] So it seemed the AWU's position opposing weekend work was based on tradition rather than the law.

Ecob's claim that rebel teams were often working outside the prescribed week day hours also had substance. Most rebel teams were prepared to work beyond 5.30 p.m. if it meant they could cut-out at the end of the week and not have to come back the following week to finish a small number of sheep. Robert Foster, who has a small farm near Wagga Wagga, spent a good chunk of his working life as a shearer. He also had a stint in the Royal Australian Air Force and operated some small businesses. During the late 1970s and early 1980s he lived in Canberra and did quite a bit of shearing in the Southern Tablelands and Monaro regions. He shore with Robert White on several occasions. Foster recalls shearing with a union team at a four-stand shed near Canberra. 'We had nine sheep left at 5.30 p.m. on a Friday afternoon, and they refused to shear them. They came back on the Monday morning and shore the nine sheep…it was ridiculous,' he said. This sort of practice was commonplace in the early 1980s – union teams were totally inflexible and simply refused to shear beyond knock-off time.

The next couple of claims elevated Ecob's letter into the realm of the bizarre. 'They [rebel shearers] try to take over small villages by force but have so far failed. They instigate fights in towns nearly every night of the week,' he wrote. Both claims were piffle and must have raised concerns about Ecob's state of mind. *The Land* printed excerpts from the letter and asked Ian Manning and Grazcos to comment on the claims. Manning said they had no basis in fact and were incredible and saddening. A Grazcos spokesman said the claims were not worthy of a response.[211]

The letter ended by imploring members, 'Stop the scabs before it is too late. Do not allow teams to settle in. Move them out of Australia.'[212] Overall, Ecob seemed to be trying to inspire union shearers to redouble their efforts to resist wide combs at all costs. But the mix of exaggerated and bizarre claims rendered it less than convincing. It was almost as if the writer was no longer confident that the union would win the dispute.

31

'Son of Wide Combs'

For the small group of people who had been closely involved in the main proceedings of the wide comb dispute, the health and safety inquiry was an appendix that became known light-heartedly as the 'son of wide combs'. Commissioner Ian McKenzie was appointed to preside over the fresh inquiry, which kicked off with a one-hour preliminary hearing in Sydney on Monday 20 June 1983.

The main purpose of this hearing was to try to sort out a time frame for a series of proposed shed inspections. However, three new parties sought and were granted permission to become involved in the proceedings – Industrial Relations Minister Ralph Willis, the New South Wales branch of the AWU, and the Shearing Contractors' Association of Australia. The minister's involvement was as an intervener – someone not directly involved in a dispute but who nevertheless has a valid interest in being made a party to the proceedings. He was represented by Bernie Frawley, who was the first assistant secretary of the Commonwealth Department of Industrial Relations, and at times by Gerry Ryan, who was the department's Melbourne-based principal executive officer. Frawley was appointed a commissioner with the Industrial Relations Commission in 1989. Given the high-profile nature of the wide comb dispute and the impact it was having on one of the nation's most important industries, the minister was keen to stay abreast of developments, however, as an intervener, he would not make any formal submissions.

The New South Wales branch of the AWU had not been directly

involved in the formal proceedings to date for two key reasons – Ernie Ecob had lambasted them and had refused to allow the branch to participate, and the union's federal branch had effectively been representing the relevant state branches. Now, with a lot at stake, the New South Wales branch also became involved as an intervener. It was represented by Mike Walton, who was an industrial officer with the union's state branch. Walton was an A-grade tennis player who later studied law and was eventually appointed a justice of the Supreme Court of New South Wales.

The Shearing Contractors' Association was a respondent to the federal Pastoral Industry Award and as such had an automatic right to participate in the inquiry. It had also been entitled to participate in the main dispute hearings, but, incredibly, had failed to do so. This was despite the fact that its members played a key role in the industry and had a direct interest in proceedings. Ivan Letchford, who was one of two people who represented the association during the secondary inquiry, was at a loss to explain the association's absence from the main hearings. All he offered was, 'We did not exercise that [right]…that was a fault of our own, I agree.'[213] Letchford, who was the association's part-time industrial officer, achieved a rare double during this inquiry – as well as making an occasional appearance as the association's legal representative, he also appeared as a witness. Indeed, his evidence was significant and is mentioned in more detail in chapter 34. The association's main representative was Carl Larsen, a shearing contractor and member of the organisation's executive committee. Larsen, from Young in New South Wales, had also been a shearer for more than 30 years.

Another interesting fact came to light during the preliminary hearing. The commissioner, it seemed, was prepared to broaden the scope of the inquiry and accept evidence on more than just health and safety aspects of using wide gear. This was something the union had been lobbying for and in correspondence from Ernie Ecob to the AWU's pastoral organisers on 14 June 1983, Ecob stated, '…I have been assured by the deputy prime minister Lionel Bowen that we will be able to argue all issues before [Commissioner] McKenzie and not be limited to those set out in the document agreed by all parties on the 10 May 1983, in the Arbitration Commission.' During the preliminary hearing, Commissioner McKenzie affirmed this when he said,

> … There is going to be no restriction on what evidence can be put forward. There is going to be no restriction on it – that could have been said last time and was not – because, quite frankly, it is the intention of the Commission that this matter has got to be tidied up and tidied up once and for all; and, therefore, we are stretching the bow to permit justice being seen to be done as well as all aspects of natural justice.[214]

This hearing ended with Commissioner McKenzie urging the parties to meet informally to draft a schedule for shed inspections that would dovetail with his availability. He wanted the inspections to start in the week beginning 25 July. However, come mid-July, the parties still had not met, let alone devised a schedule. Commissioner McKenzie called a hearing in Sydney for Wednesday 27 July. He made it clear he was not happy with the lack of progress, adjourned formal proceedings and went into conference with the parties, during which time a schedule was organised. The shed inspections were to begin in western New South Wales on 10 August.

First inspections

The inspection party flew out of Sydney at six a.m. on Wednesday 10 August on board a Piper Navajo twin-engine aircraft chartered from Hazelton Air Services. (Ansett Airlines took over Hazelton Air Services in 2001 then went into voluntary administration just months later. Regional Express took over Hazelton's passenger services in August 2002.) The 10-seater plane was full – the party consisted of Commissioner McKenzie and three staff (his associate and two court reporters), Michael Forshaw (for the federal branch of the AWU), Mike Walton (New South Wales branch of the AWU), Paul Houlihan

(NFF), Ian Manning (LGPA), Carl Larsen (Shearing Contractors' Association) and Gerry Ryan (Commonwealth Department of Industrial Relations). The destination was Trangie, a 90-minute flight almost directly west.

After landing, members of the party drove to several district properties – Merenele at Warren, Wyoming at Nevertire, Tabratong at Tottenham, and Brigadoon at Trangie. Merenele was owned by John Wild and had a four-stand shed. Kevin Kentwell, a shearer with almost 20 years' experience, was the shearing contractor. Two shearers in his team were using wide combs and the other two narrow gear. Kentwell gave evidence that the standard of shearing with wide combs was equal to the standard of work performed with narrow combs. One shearer testified that the wide comb was no more difficult to push through the fleece than a narrow comb.

At Wyoming, the shearing contractor Arthur Reid gave evidence that the six shearers in his team had started using wide combs less than a month ago. He said as a result, several shearers had been able to increase their daily tallies from roughly 90 to 100 sheep to about 120. The property's owner, Dennis Hunt, said he allowed the shearers to use wide gear conditional on there being no compromise to the quality of shearing. When he inspected the sheep during the first few runs, he told Reid he was '…terribly pleased with the job' and said, 'You just carry on.'[215] He said there had been no issue with second cuts. Carl Larsen challenged Hunt's assessment, saying he believed the quality of some of the shearing was substandard. However, he conceded that this was most likely due to the presence of several inexperienced shearers in the team.

The inspection party drove to Haddon Rig (near Warren) that afternoon to make use of the station's airstrip. The next stop was Bourke, a one-hour flight to the north-west, for an overnight stay before the next set of inspections.

Just after eight a.m. on Thursday 11 August, the inspection party left the $25-per-night Outback Motel in three vehicles and travelled about 80 kilometres west of Bourke to Romani Station, which was owned by brothers Peter and Keith Davis. The shearing contractor, Timothy O'Connor, had been working as a contractor for 15 years. He was a strong union supporter, as were the five shearers in the team. Normally narrow comb users, the shearers swapped to wide combs for one run while the inspection took place. O'Connor took detailed notes about the type of comb each shearer was using and its relative performance. He later gave evidence, saying, 'I would say the [Sunbeam] Merino comb was the one that got most of the wool off the sheep, but in doing that it did not get as much wool off as they would have with the narrow comb.'[216] O'Connor said there were safety issues with the wide combs from wool getting jammed under the cutter and the handpiece being harder to push. He also said there had been a significant increase in second cuts after the team switched to wide gear. His overall assessment was that the quality of shearing with wide combs was 'totally unacceptable'.

Several of the shearers were also interviewed, starting with Rex Layley, a South Australian who had been shearing for four and a half years. He also stated that wide gear was much harder to push. 'I think if I had to push it for a living, I would be really pushing things uphill.'[217] He also raised a new issue, saying there was a real risk with a wider comb of the shearer cutting his free hand – in fact, he had done so during the demonstration run. Layley's summary assessment of wide combs was, 'I do not think they have got anything going for them, not any assistance in shearing sheep.'[218] Ross McKay, a shearer with 11 years' experience, gave similar evidence. He said there was an excessive amount of effort required to push wide combs through the fleece. Wide combs, he said, were '...terribly hard to push... I would not want to be pushing them all day...if you had to use them all the time, if you used them for a week, I do not think you would be using them the next week because I think your arm would probably go...'[219] McKay also claimed there were potential safety issues when shearing around the horns of merino lambs – the comb was liable to catch on the horn and lock up. He did not explain why wide combs posed any greater safety risk than narrow combs, but presumably they were more difficult to manoeuvre in a relatively small, tight area. McKay also said he believed all shearers should be made to use the same gauge equipment.

The commissioner asked him, 'Why would you object [to shearers using wide combs] in view of the fact they are legal under the Award?' He replied, '…I do not think it is right in one sense that one person can use one comb and another person is using another comb, and a grazier can come along and say, "You have to use a certain type of comb" and that sort of thing…'[220]

Several other shearers gave similar evidence, particularly regarding the difficulty of pushing wide combs through the fleece. Lee Hetherington, who had 21 years' experience as a wool classer, said there had been a significant increase in the number of second cuts using wide gear – ultimately this would produce lower returns for the wool grower because the affected wool would fetch less than its real value.

Following the testimony of the shearing team, Carl Larsen made a submission in which he said his professional assessment of the sheep used in the demonstration that morning was that they were totally unsuited to wide comb shearing. This, coupled with the fact that the shearers had been using out of the box combs and cutters explained, certainly in part, some of their evidence.

Brindingabba Station

From Romani Station the inspection party drove roughly north to Brindingabba Station, located about 150 kilometres north-west of Bourke, just shy of the Queensland border. The station had been owned for the past 27 years by Anthony (Tony) Charles Marsh, who testified that the quality of shearing this year, with a wide comb team, was better than in previous years, when narrow combs had been used. He also said the daily tallies were up on the previous year. AWU organiser Fred McInerney, who shore at Brindingabba in 1980, also attended these inspections. He told the commission that Brindingabba sheep had been regarded as 'the fastest shearing sheep' in the district and tallies achieved in past years were far more than those currently being recorded – he was, in effect, giving a tick of approval to narrow gear.

New England

That evening the inspection party stayed overnight in Bourke before departing at 6.30 a.m. the following day, Friday 12 August, to fly 450 kilometres east to Armidale. From there, the party drove north to the Guyra district property Brockley, which was owned by David Rainger. Brockley was an AWU-nominated shed and the shearers were normally all narrow comb users. However, for the inspection, the five-member team used wide gear during a run and the shearing contractor, Max O'Brien, was asked to assess the quality of the shearing. He said the shearing quality was 'not as good'. '… As I think everyone could see, there is definitely a lot more wool left on them… There are definitely more second cuts too.'[221]

One of the shearers, Thomas Dalby O'Brien, of Bundarra, told the commission he had concerns about the safety of wide combs because often a shearer's free hand was moving close to the comb. O'Brien, who had 33 years' experience as a shearer, said,

> … That is the thing that has had me a bit worried… I shear very close to the handpiece. I've got chips all over my fingers from the narrow combs, but with that extra bit of width and around the head and that, you lose concentration a bit and it is very likely you will be at risk more with the wide comb.[222]

O'Brien also expressed concerns about the suitability of wide gear for crutching and other 'tight' shearing work, such as the neck area, and said the wide comb was harder to push in certain types of sheep.

Peter John Davidson, a local with 14 years' experience shearing, expressed concerns about potential damage to a shearer's arm because of the extra force required to push a wide comb handpiece. 'I have only got a skinny little arm. It started to ache in the elbow [after using a wide comb]. It is actually still aching in the elbow now.'[223]

Proceedings wound up shortly after, in time for the inspection party to drive back to Armidale, board a charter flight, and be back in Sydney by early evening. After just three days on the road and seven shed inspections, the Arbitration Commission already had a bundle of conflicting evidence – on one hand, wide combs were seen as being more efficient without compromising quality, while on the other they were panned for being harder to push, more difficult to manoeuvre, and potentially more hazardous to the shearer.

32

More Woolshed Inspections

The second set of inspections took place in the central west of New South Wales. They began on Wednesday 17 August, with a charter flight from Sydney to Orange, followed by a 30-minute drive north-west to the Molong district property Mirrabooka Station, which the AWU had nominated for inspection. At the time, Mirrabooka was owned by John O'Donnell and the shearing contractor was Les Priest. All parties were surprised when rebel shearing contractor Neil Ellery turned up to observe proceedings. He had travelled from Dubbo, which was about an hour's drive north of Molong. The LGPA quickly took advantage of his presence by asking him if he would give evidence – a move that angered the union. However, as Commission McKenzie pointed out, the AWU had done likewise during the hearings in Bourke the previous week, when it called a local grazier and renowned former shearer Arthur Buckley to testify when he had visited Romani Station to observe proceedings. Buckley, who had more than 30 years' experience as a shearer, reinforced the views of the union shearers – he said based on his observations that day, 'I do not think I would like to have my sheep shorn with them [wide combs].'[224]

Mirrabooka hearing

Several shearers testified during the Mirrabooka hearing. Gerry Olsen, from Orange, started shearing as a youngster midway through World War II. During his 40-year career, he had only ever used wide combs twice – he had tested them on a few sheep at a shed in the New South Wales Riverina at the urging of a Kiwi shearer; and the second occasion was during this inspection for the Arbitration Commission. Olsen was highly critical of wide gear, saying it was far too strenuous to push.

> I find them just to shear five or six sheep is fair enough, but if you were pushing and the pressure was on, where you have to work hard all week, you would be very, very tired by the end of the week. It would affect your back and your wrist, your arms, I mean they would ache...[225]

Olsen also claimed there were more second cuts with wide gear – if indeed the shearer bothered to go back to clip the missed wool, otherwise there would be more ridging on the sheep.

Another shearer, Malcolm McKenzie, of Cargo, used a motoring metaphor to try to describe the difference between narrow and wide combs. He said using narrow combs was like driving a Mercedes Benz, while using wide combs was like driving a Holden. Wide gear was overly difficult to push through a sheep's fleece, he said.

Neil Ellery, who at the time was one of the most experienced shearing contractors in Australia, also gave evidence. Ellery had been a shearer for 21 years (using only wide gear), and during the last 10 years, his contracting business had been responsible for shearing more than four million sheep – roughly 400,000 per year. He testified that any of his teams could have shorn the Mirrabooka flock to a satisfactory standard using wide gear.

Another one of those rare moments of humour occurred during this inspection. Given Ellery's experience as a contractor and long-time wide comb shearer, Paul Houlihan wanted to confirm a key aspect of the wool growers' case – that wide combs were in no way detrimental to the health of shearers. He asked Ellery, 'Have you ever suffered any harm or injury because you have used wide combs?' Much to Houlihan's surprise, Ellery answered, 'Yes.' Caught off guard, he sought clarification: 'What was that?' Ellery elaborated: 'We were subject to beatings by locals, [because of] the fact that we were wide comb users.'[226] Commissioner McKenzie, however, was clearly not in a jovial mood – he ruled the answer irrelevant.

Champion shearer Mel Johnston was also in the shearing team at Mirrabooka Station – he was called to give more detailed evidence to the inquiry in Sydney in mid-September. Another witness, Les Wright, who ran a rural supplies business in Orange, said since wide combs had been legalised in March that year (after the AWU's appeal failed), in his business they were outselling narrow combs 10 to one.

Dunedoo and Coolah

From Molong, members of the inspection party travelled north to Dunedoo, where they visited Mount Pleasant Station on Thursday 18 August. The station was owned by John Knott, who ran a merino flock with Haddon Rig bloodline. Mount Pleasant was a union-nominated shed and the witnesses were opposed to wide combs. They reinforced the arguments of previous wide comb opponents – that the combs were significantly harder to push and as such could be expected to cause long-term health problems, particularly for shearers' wrists and arms. An accredited shearing judge, John Cameron, also gave evidence – he said the amount of wool left on the sheep with wide combs was abnormally high and had the shearing taken place in a competition setting, the shearers would have been marked down quite significantly. (Like Mel Johnston, Cameron was also called to testify at a subsequent hearing in Sydney in mid-September.) A large portion of the inspection was taken up with a detailed explanation by AWU organiser Mick O'Shea of the workings of the individual parts of a handpiece.

The commission's next stop was the Rock Station, a Coolah district property owned by grazier Sam Stephens, who was a wide combs supporter. A Grazcos team was contracted to shear his 6,400 merino sheep and Stephens said he was pleased with the quality of the shearing that was taking place with wide gear. He described the legalisation of wide combs as '…the greatest thing that has happened for years.'[227] Most of the shearers gave evidence and all testified that wide combs were easier to use than narrow combs.

Sydney sittings

The inquiry resumed in Sydney on Tuesday 13 September for three days of hearings, much of which involved follow-up questioning of witnesses from the earlier shed inspections. John Cameron, of Wingewarra Street, Dubbo, had 35 years' experience as a shearer and 15 as a shearing judge. He had been an extremely accomplished shearer, having represented Australia in 1968 in a competition against New Zealand. Cameron had observed the shearing during the inspections at Mount Pleasant (Dunedoo) and the Rock Station (Coolah) the previous month. He described the quality of shearing at the Rock as relatively poor, saying, 'there was an extraordinary amount of wool left on the sheep'. The shearing also had been quite slow, he said, considering the quality of the sheep. (The highest tally had been 184 with wide combs.) Cameron said he could have comfortably shorn 240 with narrow combs. He described the state of the pastoral industry as

> Very unrestful; there is a lot of ill feeling and a lot of worried employers and employees…it really is heartbreaking to see the harmony that has gone out of the industry. We have been working over the last 20 years in almost perfect harmony with the employer, and these last 12 months this has all seemed practically to have vanished.[228]

This theme of harmony and the need for uniformity in shearing sheds were the key points of the AWU's argument during this inquiry. Mike Walton asked Cameron, 'Do you think there should be uniformity in the industry, in terms of combs?' He replied, 'Yes, definitely, I cannot see how they can work without uniformity.'[229] Ian Manning later asked Cameron if there was any reason why shearers who chose to use wide combs should be prevented from doing so. Cameron again emphasised the need for uniformity: 'As I said before, you have to have continuity in this industry. I do not see how we can have continuity with different types of combs.'[230]

Another interesting point arose during Cameron's cross-examination. He claimed that Grazcos was refusing to employ shearers who would not use wide combs – in other words, they were discriminating against diehard union shearers. However, when Manning drilled down, it appeared a more subtle reality was playing out. Manning asked Cameron to name any narrow comb shearers he knew who had been refused work. Cameron named one shearer from Dubbo. Manning then asked, 'Do you know if he is prepared to use his narrow comb in a wide comb team?' Cameron responded, 'I do not think he would be.'[231] The company's New South Wales shearing manager Brian Clarke later testified that Grazcos was more than happy to employ narrow comb shearers, but only if they were willing to work in mixed teams. At the time of the inquiry, they only had one shearer on their books who was willing to do so.

One of the witnesses two days later, on Thursday 15 September, was champion shearer Mel Johnston, who had shorn during the Mirrabooka Station (Molong) inspection the previous month. Johnston was a 200-a-day shearer who had won dozens of competitions and awards and had represented Australia in international competitions. His top tally was 232 merino wethers. Johnston was a loyal union shearer and only used narrow combs, although he had shorn with wide gear in New Zealand and England. At the time of giving evidence, he had been a shearer for 28 years. Johnston believed most sheep were not shaped for a wide comb and this meant it was almost impossible to shear with wide combs without leaving a ridge of wool. He too stressed the need for uniformity of gear, saying there would always be strife while different gauge combs were available. He said several times during his evidence that there had to be one comb in the industry and insisted it had to be the standard 10-tooth comb.

33

Sydney Hearings (October 1983)

The first witness to testify when proceedings resumed in Sydney on Tuesday 11 October was Richard (Dick) Duggan, one of the most accomplished shearers of his generation. Duggan, 48, from Euroa in Victoria, was known as 'the King'. And for a good reason. Duggan shore his first 100 tally at age 16, and first notched a 200 tally at 18. When he gave evidence, he had been working as a shearer for 33 years. He had won 67 open shearing championships, including two Australian open titles. Remarkably, Duggan had also won every state shearing title four times. He was among the industry's elite, a fact recognised by Ian Manning when he came to cross-examine him later that day. Manning said, 'Anyone at this bar table has got to admire a person with credentials such as yours in shearing a sheep. How many people…do you think you represent – shearers that have won an Australian championship that are still working in Australia?' Duggan replied, 'There is probably about six people.'[232]

Although he still did some shearing, at this point in his career Duggan was working mainly as a contractor. He was an avid narrow comber and he only employed narrow comb shearers. Duggan believed wide combs were inferior in almost every regard to narrow combs, except speed. However, he argued the speed advantage came at a big cost – greatly reduced quality of shearing. He told the Arbitration Commission it was almost impossible to keep the whole surface of a wide comb flat against the wrinkly skin of a merino sheep – meaning ridging was inevitable. He said 90 per cent of his wool grower clients preferred narrow combs and any wool grower who used wide combs was accepting substandard work. 'Well, quite honestly, anybody who has got wide combs shearers there, they are prepared to put up with a bad job.'[233] Duggan also expressed concern with New Zealand shearers taking work in Australia. He said he currently worked six months a year (equivalent full-time), down from about nine months a decade or so previously. He attributed the decline in work to a corresponding increase in the number of New Zealand shearers who were working in Australia. (Under cross-examination by Paul Houlihan, Duggan later conceded that some of this reduction in work could be attributed to a decrease in the national sheep flock from about 180 million to 130 million during the same period.) Duggan said he could foresee there being even less work available if the status quo continued. 'I think if this wide comb stays in Australia and we get deluged by shearers from overseas to shear our sheep at the rate they are going to be coming here, we will be working, say, two and a half to three months a year,' he said.[234]

Duggan later told Commissioner McKenzie that if the industry adopted a technology that was reportedly 14 per cent more productive, this would further reduce the amount of work that was available to shearers. 'Let us put it this way – if all the claims are true, there is a 14 per cent increase in output. I think that alone would cut down the work period of shearing,' he said.[235] However, for someone of such standing in the industry, Duggan's argument was difficult to sustain. If you accepted his reasoning, you would never adopt any new technology that resulted in increased productivity because it would effectively reduce the duration of the shearing season and cut the total number of working hours available to individual shearers. Indeed, the logical extension of his argument was to support a return to a less efficient means of shearing, such as blade shearing, to make shearers less productive – this would increase the duration of the shearing season and 'create' more work. The reality was, if shearers were more productive they would have opportunities to increase their earnings – either as a shearer if there was sufficient work available or by allowing them to spend more time working in other industries, which many shearers were doing anyway.

Duggan also repeated one of the key arguments of nearly all the union witnesses to date – that harmony was crucial to the effective operation of a shearing shed. 'You have got to have it…to do the job properly,' he said.[236]

Wide combs 'like new toy'

The following day, Wednesday 12 October, the AWU called another narrow comb supporter to testify. Malcolm Picker, from Boorowa in the south west slopes of New South Wales, had been a shearer for 14 years. He shore mainly around the Boorowa area but had worked all over New South Wales and in parts of Queensland. On occasions, he had also worked for Wellington-based contractor Kevin Humphries – he'd been part of the team Humphries put together to shear at Haddon Rig, Warren, the day after the shearers' strike ended in New South Wales earlier that year. He had also been involved in one of the commission shed inspections and wide comb trials a couple of months previously.

Picker said the wide combs were much harder to push and use than narrow combs. He said using the wide gear even briefly had caused an ongoing issue he had with his arm to flare up. Asked how he found the wide combs, he said, 'Well, I could not use them. I could not get on the skin for a start with them. I found them very hard to push and also I had to re-shear three of my sheep in the trials to get more wool off their back… I found it very hard to push in them [sic] sheep anyway… they went into the wool but from then on it was harder and harder as you went along with the… I have got a crook arm out of pushing the little ones [narrow combs]; I have been going to the doctor and getting cortisone injections in it and I can show you now, I have a bump there. When I put the wide one on and sheared three sheep, it swelled up that high…after we had the trial they said we could shear with them for the rest of the day but I took mine off.'[237]

Counsel for the AWU, Garry Johnston, asked Picker why he thought some shearers had expressed a preference for using wide combs. 'I just think a lot of them, it is like new toys to a kid, these wide combs. Mostly they are only young fellows using them who have just come in and they would not know if they were using a rake or a wide comb to be honest. It is like a new toy to them.'[238]

O'Shea testifies

The first witness called on Thursday 13 October was Mick O'Shea, the Mudgee-based AWU organiser. O'Shea's credentials were impeccable – 25 years of experience as a shearer followed by a decade as an organiser. Few people knew the shearing game as well as he did. He had attended several of the shed inspections in the central west and north-west of New South Wales during August.

Garry Johnston questioned O'Shea and soon raised the issue of harmony and uniformity in the shearing industry. He asked, 'How would you describe the industry as it is at the moment in New South Wales, having regards to the controversy over wide combs?' O'Shea responded,

> Well, I think it is in chaos myself because of the different types of combs in the industry. If one was to look and have a look at all these communities, certainly there is a big split in them. It has had a bearing on their social lives and everything else… Certainly the whole community are [sic] divided because of the different combs in the industry at the moment.[239]

And O'Shea was quick to push the union line that a single gauge was necessary for harmony. Asked how the disunity could be resolved, he said, 'In my honest opinion, as a practical man, the only way I can see it being resolved is have one standard comb in the industry.'[240]

Later, during cross-examination by Ian Manning, O'Shea repeated this point, saying, '… If there is a standard comb in the industry all this chaos would go away, and it will not go away until such time as there is.'[241] Manning later raised the issue of trials of wide combs and asked O'Shea his attitude towards a full, commercial trial. The witness responded, '… Everyone should not have to be trialling combs and making a decision on how wide the combs should be. I think it should be left to the logical people to come up with a standard comb that would suit all sheep in New South Wales.' Manning asked the obvious question, 'Who is that person, or who are those people?' O'Shea responded, 'I will volunteer for one.'[242]

O'Shea also emphasised the argument that wide combs would encourage an influx of New Zealand shearers and lead to a subsequent reduction in work opportunities for Australian shearers. He said because shearing work was seasonal and influenced by factors including the weather, most shearers, at best, could expect about 10 months of work each year. However, if more New Zealanders came, '...the sheep flock would be shorn in a much quicker time, and certainly those chaps [Australian shearers] would not gain anywhere near the amount of employment'.[243]

When Paul Houlihan cross-examined O'Shea, he slowly zeroed in on the *60 Minutes* report *Wild and Woolly*. This was a sensitive issue for O'Shea, who believed he had been badly misrepresented in the program – the union had even considered legal action at one stage. O'Shea had testified that the relationship between wool growers and the union had deteriorated following the shearers' strike. After several preliminary questions about possible causes of the poorer relationship, Houlihan asked, 'Do you think your appearance on *60 Minutes* should have had any effect on your relations with graziers?' O'Shea replied, 'I would not have a clue.' Houlihan persisted: 'Do you think the sort of comments you made on that program are the sorts of things which are likely to endear you to graziers?' O'Shea replied, '… That was only 30 minutes and I had 55 seconds prime viewing time. We were talking about two different instances completely and those tapes were cut and I was put in a jam, where two things were said within seconds. That is the story of that.'[244] During re-examination by Garry Johnston, O'Shea said he felt he had been 'crucified' by the program.

Soon after, Commissioner McKenzie adjourned the matter for further shed inspections in Tasmania, beginning on Wednesday 30 November.

34

Inspections Wrap Up

When the health and safety inquiry began, Garry Johnston, for the federal branch of the AWU, had pushed for shed inspections to be carried out in all states except Queensland.[245] (The AWU's federal Pastoral Committee had met at the union's head office in Sydney on 7 June and identified various areas and properties in New South Wales, Victoria, Tasmania, South Australia and Western Australia for inspections to take place.) Paul Houlihan, for the NFF, also supported an extensive itinerary of inspections.[246] However, by early December, Commissioner McKenzie had become concerned that the inquiry was getting bogged down and starting to lose its impetus – so he ruled out additional shed inspections in other states. (The inquiry did stage a hearing in Melbourne to take evidence, but there were no associated shed inspections in Victoria.) At this stage, there had been inspections in New South Wales, which had been chosen because of its limited involvement in the industrial proceedings to date, and Tasmania, which had effectively volunteered to be involved. On 10 July 1983, Tasmanian shearers met in Campbell Town in the state's central districts and voted to approve a series of trials of wide tooth combs. The move to stage trials, which were to be organised in conjunction with the Tasmanian Farmers' and Graziers' Association, may have seemed like an easing of the shearers' enmity toward wide combs. But it wasn't. The shearers were still very much opposed to wide combs and, outside the trials, agreed to maintain a strict narrow gear only policy. The union's state branch was not backing away from the AWU's overall position of *implacable hostile opposition* to wide combs; instead it was seeking to justify and reinforce its opposition by having its members' criticisms of wide gear tested in a controlled environment. Initially, the trials were to involve as many as 20 shearers and six sheds. However, again as a time saver, they were scaled back – eight shearers and three sheds; one shed was used to tune in brand-new Sunbeam wide comb handpieces and sets of combs and cutters over seven days; then more than 8,000 sheep of mixed varieties were shorn with the gear in two other sheds, at Mount Morrison and Merton Vale.

As well as taking evidence during the formal shed inspections in Tasmania, the Arbitration Commission took supplemental evidence from some of the people who had been involved in the union-organised trials. The formal inspections started on Wednesday 30 November at Oatlands, a convict-built village brimming with sandstone buildings about an hour's drive north of Hobart. The first stop was Spring Valley, a 2,400-hectare property running 13,000 Corriedale sheep. The inspection was the first time that wide combs had been used on the property, and one of the owners, Arthur Eyles, said he was 'quite satisfied' with the standard of shearing. Several of the shearers testified about their experiences using wide gear. In general, they echoed some of the common themes of the inspections – the combs were harder to push; they posed a greater hazard because of their extra size; and there should only be one size comb in the industry.

That afternoon, the inspection party travelled south-west to the Bothwell district property Rockford, less than half-an-hour's drive from Oatlands. Rockford covered 3,600 hectares and ran 14,000 Polwarth merino-cross sheep. It was owned by Hedley Reardon, who said he had been 'very satisfied' with the standard of shearing from a trial run of wide gear and he 'would like to see them continue'. Reardon's shearing contractor, Douglas Edwards, a local, said although he operated some mixed gear teams, he would like to see the industry standardised with a single gauge comb – whether it be a wide or narrow gauge. One of his shearers, Shane Murphy, of Cressy, about an hour's drive north of Bothwell, said he had started using wide combs following the strike so he could assess their performance himself, rather than having to rely on what the union had told him. He believed wide combs generally were harder to initially push into the wool, but then the relative ease of pushing them depended very much on the type of sheep being shorn. Murphy, a shearer with 14 years' experience, was also a supporter of a single width comb. He felt it was inevitable under a multi-comb Award that separate, lower pay rates would be introduced for wide combs, despite wool grower guarantees to the contrary. Murphy's evidence prompted Houlihan to later reiterate the wool growers' position. He said,

> The undertaking that was given was that we would not seek to use the introduction of wide combs if they created an increase in the tally, we would not seek to use that as a means of varying the tally in the formula which calculates the rates of pay. That undertaking appears, I think it is probably four times in the transcript; it is on telex to the Federal Government and to the South Australian Government, and it is quite emphatic. We will not seek to use any increase in the tally from the introduction of wide combs as a means to vary the formula.[247]

The following day, Thursday 1 December, the inquiry visited Home View, the Tunbridge district property of grazier Frederick Heazlewood. Tunbridge was in the state's midlands, midway between Hobart and Launceston, and the 400-hectare Home View housed a homestead and shearing shed that was used to clip the flocks that Heazlewood ran on several neighbouring properties. Some 3,300 Polwarth sheep from one of these properties, Black Johnny's, were being shorn with narrow gear during the Commission's inspection. One of the shearers, John Morrison, from Euroa in Victoria, was vehemently opposed to wide gear – he once walked out of a shed in Victoria because there was a wide comb user in the team. He made it clear during his evidence in chief that he thought the use of wide combs was unfair. When Paul Houlihan stepped up to cross-examine

Morrison, he naturally enough wanted to know why using wide combs was unfair. 'He is using a comb that wide [he gestured with his fingers to indicate the width of a wide comb] and I am using the comb this wide; therefore he is taking off a lot more wool with each blow. He is leaving a lot more on too.'[248] Houlihan persisted: 'How is it [unfair] given you have the right to choose the comb you want to use?' Morrison replied, 'I just think it is. It is against my belief to work with wide combs.'[249]

The Launceston leg

The inquiry resumed in Launceston the following day, Friday 2 December. Alan Jones, a sheep and wool extension officer with the Tasmanian Department of Agriculture, was first to testify. Jones, a former shearer and shearing instructor, had observed one of the union-organised trials at Mount Morrison, about 50 kilometres north-east of Hobart. Paul Houlihan asked Jones several questions about the viability of introducing wide combs to the industry. Jones said,

> There are always problems with anything new. It would be crazy to say there would not be; some people adapt quicker than others; some people do not want to adapt. From what we have seen at Mount Morrison and in sheds since, if a shearer tries hard to make them work, they will work very well…people who do not want to change will not, and do not need to, and it does not matter.[250]

Jones also revealed he favoured a single standardised comb size for the industry.

Butler testifies

A key witness during the Launceston hearings was John Butler, who had been the AWU's Tasmanian branch secretary for the past 10 years. Butler, who lived in the Hobart suburb of Lindisfarne, had a background in the mining industry – he had never shorn a sheep. As well as his senior state role with the union, he was also vice president of the AWU federal executive and a member of the AWU federal Pastoral Committee. Butler had organised the union trials in Tasmania.

During questioning by Garry Johnston, Butler said the shearers involved in the trials had been 'totally against' wide combs but they participated because their fellow shearers had endorsed the trials at the Campbell Town meeting in July. He said the main outcome of the trials was that the sheep were shorn to a satisfactory standard (according to the owners) using wide combs. Initially there had been slightly more skin cuts than would be expected with narrow combs, but this diminished during subsequent days as the shearers adjusted to the wide gear. Butler said the 'multiplicity of combs on the market' was ruining the shearing industry and there was a need for a single, standard-sized comb that could be refined for different varieties of sheep. He estimated '98 per cent' of Tasmanian shearers supported this position. He also said Award conditions were regularly being breached following the introduction of wide combs – in particular, he nominated shearers working extended hours and sleeping in substandard accommodation. However, when pressed by Paul Houlihan during cross-examination to provide examples of such breaches, Butler said he was unaware of any occurring in Tasmania but he had heard that these sorts of things were taking place in Western Australia.

Also during cross-examination, Butler revealed that the shearers involved in the trials had continued using wide gear. Houlihan asked him, 'How many shearers who took part in the trials, to your knowledge, have gone back to using narrow combs?' Butler's reply: 'None.'[251] This was significant – a small group of shearers who were vehemently opposed to wide combs, had found, after using them for a couple of weeks, that they were preferable to narrow gear.

Butler also raised a fresh concern during his testimony. He felt that, with a large variety of shearing combs on the market, insurance companies would eventually start to contest workers' compensation claims for shearers with injuries such as tendonitis on the basis that the shearers could have chosen to use a different width comb.

… Most likely the insurance company would say, 'You have the right to choose your comb, why did you not choose the other one? We will not pay you because you should have used the other comb.' I can see that happening. There is no doubt that type of thing could happen.²⁵²

Houlihan finished his cross-examination with a subtle dig at the union – he couldn't resist: 'Given your experience of the trials in Tasmania and given your position in the federal union, how much regret do you have about the union's failure to accept our [the NFF and LGPA's] proposal for trials nationally?' Butler replied, 'Do I have to answer that?' Houlihan responded, 'No, I will not press it.' It seemed Butler did not want to be put in a position of having to publicly criticise the AWU. Commissioner McKenzie adjourned proceedings to a date to be fixed.

Final shed inspections

The inquiry resumed in Sydney on Tuesday 24 January 1984, the day Apple's first Macintosh computer went on sale. This was a purely administrative hearing where the parties nutted out a rough timeline for the remainder of the inquiry. It was decided there would be two more shed inspections in New South Wales the following month, followed in March by three days of hearings in Melbourne, where final submissions were anticipated.

The extra inspections took place on Wednesday 29 February in the state's north-west at the Walgett district property Bangate Station and the Enngonia district property Lila Springs. Bangate fronts the Narran River between Lightning Ridge and Goodooga. It was owned by David Gleeson, who had purchased the property from Dalgetys in 1975. The 20,700-hectare property typically ran between 17,000 and 21,000 medium-fibre (22-micron) merino sheep and produced between 450 and 500 bales of wool per year. Gleeson also grazed some cattle and was branching into wheat cropping. Bangate was earmarked for an inspection partly because its lambs were being crutched and its stud rams were being shorn – the commission had not yet witnessed these operations taking place.

Gleeson, who had used Ivan Letchford as his contractor for the past 25 years, gave evidence that wide combs were used on his property for the first time the previous July and he had been delighted with the quality of the shearing. He said it took most of the shearers a day or two to get used to the combs. 'The quality did not change, they just shore a little slower and they were a little bit tentative with their shearing. After perhaps two days they were shearing [normally] with the wide gear and the comments I heard from the shearers were that they would not like to go back to the narrow gear after using wide gear… I was happy with the quality of the shearing. I could not tell the difference between wide and narrow,' he said.[253] Gleeson said he thought there were less second cuts in the wool with wide gear because fewer blows were required to shear the sheep. He said in terms of skin cuts, there had been no noticeable difference between wide and narrow comb shearing.

Letchford's evidence

Perhaps the most significant and powerful piece of evidence during these inspections came from Ivan Letchford, the long-time shearing contractor who had already appeared as a legal representative for the Shearing Contractors' Association of Australia during the inquiry. Letchford was in his 60s and trying to stave off baldness. He boasted a rather unlikely address for a shearing contractor – he lived in Baroona Road, Church Point, overlooking Pittwater on Sydney's northern beaches, a long way from the often harsh conditions endured by many of his clients. He had shearing contracts in the Upper Hunter, north-west and central west regions of New South Wales and his teams shore more than 180,000 sheep each year. Until the national shearers' strike the previous year (March to May 1983), Letchford had never even seen a wide comb. His first encounter with wide combs occurred on national television, during the strike, when he participated in a staged shearing demonstration broadcast on the ABC's *Nationwide* current affairs program. The presenter was the renowned Australian journalist and broadcaster Geraldine Doogue. Two shearers, one using a narrow comb and the other a wide comb, each shore a sheep in almost identical condition while Letchford gave a commentary on their progress then assessed the quality of each fleece. The wide comb shearer finished a full minute ahead of his colleague and there was no noticeable difference in the quality of shearing or the clipped fleece.

During the strike, Letchford supported a resolution adopted by the Shearing Contractors' Association for members to return to work using only narrow gear. He was quizzed about this during questioning by Ian Manning and said,

> If I had the experience I have had now I would not have supported that resolution. I was anti the wide comb for purely personal reasons that I had a lot of very difficult sheep to be shorn, particularly the wethers in the upper Hunter, and in my ignorance I thought that they are hard enough and tough enough to be shorn now with the standard gear, how are they going to push a comb that is wider. But when I had the benefit of seeing the wide comb used, I changed my opinion. In my own opinion, I could not deny a shearer or a worker of anything in my heart I thought was going to be of benefit to make his job easier.[254]

Letchford said later he believed there was no breed of sheep in Australia that could not be shorn effectively with wide combs. He also revealed every one of the shearers he employed had switched to wide gear and, as a result, their daily tallies had increased by 15 to 20 per cent. These shearers 'without exception' had also told him wide combs required less effort to use, he said.

Another key witness at the Bangate inspection was Allan Rees, a shearer from Tullamore near Parkes who boasted 22 years' experience in the industry. He had shorn all varieties of sheep in sheds throughout New South Wales, South Australia and Queensland. Rees was a long-time AWU member and had been strongly opposed to wide combs ('I swore I would never ever use one').[255] Things changed in

June 1983 when he relented to the constant nagging of a couple of graziers to at least try wide gear. He thought they would be too hard to push and use but found the opposite – they were far easier to use. In fact, he found wide gear provided him with some relief from a bad case of tennis elbow that had regularly flared up when shearing with narrow combs. After more than 20 years of shearing with narrow combs, Rees said he adjusted to using wide gear during a single run (two hours).

Lila Springs

During the early 1980s, Lila Springs Station near Enngonia, north of Bourke, covered 61,000 hectares and ran a flock of up to 20,000 merino wethers, depending on seasonal conditions. The flock would produce 300 to 400 bales of wool each year. The property was managed by John Nott and was run in conjunction with two other properties, one nearby and one across the border in Queensland. The station's flock was being shorn for the first time with 13-tooth combs and Nott said he was satisfied with the quality of the work. He said he had no preference for wide or narrow combs as long as the shearing was of an acceptable standard.

Grazcos manager testifies

Brian Clarke, the Dubbo-based New South Wales shearing manager for Grazcos, was called to give evidence during the inspection at Lila Springs, where a Grazcos team was shearing. A good chunk of his testimony turned into a defence of his employer as he found himself rebuffing various misconceptions about Grazcos' policies and operations. Clarke said of the 25 teams of shearers Grazcos had working throughout the state at that time, only one shearer was using narrow combs. However, he denied this was the result of discrimination, saying the company regularly offered work to narrow comb shearers as long as they were willing to work alongside wide comb shearers – and most weren't. He said the shearers Grazcos employed did not have to use wide gear, but it was the choice of an overwhelming majority to do so. He said he had never seen a wide comb user switch back to narrow gear. Clarke was asked about a rumour that Grazcos was trying to split the industry by trying to force narrow comb shearers to work alongside wide comb shearers. He replied,

> No. I do not know what you mean by splitting the industry. How can any company or anybody split the industry? Surely it has to be the individuals in it. Surely given that we do not demand that anyone uses wide or narrow combs, surely it must be the people that are working in the industry and their choice from then on.[256]

Clarke was also forced to deny that Grazcos only employed non-union labour. He said many of the company's shearers were AWU members and he believed there would always be an important place for the union in the shearing industry.

Wellington shearing contractor Kevin Humphries also gave evidence. After 30 years in the industry, Humphries had scaled back and was only running one, occasionally two teams of shearers. He had a run of about 60,000 mainly stud merinos in the New South Wales central west, from Quambone to Cowra. All his shearers had switched from narrow to wide gear. Humphries had obtained references from several clients about the performance of wide combs. The references were tendered as exhibits. One was from Forbes Murdoch, the manager of Haddon Rig. Murdoch's letter said, in part,

> We have found, especially in the lambs, that the shearing was carried out at a far better rate and there were far less cuts to the body. In all respects, we are completely satisfied with the [wide] gear and will continue to use it as long as it is available.[257]

Given the status of Haddon Rig in the pastoral industry, this reference was significant.

With the shed inspections now over, the health and safety inquiry was nearing completion. Proceedings were adjourned to mid-March for final submissions. After that, the industry would await Commissioner McKenzie's ruling.

35

Meanwhile, the Bitterness Continued

Away from the ordered and relatively civil proceedings of the health and safety inquiry, there had been no let-up in hostilities between the dispute's two main players. As the gathering of evidence was winding up in early 1984, the AWU and wool growers were still locked in a bitter battle. One front in this battle was occurring on the ground when encounters between wide comb and narrow comb shearers got out of hand – typically in woolsheds or small-town pubs and clubs. The other front was taking place behind the scenes and involved an equally intense propaganda campaign.

On the ground, confrontations had become more sporadic than earlier in the dispute but they were nonetheless every bit as spiteful and violent. One of the most infamous incidents of the whole dispute occurred during this period. It took place on Sunday 12 February at Galambo, a 24,300-hectare property 45 kilometres south of Bourke.

The raid on Galambo

Neil Ellery was the contractor for the Galambo shed, although he was not present when the incident occurred. His team, which included seven wide comb shearers, had started the shed the previous Monday, 6 February. Heavy rain had fallen in recent weeks and fly-strike had become widespread in the region. Some of the Galambo flock were dying in the holding yards while waiting to be shorn. It was not unusual for Ellery's teams to work on weekends, but in these circumstances the shearers readily agreed to work through to finish the contract as quickly as they could to minimise any further stock losses.

On the Saturday night, after six days of shearing, several members of the team drove into Bourke to drink and relax at the Oxley Club (the local RSL club), which was known to host both wide and narrow combers. During the evening, some of the Galambo shearers boasted to a group of union shearers that they had been working that day and intended working the next day too. This taunt started a verbal spat but, miraculously, the wide combers were able to leave before things got out of hand. However, some of the union shearers decided to confront the team about weekend work and organised an 'inspection' for the following day. They telephoned Fred McInerney, who drove across from Coonamble on the Sunday morning. McInerney was among 17 unionists who then set off for Galambo in four vehicles. So was fellow organiser Garry Jackson, a 30-year-old avid kangaroo shooter and former heavyweight boxer. Apparently, the group had some trouble locating the property – initially they drove past the turn-off and eventually had to double back. There are conflicting reports about what happened after the men arrived – the following account includes information gleaned from several sources.

One of the station owners who was at the shed met the unionists to try to avert any trouble. He spoke briefly with Fred McInerney but the rest of the group ignored him – they were set on confronting the shearers. By the time McInerney and the owner had finished speaking, the unionists, armed with wooden sticks and metal poles, had barged into the shed and demanded the shearing team stop work. There was a brief stand-off before a brawl broke out. It's not clear what triggered the brawl. McInerney said he was later told the violence started when a member of the shearing team used the removable steel handle from the Ajax woolpress to strike Garry Jackson from behind on the back of his head. Irrespective of the trigger, the ensuing scenes were wild and brutal.

The unionists attacked the shearers, who grabbed whatever was at hand to help defend themselves and try to fight back; men were wrestling and trading blows and hitting each other with improvised weapons. The violence soon spilled outside, as the outnumbered shearers tried to flee. McInerney recalled, 'They were bursting out of the shed, out of windows and doors everywhere, down the chute and there were blokes chasing other blokes across the paddocks.' One of the shearers, Ross Bryant, a close friend of Neil Ellery's from Western Australia, got about 200 metres from the shed but was caught by several union men. He was bashed and kicked while on the ground to the point of almost losing consciousness. One of his attackers tried to ram a wide comb handpiece into his mouth, but he somehow resisted and pushed it away. He was then stabbed in the neck – some accounts say with the handpiece; others suggest with a stick. Either way, the weapon pierced his jugular vein. At that point, his attackers left and regrouped with the other unionists at their cars before departing for town.

Bryant was bleeding profusely and in danger of dying. Fortunately, the team's cook had trained as a nurse and she rendered first aid until ambulance officers arrived. In all, three shearers were taken to Bourke Hospital and treated for a range of injuries, including broken and fractured bones as well as cuts and bruising. Bryant's injuries included a fractured skull. When well enough, he returned home to Western Australia to continue his recovery. He was, however, unable to work as a shearer again. Garry Jackson was later driven to the hospital by one of the unionists and received several stitches in his head.

Col Somerset, who was running a shed for Neil Ellery near Lightning Ridge at the time, recalled speaking to Ellery about the Galambo raid.

> … [Ross Bryant] got his head kicked in that badly he was never able to work again…he actually got stabbed in the neck with a handpiece…several other people in that team got quite badly hurt, there were broken arms, legs, jaws, you name it. They just stormed in there, a big heap of people and flogged the crap out of these guys.

Several unionists involved in the Galambo raid were later charged with intimidation and a range of serious assault-related offences. Some charges included assault occasioning actual bodily harm and malicious wounding. Inexplicably, given the viciousness of the attack, the charges were never prosecuted – they were no-billed by Neville Wran's New South Wales government.

Other incidents

There were numerous other incidents of violence in Bourke during early 1984. Indeed, the town, with of population of 3,600, briefly became the epicentre of the dispute. Several relatively 'minor' incidents took place in the weeks before the Galambo raid – a union shearer's car was badly damaged by a homemade bomb, a wide comber's panel van was set on fire, and there was a brawl between wide and narrow comb shearers at a local club. In early March, Greg Cleeland, the western area manager of Grazcos, was ambushed and bashed one night as he left the Oxley Club with his wife, Lindy, and two friends. Cleeland had previously received death threats because of his role with Grazcos. (The Cleelands moved to Tasmania within weeks of these events.) In mid-March, hours after a Bourke Racing Club meeting wound up, as many as 50 people converged on a house known to accommodate wide combers and started hurling rocks and assorted projectiles onto the roof. The police had to be called to disband the group. The next weekend, local AWU shearers organised a street march as a protest against wide combs – unionists who still objected to wide gear and refused to shear with wide combers had no work, and no real prospects of any shearing work. Within hours of the march, there was a fight between rival shearers at one of the three local caravan parks.

Six weeks after the Galambo incident, another local sheep station came under siege. Summerville Station was located about 35 kilometres east of Bourke on the Brewarrina Road. Grazcos was the shearing contractor and Greg Cleeland had put together a team of 11 people – two from Western Australia, two from New Zealand, with the remainder from various parts of New South Wales. The disgruntled union shearers in Bourke soon learned Grazcos had the shed and, with the main street protest fresh in their minds, they decided to pressure the owner to switch to a local, union team. About three p.m. on Saturday 24 March, eight shearers began a picket outside the property. Another dozen or so men joined them about 10 p.m. The picketers threw some fencing wire over power lines on the station's boundary – cutting the power and starting a small grass fire. They then pelted the shearers' quarters with rocks, forcing the shearing team to take refuge in the main homestead for the night. The next morning as many as 40 more men joined the picket and several police officers attended to maintain order. The police helped arrange talks between the picketers and the owner, which resulted in the Grazcos team agreeing to abandon the shed and a local union team completing the contract. The Grazcos team left the property in five cars about 2.30 p.m. with a police escort to town to allow them to fill up with petrol and leave without incident. Although this was nothing short of industrial blackmail, it was also the most straightforward way of avoiding a drawn-out and potentially violent confrontation. Certainly, from the owner's perspective, it was the most pragmatic solution to getting his sheep shorn without having to worry about more trouble.

Unfortunately for the local community, the impact of the violence was reverberating beyond those directly involved in the dispute – travellers venturing into outback regions were now avoiding Bourke and many local businesses were being affected.

And AWU shearers in Bourke were getting annoyed at what they perceived to be police bias – whenever there was trouble between local unionists and wide combers, the only people who were being arrested and charged were unionists. Peter Ballard, a local shearer and AWU member, wrote a letter to the secretary of the New South Wales Police Union, in which he claimed Bourke police had taken a stand against staunch AWU members. 'Many AWU members have been charged on various offences ranging from assault to intimidation. However, the invaders have committed the same offences and more severe offences to the extent of pulling guns. Ironically, not one of these "scabs" have [sic] been charged or bought [sic] to task,' he wrote.²⁵⁸ Garry Jackson echoed the same sentiment when he told the *Daily Telegraph* newspaper, 'There have been hotheads on both sides of the dispute but when the police come it is only the unionists who are being arrested.' In answer to that allegation, a police spokesman said the unionists were the main troublemakers.²⁵⁹

The propaganda battle

Behind the scenes, a more subtle battle was being fought. In early 1984, the farmer groups and the AWU were trying to persuade the nation's pastoral industry and many interested onlookers that they were 'winning' the dispute. The easiest way to do so was to look at the prevalence of wide shearing combs. It had been roughly 12 months since wide combs had been legalised (following the Arbitration Commission's rejection of the AWU's appeal on 23 March 1983), and the uptake of wide gear was an obvious measure of how shearers perceived the new equipment and which side had the 'upper hand'.

The NFF and LGPA were claiming that increasingly there was a move towards wide combs, suggesting that the union's continued hardline stance against the combs meant it was out of touch with both reality and its members. But the union was adamant there was overwhelming support among its members for its position (advocating narrow comb use only). It was getting very antsy with the farmer groups for spreading what it called misinformation about the prevalence of wide gear.

On 20 January, the AWU's Victorian branch secretary Ian Cuttler wrote to local committees and pastoral representatives addressing this issue. He said it was of great concern that employer representatives were alleging that most shearers were now using wide gear. He wrote,

> This is completely incorrect and in fact reports from Organisers indicate very strong support for the standard 64 mm combs at the present time. There has been pressure brought to bear on shearers to accept that wide gear use is inevitable. The original six-point agreement that was instrumental in finally ending the stoppage in

1983 clearly allowed for the union to promote its policy and allow members to continue to use standard equipment. The blatant attempt by some employer representatives to confuse the real situation can be seen only to try to influence the present proceedings before the Conciliation and Arbitration Commission. The return to work decision by the union was based on the use of standard gear by members and the union does not move away from that position. Members are to be congratulated for their support of the union's policy by sticking to the 64 mm gear in the face of some real pressures both subtly and blatantly promoting wide gear.[260]

Wide comb sales

There were signs, however, that a growing number of shearers were abandoning the union's policy. Sales figures from the main shearing comb manufacturers revealed what was really happening in the industry. During the calendar year 1983, wide combs constituted 90 per cent of Heiniger's overall shearing comb sales – narrow combs made up only 10 per cent. (Narrow comb sales dominated in small areas of Victoria, New South Wales and Queensland.) Given that the legalisation of wide combs was only confirmed towards the end of March, and this had been followed by an eight-week strike, the sales figures suggest there had been a dramatic and accelerated shift towards wide gear from the end of the strike. The company's sales projections were even more revealing. In the first half of 1984, Heiniger was expecting a sales mix of 95 per cent wide combs and only five per cent narrow combs. Then, critically, if the Arbitration Commission's health and safety inquiry found in favour of wide combs, Heiniger was anticipating 100 per cent wide gear sales by the end of the year. This major manufacturer was factoring into its production plans nil sales of narrow shearing combs after July 1984.[261]

Wide shearing combs were also dominating Sunbeam Corporation Limited's sales figures, but not to the same extent. Between 3 September 1983 and 25 February 1984, just under six months,

Sunbeam's mix of shearing comb sales was 77 per cent wide combs and 23 per cent narrow. However, the Sunbeam figures were significantly skewed and actually understated the real position – the company admitted it had been unable to produce sufficient wide combs to keep up with the market demand during this period.[262]

The other key shearing comb manufacturer, R.A. Lister Australia, did not reveal details of its sales mix, but it did say, 'Since the relaxation of restrictions on comb and cutter widths, we have noted a very rapid increase in the use of wide combs and cutters.'[263]

It was a reasonable and conservative assumption, based on the Heiniger and Sunbeam sales mix figures, that for every 100 shearing combs being sold in Australia in early 1984, more than 80 were wide combs. The union was clearly in denial about the true extent of wide comb usage in the industry. But as the final stage of the Arbitration Commission's health and safety inquiry approached, the union was turning all its attention to its end game. This involved a two-pronged push – one attacking New Zealanders for undermining Award conditions in the shearing industry, and the other emphasising the importance of there being a single gauge comb to ensure 'uniformity' in the industry.

36

The End Game

Like a balloon being inflated, the AWU's objections to wide combs slowly expanded during the course of the dispute. Initially, the main points of contention related to potential injuries to shearers and sheep, fleece damage, and fears about pay rates (see chapter 13). However, as the dispute stretched on, the AWU began to fixate on New Zealand shearers as being the key source of unrest in the pastoral industry.

An agreement between Australia and New Zealand known as the Trans-Tasman Travel Arrangement, which had been in place since 1973, allowed for the relatively free movement of tourists and workers between the two countries. Not long after the agreement was formalised, many Kiwi shearers started to travel to Western Australia for seasonal shearing work. For several years, coinciding with the wide comb dispute, the AWU had been lobbying for changes such as the introduction of a work permit system to restrict the free flow of New Zealand shearers into Australia. At one point it had even advocated for legislative reforms to give the union a role in approving the entry into Australia of all visiting shearers.

During the early 1980s, the governments of Australia and New Zealand began to negotiate a free trade agreement. The AWU only learned about these negotiations as the final touches to the agreement were being made. The Closer Economic Relations free trade agreement aimed to strengthen the economic ties between the two countries by cutting trade barriers. The union was hoping it would include tighter restrictions on labour flows across the Tasman Sea. Instead, the agreement, which came into effect on 1 January 1983, enshrined the continued open movement of workers between the two countries.

A few months later, on 18 May, the Immigration and Ethnic Affairs Minister Stewart West reaffirmed the federal government's position when he made the following statement in parliament:

> The Government has reviewed the entry of New Zealand citizens under the Trans-Tasman Travel Arrangement, which allows for the free flow of people between the two countries. This review was prompted by concern about unemployment. In coming to a decision, the Government considered both the costs and benefits of the present arrangement. Suspension of the arrangements would have serious implications for trade, foreign policy and other national interests and would be inconsistent with the recently signed Closer Economic Relations Agreement. Accordingly, the Government will allow for the continued visa free entry of New Zealanders under the Trans-Tasman Travel Arrangement, which recognises the special relationship which exists between the two countries. The requirement for New Zealand citizens to produce a passport before entering Australia will also remain. However, entry under this arrangement will be closely monitored to ensure that it remains in Australia's interests.[264]

The AWU, however, was not going to let the issue rest. During the remainder of 1983 and 1984, it ramped up its rhetoric against New Zealand shearers to try to pressure the Hawke government into making it more difficult for them to work in Australia.

Complaints against the Kiwis

The union repeatedly accused New Zealand shearers of breaching and undermining Award conditions (for example, working on weekends, working extra hours and so on), accepting below Award pay rates (of up to 30 per cent) and not paying any tax in Australia. (It was true that many New Zealand and 'rebel' wide comb shearers were prepared to work weekends and extra hours. See Robert Foster's quote, p. 265.) Although various AWU officials made these claims publicly on many occasions, the allegations were rarely documented and sent to people in authority. One exception was a letter of complaint from the Tamworth branch of the AWU written by secretary Mick Payne to federal Industrial Relations Minister Ralph Willis. The letter was undated but it arrived in Willis's office on 5 December 1983. Payne said local branch members were

> ...concerned by the harm being done to the pastoral industry by imported shearers who are breaking down established Award conditions. Examples being working outside prescribed hours and at weekends. These men are taking work from local shearers who stand a fair chance of ending up on Social Service. Also, it is a fact that New Zealand shearers obtain a work visa and on its expiry leave the country without paying tax.[265]

The minister wrote back a month later,

> ...your allegations of Award breaches by 'imported' shearers are a matter of concern. The Arbitration Inspectorate, which is responsible for federal labour inspection functions, is located within my Department. If you wish to register specific complaints – containing details of employers, locations and details of the alleged breaches – then I suggest you contact the Director (Industrial Relations) of the Department's New South Wales Regional Office... I should also point out that, under Section 119 of the Conciliation and Arbitration Act 1904, an organisation may sue for a penalty for an Award breach when its members are affected. Finally, I have had your enquiry concerning taxation arrangements applying to New Zealand shearers referred to the Treasurer's Office for reply direct to you.[266]

The reality was that the AWU had the power to investigate and prosecute Award breaches. Under the Award, organisers had a 'right of entry', which entitled them to enter a property and inspect the shearing operations and all the documentation relevant to the shearing contract, such as sign-on sheets, tally books and wages records. If there had been any substance to the union's repeated claims that New

Zealand shearers and rebel wide combers were accepting less than Award rates of pay, it could quite easily have established this and prosecuted the relevant parties for breaching the Award. Such evidence could have been presented to the Arbitration Commission to support the AWU's argument that Award conditions were being eroded.

Not only did the union fail to produce a shred of evidence that New Zealanders and rebel wide combers were accepting less than Award rates of pay, the alleged offenders emphatically denied the claim. Shearers who were challenged on this rejected the allegation outright. Two of the key protagonists, Robert White and Neil Ellery, both said they had not and would not accept less than Award rates of pay for themselves and they both quoted contract rates with wool growers that allowed them to pay their own shearers Award rates. The reason they were able to undercut narrow comb teams on contract rates came down to basic economics – their teams could shear a flock much faster than narrow comb teams and this meant a lower overall wages bill. For example, if it took four weeks for a wide comb team to shear a flock of 20,000 merinos, a narrow comb team (of the same size) might have to allow five to six weeks. Although the wages bill for the shearers would be the same for both teams (shearers were paid according to the number of sheep they shore, irrespective of how long it took to shear them), the wages bill for the shed hands in the wide comb team would be significantly less, as they would be paid for four weeks' work, while the shed hands in the narrow comb team would be paid for five to six weeks' work (rouseabouts, woolpressers and cooks were paid hourly rates). This higher wages bill for the shed hands in the narrow comb team allowed wide comb contractors to undercut narrow comb contractors.

Not paying tax? Hardly!

The claim that New Zealanders were avoiding tax was handled, in detail, by the Treasurer's office. Chris Hurford, the then Minister Assisting Treasurer Paul Keating, wrote to the Tamworth branch of the

AWU in February 1984. He completely rejected the claim – Hurford said under the tax arrangements agreed to by the Australian and New Zealand governments, workers visiting either country would pay tax in that country and not be double-taxed when they returned home. He said it was technically possible that a New Zealand worker in Australia could avoid paying tax in Australia, but it could only occur in circumstances where several very specific and narrow conditions applied. In reality, the likelihood of this occurring was negligible. Hurford summarised the normal case of a New Zealand shearer working in Australia as follows:

> In the case of a New Zealand shearer who works in this country for an Australian resident, which one would expect to be the usual situation, he would be subject to Australian tax on the wages received. In fact, he will be taxed a greater proportion of his wages as there is no tax-free threshold for foreign residents working in Australia.[267]

So not only was the union's repeated claim that New Zealand shearers were getting away without paying any tax in Australia incorrect, it completely misrepresented what was actually occurring – they were in fact paying a greater proportion of tax than Australian shearers.

But again, the union would not relent. Senior bureaucrats from the Commonwealth Department of Employment and Industrial Relations unwittingly became embroiled in this issue during 1984. On 30 April that year, two months after Chris Hurford had debunked the assertion that New Zealand shearers were paying no tax, the AWU distributed an unsigned circular to shearers highlighting the favourable tax treatment it said New Zealand shearers were receiving.

The two-page circular claimed, 'Surely it must be clear to all Australian shearers that the purpose of introducing the wide comb was to import cheap, New Zealand labour (scabs) into Australia.' It included a table comparing the weekly earnings of an Australian shearer with those of a New Zealand shearer working in Australia, before and after tax liabilities had been deducted. Assuming both shearers shore 600 sheep at the Award rate of $97.07 per hundred, each shearer would earn $582.42 before tax. It then calculated tax liabilities for the Australian shearer at $120, leaving a net income of $462.42 per week. For the New Zealand shearer, it perpetuated the union's lie that there would be no tax liability, leaving the Kiwi shearer with a net weekly income of $582.42, or $120 per week better off than his Australian counterpart. (The analysis then factored in the exchange rate and claimed the New Zealand shearer would in effect earn NZD $811.65.) The circular went on to claim, bizarrely, that 'As a result of the NZ shearer being greatly advantaged, as shown above, NZ shearers are able to go to graziers and say that are prepared to shear for well below Award rates.' Why shearers would then automatically ask to be paid less than they were entitled to is not explained.

This circular soon came to the attention of the Department of Employment and Industrial Relations. It prompted a meeting between departmental officials and members of the AWU's federal executive on 4 May to discuss several matters, including the better coordination of departmental and union resources to investigate possible Award breaches. However, the department later wrote back to the union to outline the errors in the circular. The relevant part of the response stated,

> Taxation officers have advised that in the case quoted in the circular (i.e. on income of $582.42 per week) an Australia resident, without deductions for dependents, would be liable to pay tax of $190.90, whereas a New Zealand resident similarly without deductions for dependents would be liable to pay tax of $248.35. Taxation liability where deductions are claimed for dependents would also involve proportionately higher contributions for the New Zealand resident as compared with the Australian resident. In the light of the above, the taxation information contained in the Circular of 30/4/84 is clearly wrong. These allegations have been made time and again and have contributed to disharmony in the pastoral industry… I trust the information supplied here clarifies the issue.[268]

Tax avoidance allegations

Unfortunately, it did not clarify the issue. The AWU had repeated the allegation so often it seemed it was starting to believe its own lie. With its portrayal of New Zealand shearers as tax cheats now part of its strategy to defeat the scourge of wide combs, the union was certainly reluctant to admit it was wrong. So, what did it do? It tweaked the allegation. On 6 December 1984, Gil Barr, who by this time had taken over from Frank Mitchell as federal secretary of the AWU, wrote to Prime Minister Bob Hawke to make some very serious allegations against New Zealand shearers. Key excerpts from that letter include

> The Australian Workers' Union again brings to the attention of the Government the inequitable situation that exists between the payment of income tax by Australian shearers as compared to payments made by shearers coming to Australia from New Zealand.

The AWU had been informed by both Chris Hurford and officials from the Department of Employment and Industrial Relations of the very narrow circumstances under which New Zealand shearers working in Australia would not be liable to pay income tax.[269] The union was now using this information to allege New Zealand shearers, en masse, were involved in an elaborate tax avoidance scheme. Barr said there were two main parts to the scheme:

> 1. A group of New Zealanders will come to Australia and be engaged by property owners to do the shearing, they then appoint one of their number as the contractor and he is payed [sic] all monies earned, they work under this system for any period of time they want up to the allowable 183 days, they then get a clearance from the Taxation Department and return to New Zealand without payment of any income tax.
> 2. A similar method to that described in 1 is that a group of shearers will gain employment in Australia and have all monies earned paid direct to a person who is still in New Zealand and is named as the contractor or their agent and they receive payment from that person on their return to that country.

So what evidence did the union have to support these allegations? Here's where it got a bit awkward – none! Barr admitted, 'The Union has not got specific details or proof of these alleged practices being carried out, but our members inform us that they have heard New Zealand shearers boasting about having done the above mentioned…' The only basis for these very serious allegations was the hearsay evidence of some union members who had overheard a conversation between New Zealand shearers. Incredibly, the letter also admitted union members would not hesitate to use violence 'to try and reduce the amount of work being done by them [New Zealanders]'.

…there will be eruptions of violence between our members and those who they feel are wrongfully being allowed to take away part of their livelihood.

Hawke replied six weeks later, on 21 January 1985. He said he had passed the union's concerns to the Commissioner of Taxation and the commissioner had told him he was 'unaware of any arrangements which permit New Zealand shearers to avoid payment of tax on income derived in Australia'. Referring specifically to the scheme the union had alleged was taking place, the prime minister said, 'The Commissioner said it was highly unlikely that these conditions could be met by New Zealand shearers in the circumstances you have outlined.' He added that recent inspection activity 'had generally shown that both employers and employees engaged in the industry were complying with their taxation obligations'. He finished by inviting the union to forward details of any specific cases of tax avoidance it knew about to the commissioner for investigation.

The Canberra protest

Well before the tax allegations escalated to the prime minister's office, the AWU had organised a demonstration of shearers outside Parliament House in Canberra. This rally, which was scheduled for Thursday 10 May 1984, represented a ramping up of the campaign to pressure the federal government to impose restrictions on visiting New Zealand shearers. And it took place despite the federal government having already rejected some of the union's key complaints against New Zealanders. Several hundred shearers from around New South Wales converged on the national capital to demand the government protect Australian shearing jobs from the threat of 'cheap New Zealand labour'. They arrived mainly in buses, hoping they could persuade the lawmakers to revisit the issue of work permits. They didn't. A delegation of shearers and union officials, including Canberra-based AWU southern region organiser Bill Preece, met with Immigration Minister Stewart West, Industrial Relations Minister Ralph Willis and Special Minister of State Mick Young. The ministers, however, were adamant the government would not be introducing work permits. The shearers left Canberra frustrated and angry at yet another rebuff.

Yass violence

One of the departing buses that afternoon carried about 40 shearers north of the national capital. At Yass, the group decided to 'inspect' a couple of local sheds where non-union teams were suspected to be working. The first was at the 300-hectare grazing and cropping property Drummoyne, six kilometres north-east of Yass on the Coolalie Road.

Bruce Turton, a Yass-based shearer and shearing contractor who had not participated in the Canberra protest, said the events of that afternoon became well known in the local community. He said one of the daughters of the owner spotted the bus as it was entering the property just after four p.m. She immediately alerted her father. The family called the police and several neighbours, while the owner went to meet the bus. Several unionists spoke briefly with the owner then tried to enter the shed. According to Bruce Turton, the owner's son, who was in the shed, 'booted them out of the shed and kept it locked'. While there was quite a bit of arguing, there was no violence. 'The cockies and police got there in time to avert what could have been a fairly serious situation,' he said.

The protesters retreated and headed north-west towards Harden, stopping at Kiianga, a Bowning district property owned by local grazier Richard Glover. Three unionists entered the shed and asked the four shearers in the team if they were union members. They said they were not and declined an offer to join the union. One of the unionists told Glover the Storemen and Packers' Union would black ban his wool, then returned to the bus to inform the other protesters that non-union shearers were working the shed. Meanwhile, Glover went to the homestead to call the police. When he returned, many of the occupants of the bus were inside the shed. However, he was unable to find the unionist he spoke with earlier and, with things looking highly volatile, he again called the Yass police station. When he went back to the shed, he found a diesel fuel tank tap had been turned on and fuel was draining out, and containers of drench had been poured on the ground. About this time, tensions boiled over and 15 unionists attacked the shearing team, punching and kicking several men, badly injuring some. Glover too was attacked – he was struck on the head with a piece of timber. The attackers left before the police arrived.

According to local newspaper reports which were published after the event and referenced court documents, when the unionists involved in the attack got back on the bus, they agreed to deny ever being at the property if they were questioned about this incident. Given that they were not locals, the men were confident they could not be identified. Turton said some locals were initially critical of police, believing they did not try hard enough to locate and stop the bus. However, the subsequent investigation was thorough. He said police used video footage from Parliament House security cameras and media coverage of the protest to help identify the attackers. Police later arrested and charged eight men with assault-related offences. In early 1987, the man who assaulted Richard Glover, a shearer from Young, was sentenced to 12 months' jail.

Despite the Kiianga incident, the Yass region remained relatively trouble-free during the dispute. Turton said this was partly due to the efforts of the Yass Shearing Committee, which was formed during the

1983 national strike. The committee, which comprised local shearers, contractors and graziers, aimed to ensure the local pastoral industry could continue operating as smoothly as possible during the dispute. 'We got the graziers to let us know when they were shearing so we could keep an eye out for trouble,' Turton said. 'We had phone numbers of people they could ring straight away, so people could get there quickly if needed.'

Health and safety inquiry ruling

Another area the union was focusing on in early 1984 as the Arbitration Commission's health and safety inquiry was drawing to a close was the need for a single-gauge comb in the pastoral industry. The union was exerting pressure inside and outside the inquiry for the commissioner to approve a single comb size.

In early March, Ernie Ecob wrote to both Industrial Relations Minister Ralph Willis and Commissioner Ian McKenzie to stress the importance of uniformity in the industry. He warned that '…if there is more than one size comb introduced into the industry, there will be a full exit of the professional shearers from the industry'.[270]

Another barrage of telex messages was organised to coincide with Ecob's letter, with local pastoral committees sending the commissioner messages such as: to prevent further violence in the shearing industry we urge a one size comb decision in wide comb hearing; all members call on you to introduce one comb into the Pastoral Industry Award (both from the Bourke Pastoral Committee); and, your decision to allow two combs has brought disruption, brawling, disunity to the pastoral industry; to put stability back in the industry one comb only required (Coonamble Pastoral Committee).

Proceedings in the health and safety inquiry wound up that month – final submissions were heard in Melbourne on Tuesday to Thursday 13 to 15 March, with the final day spilling over to Sydney on Thursday 22 March. Submissions for the AWU and farmer groups were of almost biblical proportions – the longer barristers talk, the more they are paid.

Garry Johnston, who presented final submissions for the federal branch of the AWU, said

> The union's submission, stripped of any emotion, can be summarised this way: that if one matter was consistent throughout the evidence the Commission took it was that there had to be standardisation and uniformity, that the industry cannot survive without that uniformity or standardisation, and in our respectful submission the Commission should revert to the standard comb of 64 millimetres.[271]

Johnston argued that the present clause had proven to be unworkable and had created disharmony, friction and violence in the industry. The farmer groups, through David Bleby QC, argued that the commission's original decision should stand. Bleby said this was really a case about technological change and the need for the pastoral industry to embrace innovation and progress.

Commissioner McKenzie handed down his decision in Sydney on the morning of Tuesday 5 June 1984. He ruled the current comb width provisions should be retained, allowing shearers to choose between standard gauge (64 mm) combs or, with the approval of the employer, wider combs. However, he also imposed a maximum comb width restriction of 92 mm (the maximum cutting arc of a wide comb handpiece). In supporting his decision, the commissioner said the use of wide combs had become entrenched in the industry; it had been clearly demonstrated that wide combs could be used to satisfactorily shear any type of sheep in Australia; and the pastoral industry could not remain impervious to technological change. However, in a concession to the union, he approved the formation of a research and development working party under the auspices of the Arbitration Commission to examine the feasibility of establishing an optimum shearing comb width and to consider future technological developments in the industry.

The commissioner found there was no evidence that wide combs had caused any occupational health and safety problems for shearers.

However, he recommended ongoing monitoring to see if any such problems emerged.

Interestingly, he also identified the fear of Award conditions and job opportunities being undermined by New Zealand shearers, not wide shearing combs, as being the most significant cause of the ongoing disharmony in the pastoral industry. He suggested the union should direct its energies towards eliminating the alleged breaches of the Award that it insisted were being perpetuated by New Zealand shearers.

So, after three Arbitration Commission cases that included hearings and shed inspections throughout Australia, roughly 3,500 pages of transcript evidence, hundreds of thousands of dollars of legal and travel expenses for the main parties, and roughly four years of industrial turmoil including a two-month national shearers' strike, an industrial dispute Robert White once said should not have lasted more than a single day, was finally over. Or was it?

37

The Aftermath

The question on the lips of just about everyone associated with this dispute was, 'How is the AWU going to react?' No one knew what to expect. Just days before the ruling was delivered, Ernie Ecob came out in the media and suggested the union was 'not going to cop' a decision allowing wide combs.[272] Paul Houlihan was not about to let this comment pass through to the keeper. He issued a statement to *The Australian* in which he slammed Ecob's obstinacy and indeed his whole handling of the dispute. The article in which he was quoted was published on the morning of the final decision, so representatives of the key stakeholders would have read his comments before proceedings began. In his typical straight-talking manner, he said if the AWU was not going to abide by its undertaking to accept the umpire's decision, should it go against them, the NFF would consider taking steps to deregister the union or cancel the Award.

> The New South Wales branch leaders have developed a neurosis against the reality of wide combs and what the shearers, their members, want to use. If the Award is going to suit only one party, then we don't see a lot of merit in it continuing to exist. The tragedy is we don't have a problem with shearers or station hands, but with a few union leaders. We have been through three hearings in three years covering 3,300 pages of transcript and I'm yet to be let in on the secret of the real reason behind the dispute.[273]

Although most parties, including the federal government,

welcomed the decision, the future of the pastoral industry hinged on the union's response. The AWU's federal Executive Council met within hours of Commissioner McKenzie's ruling to consider its position. Federal president Allan Begg said the union was disappointed with the ruling and he anticipated members would also be upset. He doubted the decision would ease the animosity and disharmony in the industry. However, the AWU was once again in an awkward position – although it did not like the ruling, it had given an undertaking that it would accept the outcome. It had little choice but to recommend to its members that they accept the ruling, and so passed a resolution to this effect. The resolution conceded that the practical effect of the original ruling in the dispute, on 10 December 1982, had been 'to force many shearers to use combs wider than 64 millimetres in order to remain in employment'. The AWU reserved a decision on participating in the proposed research and development working party until its members had had time to consider the ruling.

So, was the dispute now over? Robert White, who had travelled to Sydney to hear Commissioner McKenzie's final decision, summed it up best. He told the *Sun* newspaper that day the wide combs issue had mostly died down in the bush, 'although there will always be a few diehards'.[274] Most shearers, it seemed, had changed camps. The best estimate at the time was that 80 to 90 per cent of shearers were using wide gear. In a report prepared for a meeting of AWU delegates in early 1985, Errol Hodder, the AWU's Queensland branch secretary, estimated that up to 90 per cent of the New South Wales flock was being shorn with wide gear when Commissioner McKenzie handed down his findings in June 1984. These figures are in line with the comb manufacturers' sales figures and projections discussed earlier. And Sunbeam, which only a few months earlier revealed a sales mix of 77 per cent wide and 23 per cent narrow (between September 1983 and February 1984), was now selling 90 per cent wide gear.[275]

Nevertheless, it was not long before the parties were again at loggerheads. A little over a week after the final ruling, the AWU, which still had black bans in place on several properties, became incensed that some of its members were effectively being black-banned. Graziers in some areas of New South Wales, including Yass and Moree, were declining to directly employ or allow their contractors to employ union shearers they knew had been involved in violence and intimidation. Ernie Ecob went ballistic. He wrote to Commissioner McKenzie on 13 June to notify a dispute, saying,

> The disputation in the industry concerns actions either initiated by or taken by members, officials and officers of the Livestock and Grain Producers' Association of New South Wales, the National Farmers' Federation and the Shearing Contractors' Association of Australia by means of bans and limitations and by other means of conspiracy of their members to prevent Australian Workers' Union members from the acceptance of, offering for and/or performance of work in accordance with the Pastoral Industry Award 1965. The union further contends that members, officials and officers of those employer organisations named in this notification have taken actions which victimise members of the Australian Workers' Union in their employment.[276]

Commissioner McKenzie called a conference of parties in Sydney on 21 June, at which he said it was time to bury the hatchet ('not in each other's heads but in the ground')[277] and put an end to the animosity and violence that had been permeating the industry. 'Unless we do, we are going to continue this senseless fighting,' he said.[278] The commissioner recommended both parties immediately lift all bans and move on.

The Coleraine gun battle

However, after such a spiteful few years of conflict, it was always going to be difficult for everyone to simply move on. And in October 1984, tensions once more boiled over. This time in Coleraine, a sleepy town with a population of roughly 1,200, about 350 kilometres west of Melbourne and 35 kilometres north-west of Hamilton.

The dramas began on the afternoon of Saturday 6 October, when a New Zealand shearer went to the Hamilton TAB (a betting shop) and was assaulted by three men. He suffered injuries to his face but declined to press any charges. Later that day, about six p.m. in Coleraine, two New Zealand shearers became involved in a brawl with four local shearers. The brawl was broken up by one of the town's two stationed police officers, with the aid of a 44-year-old local man, who stepped in and struck several men involved in the fight with a fence paling. The local man got caught up in the fighting, was injured and had to miss two weeks of work. He was later charged with several assault offences. However, the charges were withdrawn in court when the prosecution acknowledged he had come to the aid of the policeman. The four Coleraine shearers were charged with various assault offences, for which they were later convicted, fined and placed on good behaviour bonds.

This 'minor' scuffle, however, was just a prelude to the main event. The following day, tensions ramped up even more – there were reports that the two groups involved in the previous day's fighting were looking to 'meet up' again. About 9.30 p.m., two cars full of New Zealand shearers drove to a house in Winter Street, Coleraine, where several local union shearers and their families were having a barbecue. Apparently, the occupants of the house had been warned via a telephone call that the Kiwis were on the way. When they arrived, the New Zealanders fired guns from their cars towards the house. As well as several shearers and their wives, there were six children inside the house. The women and children flung themselves to the floor, while the shearers armed themselves and returned fire. A gun battle broke out in which 14 or 15 shots were fired. Two men in the front of one of the vehicles, a panel van, were struck and injured by shots fired through the windscreen. One was hit in the forehead by a .22 calibre rifle shot; the other was struck in the arm by a shotgun pellet. Both men had to be treated in hospital. A police spokesman said, 'The two wounded men were sitting alongside each other in the front seat of the panel van. If it hadn't been for the windscreen, this could have been a matter for homicide.'[279]

Following this incident, one of the shearers inside the house was charged with causing grievous bodily harm and five counts of criminal damage. However, the charges were dropped in January 1985, when the two New Zealand victims, who had returned home, failed to appear in court. The police prosecutor told the court both men were unlikely to return to Australia as they could face charges over the incident if they did.

Understandably, this incident sparked widespread anger and condemnation from community and political leaders as well as representatives of the AWU and farmer groups. A shoot-out in a sleepy country town was outrageous. Many leaders called for calm and an end to the lingering violence – the dispute had been finalised in the Arbitration Commission and it was time for this to be reflected on the ground. Perversely, the Coleraine gun battle may have had a calming effect, by making people realise just how out of hand the situation had become. Any escalation from this sort of incident would almost certainly lead to people being killed, so the protagonists seemed to back down.

Shearers abandon AWU

It's difficult to pinpoint the end of the dispute – it just petered out after the Arbitration Commission's final ruling on 5 June, with the Coleraine violence a blip. It was clear, however, that the end was near when the AWU organised a meeting at the Dubbo Golf Club on 24 November. Significantly, this was a pastoral industry delegates' meeting, not a meeting of rank and file shearers. Why? As Ernie Ecob explained, there had been '…a turn-down in solidarity in the industry…big numbers of shearers had abided [by the] employers' request regarding the use of wide combs instead of abiding by their own rank and file decision of May 1983'.[280]

However, the notion that employers were somehow coercing shearers to use wide gear was utterly false. Shearers could choose which combs to use and by now most had discovered that wide combs were better. As a result, rank and file members had abandoned the union in droves and were out shearing with wide combs. The meeting called for the establishment of a standard gauge 86 mm comb. But no one was listening any more.

There were a few more relatively minor incidents early in 1985 (shearing sheds being burnt down in the Young and Hay districts of New South Wales). However, by the end of that year, the dispute was effectively over, and the union had lost about 60 per cent of its pastoral members (more than 8,000 shearers). Many of the diehards who remained struggled to find work because they refused to shear in the same shed with wide combers. A small portion left the industry or retired.

Relentless campaign

Having lost the wide comb dispute and most of its pastoral industry members, the AWU wanted someone, other than itself, to blame for its predicament. And who better than the New Zealand shearers? In early 1985, it turned its attention once more to campaigning for the introduction of work permits to limit the number of New Zealanders who could work as shearers in Australia. This time the campaign emphasised the impact on local jobs – the union argued the New Zealanders were effectively putting a large number of Australian shearers out of work and onto social welfare. It persisted with this campaign for six or seven years, into the early 1990s, when it quantified the problem – arguing variously that 42 per cent of the Australian sheep flock was being shorn by New Zealanders or that New Zealanders now comprised 42 per cent of Australia's shearing workforce. (Just how the figure of 42 per cent was derived became the subject of discussion at a subsequent Senate inquiry.) It's true a large number of Australian shearers were out of work in the late 1980s and early 1990s, but there were many factors at play.

The AWU also refined its tax-related objections to New Zealand shearers. It was now arguing visiting New Zealand shearers who stayed in Australia for less than six months could claim a 100 per cent refund of tax paid in Australia when they returned to New Zealand. This claim effectively scuppered the union's previous claims that New Zealand shearers were not paying any tax in Australia or that they were engaged en masse in elaborate tax avoidance schemes.

The federal government was resisting the push to make changes, arguing the two-way open door labour market arrangements between Australia and New Zealand via the Closer Economic Relations agreement were mutually beneficial and had been working well for many years. It refused to restrict the movement of New Zealand shearers into Australia.

However, by 1992, the AWU campaign was in overdrive. In late March, shearers set up tents on the lawns in front of Parliament House in Canberra and each day lobbied members of parliament and members of the public, trying to convince them of the need for legislative reforms to protect the jobs of Australian shearers. A core group of about 50 shearers camped there for several months. In early June, when the Canberra winter set in, the group dispersed. During this 'Capital Hill Camp', the Victorian branch of the AWU handed out leaflets in which it was claimed that

- Over 50 per cent of Australian shearers and shed hands were not working;
- Over 42 per cent of the Australian wool clip was shorn by New Zealand shearers;
- New Zealanders received NZ$1.35–$1.40 for every Australian dollar when returning home;
- Visiting New Zealand shearers here less than six months received a 100 per cent refund on all income tax paid in Australia when they returned home.

Incredibly, some members of parliament treated some of these claims as axioms and used them in speeches. For example, Colin Hollis, the member for Throsby (Labor, 1984–2001), addressed the House of Representatives on Tuesday 31 March.

Mr Deputy Speaker, do you realise that over 42 per cent of the Australian wool clip is shorn by New Zealand shearers? Unless action is taken, in a few years the total Australian wool clip will be shorn by New Zealand shearers. Australia will have lost yet another skill. Honourable members may have noticed tents outside the front of Parliament House. Australian shearers have come to Parliament House to highlight to politicians and to the general public the plight of Australian shearers. Today, more than 50 per cent of Australian shearers are out of work… I have been told that New Zealand shearers receive between NZ$1.35 and NZ$1.40 for every Australian dollar when returning home. If visiting New Zealanders have worked here for less than six months, they receive a 100 per cent refund on all income tax paid in Australia… It's a tax rort. The sum taken out of Australia by visiting New Zealand shearers is approximately $130 million.[281]

In September 1992, the government finally conceded some ground when it asked the Senate Standing Committee on Rural and Regional Affairs to conduct an inquiry into 'the employment of visitors to Australia in the shearing industry'. The terms of reference covered the social and economic implications for rural communities, taxation arrangements, immigration regulations, international agreements, and industrial relations.

New Zealand shearers inquiry

Thirteen public hearings were held throughout Australia during the next eight months. The committee heard evidence from 124 witnesses and received 90 submissions. It tabled its report in parliament in February 1994. The key findings included:

- The main factors that had led to a decline in job opportunities for Australian shearers were a substantial decrease in national flock size, the effects of recession and severe droughts, and increased 'cocky shearing'.
- New Zealand born workers comprised just 6.6 per cent of Australia's shearing industry workforce. A substantial number of these New Zealanders were now permanent residents of Australia.

- There was no evidence of a systematic disregard for Award conditions by New Zealand shearers. Where Award breaches were occurring, they were just as likely to involve Australian shearers and contractors as their New Zealand counterparts.
- New Zealand shearers who returned home after working in Australia for less than six months could not obtain refunds of the tax they paid in Australia.
- There was no evidence of widespread tax evasion in the shearing industry. Where it was occurring, it was just as likely to involve Australian shearers as New Zealand shearers.[282]

The committee recommended the establishment of a shearing industry taskforce to develop strategies for revising the federal Pastoral Industry Award, and ensuring industry compliance in relation to Award pay and conditions, as well as taxation and superannuation obligations.

The committee's findings were another blow for the AWU. It had spent years campaigning to rid the shearing industry of New Zealanders, and indirectly, to try to re-establish some standing and authority in the industry. But evidence from the inquiry clearly showed the campaign had been based almost entirely on false assumptions. The union's credibility was shot.

Afterword: Cut-out

Robert White's legacy

On the afternoon of Sunday 16 March 1986, Robert White was home at his Mandurama property Robayle working on a car with a friend. The two men were using a block and tackle to place a rebuilt V8 engine into a black HJ Holden ute. At one point, White had to get under the vehicle to help guide the motor into the correct position as it was being lowered into the engine bay. As he did, catastrophe struck – the chain supporting the engine broke and the engine dropped onto White, crushing him. His friend managed to reattach the chain, lift the engine and drag White's body from under the vehicle, but tragically he had died from the injuries he received.

White was just 42. He was survived by his wife Gayle and four children. His contribution to Australia's shearing industry was substantial. However, it has gone largely unnoticed. Although several shearers advocated for wide combs during the early 1980s, none were as strategic, vocal, single-minded, and undeterred as White.

It was no accident that White became embroiled in a fight to have wide combs introduced into the shearing industry. Based on his experience in Western Australia, he knew wide combs were superior to the standard gear that had been used in the industry for decades. Depending on the skill of the shearer, they could boost their daily tallies by 20 to 40 sheep. This equated to a massive pay increase for workers who toiled harder than anyone else. He could not believe they were not being used more extensively. Recognising the potential benefits for shearers and wool growers alike, he deliberately set out to try to reform and modernise the wool industry.

Frank Myers, who shore for White until late 1981, when he was convicted of using wide gear, recalled having a beer with White in a Bathurst pub towards the end of 1980, when the dispute was just starting. White told him he was going to come out as a wide comb user, defy the union and provoke a confrontation over wide gear. He had thought it through and knew the AWU would resist. He knew too that he would face fierce opposition and potentially be targeted by radical unionists, but he didn't care – he believed it was the right thing to do.

During the early 1980s, anyone who dared defy the AWU was asking for trouble. The union went to great lengths to try to silence White – he was bashed several times, his shearing teams were ambushed and beaten up, his family was threatened and harassed, and for several years his life was on the line. Some nights he had to sleep in police lock-ups for his own safety. At times his wife and family lived under a police guard. Occasionally they had to leave home for brief periods to avoid being attacked.

Most of the shearers who shore for White shared his conviction and passion for wide combs and also deserve credit for their courage in advocating for change in the face of violent opposition. Many of them too were beaten and harassed, and their families were threatened.

After the dispute ended, Paul Houlihan said Robert White's tenacity led to wide combs being introduced a decade or so sooner than they otherwise would have been. White never set out to destroy the union – he was a strong supporter of the union. The AWU initiated its own demise when it failed to recognise the potential of wide comb technology to benefit its members. Then it tried to blame everyone but itself for its downfall. In the end, most shearers worked out who was to blame when they abandoned the union and rendered it impotent and irrelevant to the industry.

Like so many people who have made a difference, Robert White was a rebel. He refused to conform to shearing industry norms. This slightly built, unassuming gun shearer, realised wide shearing combs would revolutionise his vocation. And for the role he played in having them approved, he surely ranks as an unsung hero of Australia's iconic shearing industry.

Glossary

Blow: the stroke or movement of the shearer's handpiece along the sheep's body while the sheep is being shorn.

Board: the floor area of the woolshed where the sheep are shorn.

Cheesy gland: a contagious bacterial disease in sheep (and goats) that produces abscesses in the lymph glands throughout the body.

Cocky: a nickname used by shearers for a farmer.

Crutching: shearing the wool around a sheep's crutch to reduce the risk of fly-strike (see definition below).

Cutter: the four-pronged steel plate that fits into the shearer's handpiece and oscillates against the shearing comb. It is this back-and-forth movement of the cutter that cuts the wool as the shearer moves the handpiece through the sheep's fleece. (Cutters for narrow gauge combs have three prongs.)

Cut-out: the completion of the shearing contract at a particular woolshed.

Fly-strike: a potentially fatal condition in sheep caused by the Australian sheep blowfly (*Lucilia cuprina*). Female flies lay their eggs in a sheep's fleece, near the skin. When they hatch, the maggots eat damaged skin and create a wound that attracts more flies. This condition is a major cause of lost production in the Australian wool industry. (Also called blowfly-strike.)

Handpiece: the mechanised tool used by shearers to shear a sheep. It resembles a large pair of hair clippers and features a comb and a cutter, which together collect and cut the sheep's fleece as the shearer guides the handpiece through the sheep's wool.

Pulled combs: shearing combs that have had their outside teeth slightly bent to extend the overall width of the combs.

Presser/woolpresser: the worker who operates the shearing shed's woolpress.

Ridges: narrow strips of wool left on a sheep after shearing. Experienced wool growers and shearers can tell by the ridges what sort of shearing combs were used on the sheep.

Rouseabout: a woolshed worker who has a variety of roles. (Also called roustabout.)

Scab: a shearer who was prepared to defy AWU directives and work during a strike. To be labelled a 'scab' was highly derogatory. In colonial times, scabs were sometimes called 'blacklegs'.

Second cuts: short portions of wool staples resulting from the shearer making two blows over the same area.

Skin cuts: a nick or cut to the sheep that occurs during shearing, often caused by the sheep moving or excessively wrinkled skin.

Stand: the area on the board allocated to shearers for them to shear the sheep.

Standard gauge/narrow combs: shearing combs that have 10 steel teeth and are no wider than 64 mm (measured between the outside two teeth).

Wide combs: combs that have 13 steel teeth and are roughly 20 mm wider than narrow combs.

Wool classer: a person qualified to sort, classify and grade raw wool based on factors such as the length, thickness, quality, colour, srength and cleanliness of the wool.

Woolpress: an electrical machine used to compact wool into bales.

Timeline

1888: Mechanical shears debut (in a full-scale commercial setting) at Dunlop Station along the Darling River near Bourke in north-west New South Wales. They rapidly replace hand shears and within a few years are being used by almost every shearer in Australia.

1891–1894: This period bookends two significant shearers' strikes, which focused on pay rates. These strikes played a crucial role in the formation of the Australian Labour Party in February 1894.

1907: The federal Pastoral Industry Award is established, guaranteeing shearers a minimum rate of pay and working conditions.

1910: The AWU approves a rule banning the use of wide gauge shearing combs or double bent or 'pulled' narrow combs.

1926: The Commonwealth Conciliation and Arbitration Commission agrees to an application by wool growers to vary the Award to restrict the width of shearing combs to two and a half inches (64 mm). This variation formalises the union's ban on wide combs. At the time wool growers argued wide combs caused more second cuts and equipment breakages.

1927: The union tries unsuccessfully to have the commission relax the ban on double bent or pulled combs. The commission said that pulled combs 'injure sheep and ridge the wool'.

1948: The Award is varied to prohibit employers from allowing their employees to use combs wider than two and a half inches. (The words 'nor shall the employer permit a shearer to use' were added to the width restriction clause.)

1956: Queensland and New South Wales shearers go on strike after their pay rate is cut through separate industrial court rulings. Following a lengthy and bitter dispute, the shearers succeed in having their previous pay rates reinstated. (This strike is the subject of the iconic 1975 Australian film *Sunday Too Far Away*, which starred Jack Thompson.)

Early 1970s: The Australian Wool Corporation conducts limited trials on different shearing combs as part of its Australian Wool Harvesting Program and finds wide combs could offer advantages to both wool growers and shearers.

July 1979: The National Farmers' Federation is formed to be the peak body representing Australian agriculture.

October 1979: Researchers from the Western Australian Department of Agriculture publish the results of preliminary research trials into the use of wide combs. Two trials demonstrated significant productivity improvements through the use of wide combs. The researchers recommended larger, commercial-scale trials involving different shearing combs.

January 1980: The AWU seeks to extend the ban on the use of wide combs to Western Australia, where the shearing industry has been mostly unregulated.

14 May 1980: The LGPA applies to the Arbitration Commission to have the Pastoral Industry Award varied to allow a series of controlled commercial field research trials on the use of different combs. The application was set down for hearing in July 1980 but was adjourned indefinitely to allow the parties more time to discuss the use of different combs.

June 1980: An AWU meeting in Dubbo rejects the LGPA proposal to conduct field trials to test the effectiveness of wide combs. Conferences between representatives of the wool growers and the AWU were held to discuss the proposed trials, but the union refused to cooperate with any trials, regardless of whether the Award was varied to allow trials to proceed.

17 July 1980: Mandurama shearer Robert White attacks the AWU for its stand against the use of wide combs, saying the union's stance threatened to disrupt the industry.

22 September 1980: Shearers meeting in Orange vote to black ban Robert White, as well as any shearers using wide combs and properties where wide combs are used.

9 October 1980: Australian Workers' Union organiser Laurie (Bluey) Rodwell is allegedly assaulted on a Cumnock property he attends to investigate alleged breaches of the federal Pastoral Industry Award.

26 October 1980: About 200 shearers attend an AWU meeting in Dubbo and pass a motion condemning the use of wide combs. The meeting resolves to instigate a statewide stop work meeting immediately if the union becomes aware of wide combs being used in New South Wales.

December 1980: Paul Houlihan is appointed the new Industrial Director of the National Farmers' Federation.

27 April 1981: The AWU catches Robert White's shearing team using wide combs at the Canowindra district property, Canomodine. This breach of the Award prompts the AWU to organise a stop work meeting in Dubbo for 1 June.

13 May 1981: The AWU black bans Canomodine, where 20,000 sheep need feed during a drought.

1 June 1981: Shearers and pastoral workers attending an AWU meeting in Dubbo instruct the union 'to explore all avenues to peaceful settlement by negotiations with all interested organisations to settle this dispute by 1 August 1981, provided that such settlement brings about a situation where wide combs will not be tolerated'.

Mid-July 1981: At its annual conference in Sydney, the LGPA passes the following motion: 'That LGPA continues to seek, by negotiation, Australian Workers' Union consent to variations in the Pastoral Industry Award which would permit the conduct of field research trials on the use of different combs.'

1 August 1981: Ernie Ecob is quoted in the *Central Western Daily* as saying the AWU would not consent to trials on the use of different combs.

20 August 1981: The LPGA writes to the AWU seeking assurances that the union will still support field research trials on wide combs.

9 September 1981: Ernie Ecob replies to the LGPA, assuring the association that the union was prepared to negotiate over the proposed research trials.

Late September 1981: Behind the scenes 'negotiations' take place between the AWU and LGPA in a bid to have all black bans removed. However, a stalemate ensues and culminates in Paul Houlihan contacting the commission on 28 September and asking for the LGPA trials application to be relisted.

29 September 1981: Commissioner Ian McKenzie orders the AWU to lift all black bans on properties and contractors using wide combs. This order was mistakenly reported by some media outlets as being a lifting of the ban on wide combs.

26 October 1981: The Wool Council of Australia enters the debate, with president Ian McLachlan warning that unless the AWU immediately consents to the conduct of field research trials on wide combs, there would be an inevitable escalation of the wide comb dispute.

2 November 1981: A union meeting in Dubbo reinforces black bans on properties where wide combs have been used. These bans will become part of further Arbitration Commission hearings.

8 November 1981: A meeting of AWU pastoral workers at Bendigo, Victoria, resolved to call on the AWU to negotiate with wool growers for the introduction of research trials on the use of wide combs. The vote took union officials by surprise and they scrambled to organise another meeting a week later to overturn the decision.

13 November 1981: Bathurst magistrate Clive Werry begins hearing an AWU prosecution of Robert White and his team of shearers for using wide combs at Canomodine and Millambri earlier in the year.

1 December 1981: Wool growers withdraw their trials application from before the Arbitration Commission and submit a new application seeking the removal from the Award of the ban on the use of combs wider than 64 mm. This application was joined to the AWU application to extend the ban on wide combs to Western Australia.

2 December 1981: The LGPA organises a wide comb shearing demonstration for the commission at the Sydney Showground. And in something of a 'covert' operation, it organised a separate demonstration for the media. In doing so, it infuriated the union and incurred the wrath of Commissioner Ian McKenzie.

16 December 1981: The wide combs case resumes before the Arbitration Commission, which agrees to an AWU request to carry out a series of shed inspections in Victoria, South Australia and Tasmania. The wool growers successfully seek an extension of the inspections to Western Australia.

Late January 1982: AWU members meeting at the union's annual convention resolve to endorse a one-day national shearers' strike on 28 February to protest the LGPA's campaign to introduce wide comb shears. The stoppage will affect more than 15,000 pastoral workers.

Early February 1982: Arbitration Commission inspections and hearings take place on properties in Tasmania and Victoria.

13–17 February 1982: Arbitration Commission inspections and hearings take place on properties in South Australia.

21 February 1982: AWU pastoral workers meet at Dubbo and resolve to black ban Sunbeam (the key manufacturer of wide combs) and authorise New South Wales secretary Ernie Ecob to call an immediate stoppage if the commission legalises the use of wide combs.

Late February–mid March 1982: Inspections and hearings take place in Western Australia.

26 March 1982: Shed inspections are finalised and the commission invites evidence from shearing comb manufacturers and the New South Wales branch of the AWU.

Mid-April 1982: The AWU says it will not take part in the hearings when they resume on 27 April. New South Wales branch secretary Ernie Ecob says, 'We will not be party to the hearing – we will not lower ourselves to be associated with such a scabby turnout.'

27 April–1 June 1982: The Arbitration Commission hearings resume and conclude after 50 sitting days.

10 December 1982: Commissioner Ian McKenzie hands down his decision, ruling that wide combs can be used. He varied the Award to allow shearers to use combs wider than 64 mm if they wanted to, provided the shed owner agreed to their use and that the combs were not modified or 'pulled' from their manufactured specifications. The union immediately calls a national shearers' strike.

21 December 1982: The strike ends after the AWU is granted a stay of the decision pending an appeal.

January 1983: The AWU asks wool growers to sign a petition undertaking that they will never allow the introduction of wide combs on their properties. It had planned to present the petition as part of the appeal hearings, and although the union claimed publicly that hundreds of wool growers had signed the petition, it did not tender the document during the appeal.

8 February–9 March 1983: The full bench of the Arbitration Commission hears the union's appeal against its decision allowing the use of wide combs.

23 March 1983: The full bench hands down its decision (just weeks after Bob Hawke became prime minister), rejecting the union's appeal. In doing so, the commission states, 'The attitude of the AWU was hedged by conservatism and tinged with hysteria.'

23 March–6 May 1983: Soon after the decision is handed down, the AWU calls a national shearers' strike. In early May, a deal is struck with the union to end the dispute. It involves the establishment of an investigation by Commissioner McKenzie into possible health and safety risks associated with the use of wide combs.

18 April 1983: The LGPA organises a series of meetings throughout the state (Coonamble, Walgett, Armidale) to clarify its position on wide combs. It says it is not seeking to enforce their use by all shearers and it also gives public assurances that it will not attempt to breakdown the shearers' Award or reduce pay rates.

10 August 1983: Hearings begin in the inquiry into possible health risks from using wide combs.

September–October 1983: The AWU organises black bans against those properties that allowed rebel shearers to use wide combs to try to break-up the national strike earlier in the year.

5 June 1984: The inquiry into possible health risks associated with wide combs wraps up, finding no evidence of any detrimental impacts. This is the final decision made on wide combs.

16 March 1986: Robert White, the key shearer advocate of wide combs, dies in a farm accident on his property at Mandurama.

September 1992–February 1994: The Australian Senate's Standing Committee on Rural and Regional Affairs conducts an inquiry into the impact of the employment of New Zealand shearers in Australia on the Australian shearing industry.

Acknowledgements

I met Paul Longhurst in the Orange courthouse in 2001. At the time I was the court reporter for the local newspaper, the *Central Western Daily*, and was covering the day's Local Court proceedings. Paul, a solicitor and partner in the local law firm Boyd & Longhurst, was representing some clients. The court building, built in 1883, was undergoing renovations. As a result, the Local Court was sitting in a cramped back room. I'd seen Paul a few times, in court and around town, but it was in this confined space during a morning tea break that our paths first crossed.

There was nothing pretentious about Paul. He had grey hair with matching beard and moustache, and wore a woollen sports jacket, neat trousers and chestnut-coloured RM Williams boots – typical country business attire. Although he was neatly dressed, he managed to look a bit scruffy. He came across as down-to-earth and likeable. Our conversation meandered before it somehow arrived at the wide comb shearing dispute, which had roughly coincided with my university years. I could recall reading about it in various newspaper articles but had not followed it closely. Paul had and was soon telling me about many of the local people who had been involved as well as key local events. He mentioned Robert White as being the 'champion' of the wide comb; the fact that many of the union meetings and developments occurred in Dubbo; and the role that a union black ban on a Canowindra district property played in escalating the dispute. I wanted to ask lots of questions, but the brief adjournment in court proceedings drew to a close. And our conversation ended rather hurriedly with Paul saying, 'It's a great story. Someone should write a book about it.'

At the time, I had no plans to write a book. I was working full-time and busy, with my wife Linda, raising two daughters. We were heavily involved in our church and the girls' school – spare time was scarce. But that conversation stuck in my mind and soon I began researching the dispute. My search for information quickly gained momentum and within months I knew this was a story that had to be documented. Writing this book has been a frustrating, time-consuming and costly quest. But it has also been an incredibly rewarding journey. The process of transitioning from print journalism to long-form writing has been challenging but immensely satisfying. I want to thank Paul Longhurst for inadvertently starting me on that journey. I hope, if he reads this book, he is satisfied with the result.

While researching this book, I spoke to hundreds of people. I extend my sincere thanks to the following people, who agreed to be formally interviewed: David Kingham, Bruce Turton, Brian Clarke (Dubbo), Brian Clarke (Eaglehawk), Graeme Pora, Paul Houlihan, John Ecob, Frank Myers, Arthur Watson, Col Somerset, Seymour Maere, Mel Johnston OAM, Mick O'Shea, Allen Murphy, John Frazer, Andy Newstead, Peter White, Paul Woollaston, Michelle Lees, Cliff Healey, Ian McLachlan AO, Paul McGaw, Fred McInerney, Allan and Betty Watt, Robert Foster, John Schick, Joe Nobes, Gary Doyle, John Conlan, Mark Shiels, Geoff 'Andy' Anderson, George Mack, and Laurie Polomka. As well as sharing details of their experiences and recollections, many also supplied me with copies of newspaper clippings and personal correspondence related to the dispute. This material proved invaluable.

I spoke at length with Ian Manning and Paul Houlihan, who both helped me greatly. Ian Manning kindly gave me access to an archive of material relating to the LGPA's industrial case. Ken Prato and Peter O'Brien provided me with copies of some of their writings and reflections on the wide comb dispute. This material has also been of great assistance and I offer them my sincere thanks. Keith Capps wrote to me about various incidents that took place in the New South Wales central west during the dispute. Mick Madden, a former shearer and

AWU organiser, offered sound advice and connected me to several key former union officials.

I accessed the newspaper collection at the National Library of Australia in Canberra. This library is a fantastic resource and I extend my thanks to the staff for their help.

Staff in the Canberra registry of the Fair Work Commission were helpful with documents relating to the wide comb dispute hearings that were held before the former Arbitration Commission. Janica Barbosa deserves mention for her assistance with archival material.

An unexpected source of information was the Tamworth Regional Film & Sound Archive, which houses more than 8,000 cans and cassettes of locally produced film and audio material. I would like to thank the archive's volunteers for their help in locating and sending me several items relating to the wide comb dispute. I would also like to thank the volunteers at the Hamilton History Centre in country Victoria, who sent me copies of archival material relating to an incident that took place at nearby Coleraine in October 1984.

My close friend Dr Richard Stanton played an important role in this manuscript taking shape. A former journalist, he recognised the significance and potential of this story and more or less challenged me to write this book. Richard offered encouragement, sound advice and valuable feedback at each stage of the process. He and his wife Lorraine even invited me to use their holiday home as a writing retreat. Richard and Lorraine's generosity and support have been invaluable, and I want to acknowledge their contribution to this project.

Another dear friend, Professor Phil Dolan, also made an important contribution. Phil kindly wrote the foreword, which highlights the fact that the historical events of the wide comb dispute are closely linked to the broader issue of technological change and how such change affects workers and society. Indeed, the dispute serves as a classic case study of the impact technological change can have on a specific agricultural industry and its workforce, and the different reactions of workers to change. Phil's insightful comments provide a bigger picture perspective from which to view and interpret the events of the wide comb dispute and I thank him for his generous contribution.

Many friends and colleagues have contributed indirectly to this book by helping me with contacts and simply encouraging me to press on – two people I should mention are Jeff Haydon and Arthur White.

Finally, and most importantly, I must thank my immediate family. It was a conversation with my eldest daughter Lauren in late 2015 that convinced me it was time to write this manuscript. Lauren told me she had been scouring various websites to try to find some writing scholarships I could apply for, so I could devote more time to writing. She said, 'Dad, you need to make some time for yourself and finish your book.' My youngest daughter Nicole was more forthright, advising me to resign from my job so I could have more time for writing.

Crazy as it might seem, that's what I did. At that stage, Linda had been offered a full-time teaching role, which meant we would survive financially. Linda, as always, has been patient, supportive and encouraging. She generously and unselfishly allowed me the time I needed to research and write this manuscript – sacrificial love in action! Linda has an English major and a love of languages. We often talk about words and phrases, writing and grammar. Her keen eye for detail and solid grasp and knowledge of the many nuances of the English language have helped refine the text in this book. I'm forever grateful.

Disclaimer

I have never shorn a sheep and doubt I could do so without causing injury or trauma to both the sheep and me. I cannot claim to have any expert knowledge of farming. I did spend a year living on a dairy farm near Bega on the far south coast of New South Wales, but it was the first year of my life. My family moved into town just after I turned one. I have not approached this history as a wool industry expert or an academic or a shearer or trade unionist (although I am an honorary member of the Media Entertainment and Arts Alliance). Rather, I have approached it as a journalist. My sole aim has been to explain in detail the events that took place during the wide comb shearing dispute from the viewpoint of the people and parties involved and to try to make some sense of why these events occurred. Many people I initially approached for information or to interview wanted to know what 'side' I was taking. I tried to explain that I wasn't taking sides; that I simply wanted to compile an objective account of what happened during those tumultuous years of the early 1980s. I have to say, however, that having interviewed 40 people and read through thousands of pages of archival documents, I think it is almost impossible for any reasonable and fair-minded person to examine this industrial dispute in detail and not be critical of the Australian Workers' Union for the way it handled the dispute.

When you set out to document a history such as this, you soon realise there are significant limitations to what you can achieve. In the early 2000s, I sent a letter to the editors of numerous rural newspapers throughout the eastern states inviting readers to contact me if they had been involved in the dispute or had some interesting stories to tell about the events of those years. I was overwhelmed with the response – dozens of people contacted me from all over New South Wales, Victoria and Queensland. I tried to follow up all these people but unfortunately there were several I did not. To them I offer my humble apologies. There comes a time when you have to decide you have sufficient information and get on with writing. As a result, this is far from being, and was never intended to be, a definitive account of the dispute.

People recall events differently. I interviewed many people who gave slightly varying accounts of the same event. The variations did not amount to major discrepancies; they were almost always to do with the minutiae. For example, the colour or model of vehicle a person drove, who was present in a shearing shed at a particular time, which shearer moved a particular motion at a meeting and so on. Of course, such discrepancies did not arise from any intentional distortion of the truth – it was simply human nature at work. We all see things through different eyes, notice different things, absorb varying amounts of detail, and interpret what we see and hear in slightly different ways. Add in the passage of time, in this case 25 to 35 years, and invariably you get differing accounts of events. In such cases, I have tried as far as possible to verify information through other source material. Where that has not been possible, I have at times preferred one version over another. In doing so, I concede that some of the minutiae may in fact be inaccurate. However, I have tried my best to make sure all the key aspects of the events described in this book are correct. I am wholly responsible for any errors, factual or grammatical. I welcome feedback from readers via mfilmer@mac.com.

Notes

1. 'Bare Belted Ewe', ABC TV, *Landline*, Report by Sean Murphy, broadcast 2 February 2014.
2. Although wide combs were banned in 1926, they could still be used with the consent of the employer. The total ban came into effect on 1 August 1939 following an amendment to the Award by Mr Justice Dethridge.
3. Minutes of the Australian Workers' Union Pastoral Committee meeting, Sydney, Tuesday 7 June 1983, p. 1.
4. ABC radio, *Country Hour*, Wednesday 13 May 1981.
5. Ibid.
6. Ibid.
7. 'Black-banned for using wide combs', Tony Sarks, *The Land*, Thursday 21 May 1981, p. 7.
8. Ibid.
9. Minutes of the meeting of Australian Workers' Union pastoral workers, Dubbo Civic Centre, Sunday 26 October 1980, chaired by Mick O'Shea.
10. ABC Radio 2CR Orange, *Country Breakfast Show*, Tuesday 2 June 1981.
11. White's team also shore with wide combs at the Canowindra district properties Rockdale and Millambri during the autumn 1981 shearing season.
12. Minutes of the meeting of Australian Workers' Union pastoral workers, Dubbo Civic Centre, Monday 1 June 1981, chaired by Mick O'Shea.
13. ABC radio, *Country Breakfast Show*, Tuesday 2 June 1981.
14. 'Shearers to meet over AWU assault', Barbara Davis, *Daily Liberal* (Dubbo), 9 October 1980.
15. Australian Workers' Union circular to all pastoral industry workers, 23 September 1980, under the names Ernie Ecob and Charlie Oliver, signed by Ernie Ecob.
16. Personal interview, 13 November 2004, Mudgee.
17. 'AWU blames shearing dispute on graziers', Malcolm Brown, *Sydney Morning Herald*, 26 March 1984, p. 14.
18. 'Obituary: Ernie Ecob AM, union leader', Marilyn Dodkin, *Sydney Morning Herald*, 6 September 2000, p. 39.

19. 'Big Charlie Oliver: new power in the ALP?', Craig McGregor, *Sydney Morning Herald*, 4 September 1964, p. 2.
20. 'Big Charlie, key man in plugging the state's fuel flow', Andrew Watson, *Sydney Morning Herald*, 20 May 1979, p. 7.
21. 'Why Big Charlie is smiling at a strike', Andrew Casey, *Sydney Morning Herald*, 24 February 1987, p. 3.
22. A brief history of the wide comb dispute in the Pastoral Industry Award, Paul Houlihan, address to the H.R. Nicholls Society, August 1988.
23. O'Malley, T.R. (2013). *Mateship and Moneymaking. Australian shearing: The clash of union solidarity with the spirit of enterprise 1895–1995*, Xlibris Corporation, p. 296.
24. 'Shearers' strike brings old dispute full circle', Patsy Adam-Smith, *The National Times*, 8 April 1983, pp. 9–10.
25. Raddling was the practice of wool growers marking sheep that had not been properly shorn with an ochre mark. Shearers would not be paid for these sheep. For more details, see chapter 7.
26. Minutes of the meeting of Australian Workers' Union pastoral workers, Royal Hotel Dubbo, 23 March 1980.
27. Commonwealth Reporting Service, Australian Conciliation and Arbitration Commission, C No 3221 of 1981, Transcript of Proceedings, Sydney, Thursday 3 December 1981, p. 122.
28. The Australian Wool Board was a Commonwealth government statutory agency with a primary focus on wool marketing and promotion. Between April 1953 and 1962, the board was named the Australian Wool Bureau, and in January 1973 it amalgamated with the Australian Wool Commission to form the Australian Wool Corporation.
29. *The Land* (Central and Western Extra), 17 July 1980, p. 1.
30. ABC Radio 2CR Orange, July 1980.
31. *The Land* (Central and Western Extra), 17 July 1980, p. 1.
32. Australian Workers' Union New South Wales branch, letter from Ernie Ecob to Peter White, 23 November 1981.
33. Commonwealth Reporting Service, Australian Conciliation and Arbitration Commission, C No 3221 of 1981, Transcript of Proceedings, Thursday 3 December 1981, Sydney, p. 132.
34. Massy, C. (2011). *Breaking the sheep's back: The shocking true story of the decline and fall of the Australian wool industry*, University of Queensland Press, p. 382. (This book provides a comprehensive account of the operation and eventual failure of the Reserve Price

Scheme. Massy examines in detail the players involved, the political machinations affecting the industry during these years, as well as the disastrous and tragic consequences of the scheme's demise for wool growers. A compelling read.)

35. Included in this total was $376,000 of private sector funds.
36. Richardson, A. (1973). 'Wool harvesting'. *Wool Technology and Sheep Breeding*, 20 (1), p. 14.
37. In his research report, Richardson actually reported there were 188.5 million sheep in Australian in 1971. However, this was a mistake. Australia's sheep flock peaked at 180 million in 1970 and has mostly declined since then. This means too his calculation of the number of sheep per shearer in 1971 was also incorrect. He reported it was one shearer per 30,000 sheep, when it fact it was one per 28,000.
38. Richardson, A. (1973). 'Wool harvesting'. *Wool Technology and Sheep Breeding*, 20 (1), p. 12.
39. 'Shears click', Ted Cavey, *The Age*, 8 July 1980, p. 11.
40. The provisions of the Federal Pastoral Industry Award did not apply to research settings.
41. Lightfoot, R.J., Ingleton, A.M., Mills, R.A., Marney, N.M., D'Antuono, M. (1979). *A Preliminary Investigation of Shearing Merino Sheep With Combs of Varying Width*.
42. Cheesy gland (*caseous lymphadenitis*) is a bacterial disease of sheep that causes abscesses in the lymph nodes of the body and various organs, especially the lungs. It can result in lost wool production.
43. Hearn, M. & Knowles, H. (1996). *One big union: A history of the Australian Workers' Union 1886–1994*. UK: Cambridge University Press, p. 26.
44. Blainey, Geoffrey, *A Land Half Won*, Sun Books, 1983, p. 263.
45. Hearn, M. & Knowles, H. (1996). *One big union: A history of the Australian Workers' Union 1886–1994*. UK: Cambridge University Press, p. 83.
46. Massy, C. (2011). *Breaking the sheep's back: The shocking true story of the decline and fall of the Australian wool industry*. Australia: University of Queensland Press, p. 3.
47. Watson, A.S., 'Wool in 1980', Australian Journal of Agricultural Economics, August 1980, vol. 24, no. 2, p. 80.
48. Laurie, A. Alderman, The Shearers' and Bushworkers' Strike of 1891, paper/speech presented to a meeting of the Historical Society of Queensland, 25 October 1938.
49. Woldendorp, R., McDonald, R. & Burdon, A. (2003). *Wool: The Australian Story*. Australia: Fremantle Arts Centre Press, p. 29.
50. Hearn, M. & Knowles, H. (1996). *One big union: A history of the Australian Workers' Union*

1886–1994. UK: Cambridge University Press, p. 26.
51. Ibid, p. 107.
52. Ellis, R., *Sheep and Shearing: Their Evolution and Contribution to Australia*, 2010, self-published by Robert Ellis, p. 80.
53. Sullivan, R.J. & R.A., 'The Pastoral Strikes, 1891 and 1894', in *The Big Strikes, Queensland 1889–1965*, Edited by D.J. Murphy, University of Queensland Press, 1983, p. 80.
54. Laurie, A. Alderman, The Shearers' and Bushworkers' Strike of 1891, paper/speech to the Queensland Historical Society. 25 October 1938.
55. Sharman, R.C., Shearers on Strike, paper/speech to the Queensland Historical Society. 22 November 1962.
56. Many unemployed labourers joined the camps during the strike because it gave them access to free food and tobacco.
57. Sharman, R.C., Shearers on Strike, paper/speech to the Queensland Historical Society. 22 November 1962.
58. Sullivan, R.J. & R.A , 'The Pastoral Strikes, 1891 and 1894', in *The Big Strikes, Queensland 1889–1965*, Edited by D.J. Murphy, University of Queensland Press, 1983, p. 84.
59. Laurie, A. Alderman, The Shearers' and Bushworkers' Strike of 1891, paper/speech to the Queensland Historical Society. 25 October 1938.
60. Harris, W.J.H., *First Steps – Queensland Workers' Moves Towards Political Expression, 1857–1893*, Australian Society for the Study of Labour History, 1966, p. 14.
61. Docherty. J.C., van der Velden, S., & van der Velden, J.H.A. (2012). *Historical Dictionary of Organized Labor*. Scarecrow Press, p. 39.
62. Machine shearing was introduced in the late 1880s, and during the early 1890s there were still many properties where machine shearing equipment had not yet been installed.
63. Adam-Smith, P., *The Shearers*, 1982, Australia, Thomas Nelson, p. 134.
64. Hearn, M. & Knowles, H. (1996). *One Big Union: A History of the Australian Workers' Union 1886–1994*. UK: Cambridge University Press, p. 75.
65. The Australian Labor Party changed the spelling of 'Labour' to 'Labor' in 1912.
66. *The Federation Drought of 1895–1903, El Niño and Society in Australia. Common Ground: Integrating the Social and Environmental in History*. Cambridge Scholars Publishing 2010, p. 275.
67. 'Dry and drier', Geoffrey Blainey, *The Australian*, 30 December 2006.
68. Hendrickson, K.E. (2014). *The Encyclopaedia of the Industrial*

Revolution in World History. Rowman & Littlefield Publishers, p. 1054.
69. O'Malley, T.R. (2013). *Mateship and Moneymaking: Australian shearing: The clash of union solidarity with the spirit of enterprise, 1895–1995*, Xlibris Corporation, p. 42.
70. 23 Commonwealth Arbitration Reports pp. 468–469.
71. 25 Commonwealth Arbitration Reports p. 660.
72. 36 Commonwealth Arbitration Reports p. 299.
73. 39 Commonwealth Arbitration Reports pp. 628, 648.
74. 61 Commonwealth Arbitration Reports p. 279.
75. 121 Commonwealth Arbitration Reports p. 454.
76. The Commonwealth Court of Conciliation and Arbitration changed its name to the Commonwealth Conciliation and Arbitration Commission in 1956, then to the Australian Conciliation and Arbitration Commission in 1973. From 1988 it was known as the Australian Industrial Relations Commission. Between 2009 and 2012 it was called Fair Work Australia, and since 2013 it has been called the Fair Work Commission.
77. ABC Radio 2CR Orange, *Country Breakfast Show*, June 1980.
78. ABC radio, *Country Hour*, 5 July 1980.
79. Ibid.
80. Ibid.
81. The Wool Council of Australia was formed in 1979 as the peak body representing Australia's wool growers on wool industry issues. It was responsible for developing and implementing wool grower policy. Wool Producers Australia replaced the Wool Council in July 2001.
82. 'Arbitration system needs overhaul', *The Land*, 26 February 1981.
83. 'Shearers told to lift bans', *Sydney Morning Herald*, 30 September 1981; 'Union told to lift bans on wider combs', *The Australian*, 30 September 1981; 'Wide combs ban lifted', *The Land*, 1 October 1981.
84. 'LGPA might opt out', *The Land*, 15 October 1981.
85. Commonwealth Reporting Service, Australian Conciliation and Arbitration Commission, C No 3221 of 1981, Transcript of Proceedings, 3 December 1981, pp. 145–146.
86. ABC Radio 2CR Orange, *Country Breakfast Show*, June 1980.
87. 'Sayings of the week', *Sydney Morning Herald*, Saturday 2 April 1983, p. 14.
88. ABC radio, *Country Hour*, July 1980.
89. 'Shearers vote for black ban', *Central Western Daily* (Orange), 22 September 1980.
90. ABC Radio 2CR Orange,

Country Breakfast Show, 27 October 1980.
91. Ibid., 2 June 1981.
92. Transcript of extract from television news broadcast, Channel 10, 2 December 1981.
93. ABC radio, November 1981.
94. Ecob, E., Australian Workers' Union New South Wales branch, letter to Robert White, 26 November 1981.
95. Ecob, E., Australian Workers' Union New South Wales branch, circular to organisers, committees and members of the union in the pastoral industry, 3 December 1981.
96. 'Graziers hit AWU combs move', Don Story, *Stock and Land*, 13 January 1983.
97. Hodder, E. (1983). 'The wide comb dispute in the Australian shearing industry'. *Queensland Digest of Industrial Relations*, 2(2), pp. 1–8.
98. ABC Radio 2CR Orange, *Country Breakfast Show*, 27 October 1980.
99. Minutes of the meeting of the Australian Workers' Union New South Wales branch pastoral workers, Dubbo Civic Centre, 26 October 1980, p. 8.
100. Helen Riseborough, *Shear Hard Work*. Auckland University Press, 2010, p. 1.
101. Some mining jobs are also very physically exhausting, but these roles are usually performed in more amenable conditions than a shearing shed.
102. Richardson, A. McDonald, *Wool Technology and Sheep Breeding Journal*, Vol. 20, Issue 1, July 1973.
103. Commonwealth Reporting Service, Australian Conciliation and Arbitration Commission, C No 3221 of 1981, Transcript of Proceedings, 3 December 1981, p. 137.
104. Commonwealth Reporting Service, Australian Conciliation and Arbitration Commission, C No 3105 of 1980, C No 3221 of 1980, Transcript of Proceedings, Sydney, Tuesday 11 October 1983, pp. 1863, 1865–1867.
105. Worksafe Australia was the short name used for the National Occupational Health and Safety Commission, which the Commonwealth government established in 1985 to develop, facilitate and implement a national approach to occupational health and safety. It comprised representatives of the peak employee and employer bodies – the Australian Council of Trade Unions and Confederation of Australian Industry, as well as the Commonwealth, state and territory governments. Since 2008, this role has been performed by Safe Work Australia.
106. Culvenor, J. et al., 1997. 'The Ergonomics of Sheep Shearing', in *Productivity Ergonomics and Safety, The Total Package*, international Workplace Health Safety Forum and 33rd Ergonomics Society of Australia Conference, Gold Coast,

107. Gmeinder, G.E., 1986. 'Back complaints among shearers in Western Australia: A pilot study'. *Australian Journal of Physiotherapy*, 32(3), pp. 139–144.

108. McKenzie, Robin Anthony (1981), *The Lumbar Spine, Mechanism, Diagnosis and Treatment*, New Zealand Spinal Publications, Waikanae.

109. ABC radio, *The World Today*, Rachel Mealey, Friday 25 February 2000.

110. Bishop, D., Edge, J. & McGawley, K. (2005). 'Physiological responses during a 9h sheep shearing world record attempt: A case study'. *Journal of Science and Medicine in Sport*, vol. 8: Supplement, p. 59.

111. Prime Minister Bob Hawke, opening address to the National Farmers' Federation annual conference, 17 May 1983, Canberra.

112. Stevens, G., address by the Governor of the Reserve Bank to the Inaugural Faculty of Economics and Business Alumni Dinner, The University of Sydney, Sydney, 15 May 2008.

113. Trebeck, D., No Ticket, No Start – No More: The Industrial Significance of the 1978 Live Sheep Export Dispute, address to the H.R. Nicholls Society annual conference, February 1989.

114. McLachlan. I.M, No Ticket, No Start – No More: The Live Sheep Dispute – Some Personal Reminiscences, address to the H.R. Nicholls Society annual conference, February 1989.

115. McLachlan, I.M., We used to run this country, and it wouldn't be a bad thing if we did again: In praise of a 'comrade', address to the H.R. Nicholls Society, October 2007.

116. ABC radio, *Country Hour*, transcript of interview with Ian Manning and Ernie Ecob, 26 January 1982.

117. Ibid.

118. MacKenzie, A.J. & Field, B. W. (1982). 'Comparison of dimensions of Australian shearing combs with the requirements of Clause 32 of the Federal Pastoral Industry Award'. *Wool Technology and Sheep Breeding*, 30(3), pp. 133–137.

119. Commonwealth Reporting Service, Australian Conciliation and Arbitration Commission, C No 3105 of 1980, C No 3221 of 1980, Decision, Melbourne, 10 December 1982, p. 14.

120. Taken from the transcript of the Channel 9 Sydney evening news broadcast, Wednesday 2 December 1981.

121. Taken from the transcript of the Channel 10 Sydney evening news broadcast, Wednesday 2 December 1981.

122. Commonwealth Reporting Service, Australian Conciliation and

Arbitration Commission, C No 3221 of 1981, Transcript of Proceedings, 3 December 1981, pp. 105–107.

123. As well as black-banning Ian Manning's farm at Vittoria, between Bathurst and Orange, Ecob also organised a black ban on a property at Yass owned by John White, chief executive officer of the Livestock and Grain Producers' Association.

124. Commonwealth Reporting Service, Australian Conciliation and Arbitration Commission, C No 3221 of 1981, Transcript of Proceedings, 3 December 1981, pp. 112–113.

125. Wide comb shearing demonstration makes history, Livestock and Grain Producers' Association news release PR 102181, issued Friday 4 December 1981.

126. Commonwealth Reporting Service, Australian Conciliation and Arbitration Commission, C No 3221 of 1981, Transcript of Proceedings, 3 December 1981, pp. 115–119.

127. The committee comprised representatives from wool growers, wool brokers, the Australian Workers' Union, shearing contractors, the Australian Wool Corporation, and federal and state government departments.

128. Letter from Frank Mitchell of the Australian Workers' Union Executive Council to Australian Workers' Union Victorian branch secretary Ian Cuttler, 4 August 1982.

129. 'Violence feared in shearers' strike', Joseph Glascott, *Sydney Morning Herald*, 31 March 1983, p. 3.

130. Minutes of the meeting of Australian Workers' Union pastoral workers, Dubbo Golf Club rooms, Sunday 21 February 1982.

131. Commonwealth Reporting Service, Australian Conciliation and Arbitration Commission, C No 3221 of 1981, Transcript of Proceedings, Sydney, Thursday 3 December 1981, p. 142.

132. Sunbeam memo to rural division staff, dated 2 May 1982, signed by John Allan, General Manager.

133. Letter from Sunbeam rural division to the federal secretary of the AWU, Frank Mitchell, 4 May 1982.

134. Minutes of the meeting of Australian Workers' Union pastoral workers, Dubbo Golf Club, Sunday 31 October 1982, p. 6.

135. 'AWU refuses talks on combs', *The Land*, 15 April 1982, p. 16.

136. Australian Workers' Union Business Paper, 96th Annual Convention, 149 Castlereagh Street, Sydney, 18 January 1982, federal secretary Frank Mitchell's address to delegates.

137. 'Shearers strike over wide comb', *Sydney Morning Herald*, 27 February 1982, p. 1

138. Minutes of the meeting of Australian Workers' Union pastoral workers, Dubbo Golf Club, 29 September 1982, p. 3.
139. Ibid., p. 4.
140. Minutes of the meeting of Australian Workers' Union pastoral workers, Dubbo Golf Club, Sunday 31 October 1982, p. 2.
141. 'Violence may follow comb ruling-Union', Jack Taylor, *Sydney Morning Herald*, 11 December 1982, p. 3.
142. 'Shearer clash looms on wide comb', Martin Summons, *The Land*, 16 December 1982.
143. Australian Conciliation and Arbitration Commission, C No. 4189, Transcript of Proceedings, Sydney, 9 February 1983, p. 164.
144. Ibid., pp. 78–79.
145. Australian Conciliation and Arbitration Commission, C No. 4189, Decision in appeal by Australian Workers' Union, Melbourne, 23 March 1983, p. 4.
146. Ibid., pp. 4–5.
147. Ibid., p. 5.
148. 'Woolgrowers welcome wide comb decision', Livestock and Grain Producers' Association media release PR27, Wednesday 23 March 1983.
149. 'Shearer walk-out as appeal fails', *The Land*, Thursday 24 March 1983.
150. Minutes of the meeting of Australian Workers' Union pastoral workers, Dubbo Golf Club, Thursday 24 March 1983, p. 3.
151. 'Shearers threaten to starve sheep…and the Ministers refuse to comment', Heather Jeffery, *Daily Liberal* (Dubbo), Friday 25 March 1983, p. 1.
152. 'LGPA president slams shearers: We face industrial anarchy', Heather Jeffery, *Daily Liberal* (Dubbo), 28 March 1983.
153. Wide Comb Shearing, news release, Shadow Minister for Primary Industry, Tom McVeigh, 28 March 1983.
154. Wide combs dispute, *The Australian Worker*, Thursday 31 March 1983, p. 1.
155. 'AWU: heads in the sand', *The Land*, 31 March 1983, p. 6.
156. 'Most graziers can't shear', David Ellery, *Daily Liberal* (Dubbo), 28 March 1983.
157. 'Shearers seek intervention', *Canberra Times*, Tuesday 29 March 1983, p. 7.
158. 'Shearing waits on strike talks', David Kelly, *The Land*, 31 March 1983, p. 3.
159. Ibid.
160. 'Rebels weaken strike', *The Land*, 7 April 1983.
161. 'Wagga meeting says "Let us choose": Rebel shearers to break strike', *Daily Advertiser*, Thursday 7 April 1983, p. 1. The report mistakenly said there were 1,500 shearers in Australia. There were actually about 15,000 at that time.
162. 'Rebel shearers to resume',

Sydney Morning Herald, Thursday 7 April 1983, p. 1.
163. 'Showdown at Wagga this weekend: Shearers prepare for confrontation', Maree George, *Daily Liberal* (Dubbo), Friday 8 April 1983, p. 1.
164. Ibid.
165. 'Rebel shearer hides in Dubbo motel room', Maree George, *Daily Liberal* (Dubbo), Friday 8 April 1983, pp. 1–2.
166. 'Striking shearers meet: 'Scabs' tossed out, plenty of abuse', Guy Freeman, *Daily Advertiser* (Wagga Wagga), Monday 11 April 1983, pp. 1, 10.
167. *Wild and Woolly*, Ian Leslie, *60 Minutes*, Channel 9, broadcast on Sunday 17 April 1983.
168. National Farmers' Federation letter from Paul Houlihan to Commissioner Ian McKenzie, headed Application No 3105 and 3221 of 1980, 11 April 1983.
169. Commonwealth Reporting Service, Australian Conciliation and Arbitration Commission, C No 3105 of 1980, C No 3221 of 1980, Transcript of Proceedings, Sydney. 11 April 1983, p. 1387.
170. lbid., p. 1391.
171. 'Industrial anarchy: Commissioner', The Barrier Daily Truth (Broken Hill), Friday 22 April 1983, p. 1.
172. 'Shearing "anarchy" has to stop: Commissioner', *Adelaide Advertiser*, Friday 22 April 1983.
173. 'Industrial anarchy: Commissioner; Shearing dispute going back to arbitration', *Canberra Times*, Friday 22 April 1983, p. 3.
174. Minutes of the meeting of Australian Workers' Union pastoral workers, Dubbo Golf Club, Tuesday 12 April 1983, p. 3.
175. 'Shearers attacked', *The Barrier Daily Truth* (Broken Hill), 16 April 1983.
176. 'Station workers in brutal attack', *The Land*, Thursday 21 April 1983.
177. 'Gang attacks working SA shearers', *Sydney Morning Herald*, Friday 15 April 1983, p. 4.
178. 'Shearers attacked', *The Barrier Daily Truth* (Broken Hill), 16 April 1983.
179. 'LGPA challenges shearers' strike', Livestock and Grain Producers' Association press release, PR/31, 14 April 1983.
180. 'Bodyguards formed for rebel shearers', *Daily Liberal* (Dubbo), 15 April 1983.
181. 'LGPA sets the record straight on wide comb dispute', Livestock and Grain Producers' Association press release PR/33, 18 April 1983.
182. 'Shearers, graziers meet at Coonamble: LGPA seeks peace over wide combs', Maree George, *Daily Liberal* (Dubbo), Monday 18 April 1983, p. 1.
183. 'Strike-breaking shearers are armed for possible attack', Martin

Daly, *Adelaide Advertiser*, Wednesday 20 April 1983, p. 1.

184. Minutes of the meeting of Australian Workers' Union pastoral members, Dubbo Golf Club, Tuesday 26 April 1983, pp. 6–7.

185. Government abrogates responsibility in wide combs dispute, statement by the Hon. T. McVeigh, Shadow Minister for Primary Industry, Canberra, 22 April 1983.

186. News release, federal Minister for Employment and Industrial Relations, Ralph Willis, MP, 29 April 1983.

187. 'Shearing goes on in all states', *The Land*, Thursday 5 May 1983, p. 3.

188. Ibid.

189. Ibid.

190. Shearing Contractors' Association of Australia, confidential two-page letter with attachment, addressed to the AWU general secretary, 5 May 1983, signed by K.J. Crawford.

191. 'Coonamble festivities turn sour with violence', Bruce Hextell, AAP, *Daily Liberal* (Dubbo), Monday 16 May 1983.

192. 'Shearers storm "rebels" in shed', *Canberra Times*, Tuesday 10 May 1983, p. 3. The report included a direct quote from Russell Smith in which he said there were only seven men sheltering in the shed. However, with six shearers in the team, there would almost certainly have been additional workers present too, such as rouseabouts, shed hands, a wool classer, a woolpresser and so on.

193. 'Policeman threatens to shoot shearers at Coonamble protest', *Daily Liberal* (Dubbo), Tuesday 10 May 1983, pp. 1, 3.

194. 'Siege at shearing shed', Jim Tennison, *Sun News Pictorial*, Tuesday 10 May 1983, p. 1.

195. 'Shearers storm "rebels" in shed', *Canberra Times*, Tuesday 10 May 1983, p. 3.

196. 'Shearing war erupts', Arthur Stanley and Grantlee Kieza, *Daily Telegraph*, Tuesday 10 May 1983, pp. 1–2.

197. 'Shearer row no closer to a settlement', *Barrier Daily Truth* (Broken Hill), Friday 13 May 1983, p. 1.

198. 'Strike continues so does shearing', *The Land*, Thursday 12 May 1983, p. 3.

199. The content of the telex was made public in a news release to make the federal government's position clear. Wide combs dispute, 13 May 1983, 72/83, federal Minister for Employment and Industrial Relations, Ralph Willis, MP.

200. Minutes of the meeting of Australian Workers' Union pastoral workers, Victoria Park Oval, Dubbo, Monday 16 May 1983, p. 2.

201. 'Harvest threat follows wide

comb ceasefire', *The Land*, 19 May 1983.
202. All the quotes relating to these incidents in Walgett were from 'The night Aussie and Kiwi shearers fought toe-to-toe…and the Kiwis won; It was like a night in wild west', *Daily Liberal* (Dubbo), Tuesday 31 May 1983, p. 1.
203. 'Uneasy quiet over "wild" wool town', Mark Voisey, *The Sun*, 6 June 1983.
204. Ibid.
205. 'Police escort for shearers', Chris Thomas, *Moree Champion*, Tuesday 7 June 1983.
206. 'Shearers object to 'bad guy' image', *Moree Champion*, Thursday 9 June 1983.
207. Notice to all AWU pastoral workers, authorised by Ernie Ecob, branch secretary, New South Wales, 21 June 1983.
208. 'Strikebreaker', Greg Hunter, *Penthouse*, September 1984, p. 40.
209. Details of this judgement are contained in a federal Department of Employment and Industrial Relations Minute, 8411105, Pastoral Industry Award 1965, Clause 20, Hours of Work of Shearing Employees, signed B.W. Lewis, Assistant Secretary Arbitration Inspectorate (Technical Branch), 9 July 1984.
210. Legal opinion from the Australian Government Solicitor, Melbourne, to Mr B.W. Lewis, Assistant Secretary (Technical Branch), Department of Employment and Industrial Relations, Melbourne, 19 November 1984.
211. 'Shearing 'takeover' claim', Ted O'Kane, *The Land*, Thursday 7 July 1983.
212. Notice to all AWU pastoral workers, authorised by Ernie Ecob, branch secretary, New South Wales, 21 June 1983.
213. Commonwealth Reporting Service, Australian Conciliation and Arbitration Commission, C No 3105 of 1980, C No 3221 of 1980, Transcript of Proceedings, Sydney, Monday 20 June 1983, p. 1416.
214. Ibid., p. 1414.
215. Commonwealth Reporting Service, Australian Conciliation and Arbitration Commission, C No 3105 of 1980, C No 3221 of 1980, Transcript of Proceedings, Warren and Tottenham, Wednesday 10 August 1983, p. 1459.
216. Commonwealth Reporting Service, Australian Conciliation and Arbitration Commission, C No 3105 of 1980, C No 3221 of 1980, Transcript of Proceedings, Bourke, Thursday 11 August 1983, p. 1467.
217. Ibid., p. 1477.
218. Ibid., p. 1481.
219. Ibid., p. 1482.
220. Ibid., p. 1485.
221. Commonwealth Reporting Service, Australian Conciliation and

Arbitration Commission, C No 3105 of 1980, C No 3221 of 1980, Transcript of Proceedings, Guyra, Friday 12 August 1983, p. 1512.
222. Ibid., p. 1520.
223. Ibid., p. 1524.
224. Commonwealth Reporting Service, Australian Conciliation and Arbitration Commission, C No 3105 of 1980, C No 3221 of 1980, Transcript of Proceedings, Bourke, Thursday 11 August 1983, p. 1493.
225. Commonwealth Reporting Service, Australian Conciliation and Arbitration Commission, C No 3105 of 1980, C No 3221 of 1980, Transcript of Proceedings, Molong, Wednesday 17 August 1983, p. 1541.
226. Ibid., p. 1559.
227. Commonwealth Reporting Service, Australian Conciliation and Arbitration Commission, C No 3105 of 1980, C No 3221 of 1980, Transcript of Proceedings, Coolah, Thursday 18 August 1983, p. 1597.
228. Commonwealth Reporting Service, Australian Conciliation and Arbitration Commission, C No 3105 of 1980, C No 3221 of 1980, Transcript of Proceedings, Sydney, Thursday 14 September 1983, pp. 1762–1763.
229. Ibid.
230. Ibid., p. 1765.
231. Ibid., p. 1766.
232. Commonwealth Reporting Service, Australian Conciliation and Arbitration Commission, C No 3105 of 1980, C No 3221 of 1980, Transcript of Proceedings, Sydney, Tuesday 11 October 1983, p. 1847.
233. Ibid., p. 1835.
234. Ibid., p. 1842.
235. Ibid., p. 1870.
236. Ibid., p. 1843.
237. Commonwealth Reporting Service, Australian Conciliation and Arbitration Commission, C No 3105 of 1980, C No 3221 of 1980, Transcript of Proceedings, Sydney, Wednesday 12 October 1983, p. 1958.
238. Ibid., p. 1965.
239. Commonwealth Reporting Service, Australian Conciliation and Arbitration Commission, C No 3105 of 1980, C No 3221 of 1980, Transcript of Proceedings, Sydney, Thursday 13 October 1983, p. 1994.
240. Ibid., p. 1995.
241. Ibid., p. 2008.
242. Ibid., p. 2011.
243. Ibid., p. 1998.
244. Ibid., p. 2035.
245. Commonwealth Reporting Service, Australian Conciliation and Arbitration Commission, C No 3105 of 1980, C No 3221 of 1980, Transcript of Proceedings, Sydney, Monday 20 June 1983, pp. 1411–1412.
246. Commonwealth Reporting Service, Australian Conciliation and Arbitration Commission, C No 3105 of 1980, C No 3221 of 1980, Transcript of Proceedings,

Launceston, Friday 2 December 1983, p. 2135.
247. Commonwealth Reporting Service, Australian Conciliation and Arbitration Commission, C No 3105 of 1980, C No 3221 of 1980, Transcript of Proceedings, Oatlands, Wednesday 30 November 1983, p. 2078.
248. Commonwealth Reporting Service, Australian Conciliation and Arbitration Commission, C No 3105 of 1980, C No 3221 of 1980, Transcript of Proceedings, Oatlands, Thursday 1 December 1983, pp. 2102–2103.
249. Ibid., p. 2104.
250. Commonwealth Reporting Service, Australian Conciliation and Arbitration Commission, C No 3105 of 1980, C No 3221 of 1980, Transcript of Proceedings, Launceston, Friday 2 December 1983, pp. 2124–2125.
251. Ibid., p. 2149.
252. Ibid., p. 2150.
253. Commonwealth Reporting Service, Australian Conciliation and Arbitration Commission, C No 3105 of 1980, C No 3221 of 1980, Transcript of Proceedings, Walgett, Wednesday 29 February 1984, p. 2178.
254. Ibid., p. 2184b.
255. Ibid., p. 2198.
256. Ibid., p. 2210.
257. Australian Conciliation and Arbitration Commission, C No 3105 of 1980, C No 3221 of 1980, Exhibit K.H.1., Letter from Haddon Rig, Warren, to Kevin Humphries, Wellington, 27 February 1984, signed by F.M. Murdoch.
258. Letter from Peter Ballard, Merlin Street, Bourke, to the secretary of the New South Wales Police Union, undated, but believed to be written in April 1984.
259. 'Violence putting families to flight', *Daily Telegraph*, Monday 5 March 1984, p. 3.
260. Circular letter to Australian Workers' Union local committees and pastoral representatives, Victorian branch secretary Ian Cuttler, 20 January 1984.
261. These figures are contained in a letter from John Allan of Heiniger Australia Pty Ltd to Livestock and Grain Producers' Association industrial officer Ian Manning, 24 February 1984. By this time John Allan, previously managing director of Sunbeam Corporation Limited, had moved to Heiniger Australia. He later had a period working for R.A. Lister Australia too.
262. The company's sales figures were contained in a letter from Sunbeam's general manager rural division Ted McAfee to Commissioner Ian McKenzie, 7 March 1984.
263. Letter from David Nankervis, R.A. Lister Australia Divisional Manager Agriculture, to Ian Manning,

New South Wales Livestock and Grain Producers' Association industrial officer, 21 February 1984.

264. Ministerial statement to the House of Representatives by the Minister for Immigration and Ethnic Affairs, Stewart West, 18 May 1983, on Australia's immigration policy and program, extract re Trans-Tasman migration. Used as an exhibit (R5) in the Wide Combs Health and Safety Inquiry, 14 March 1984.

265. Handwritten letter from the Tamworth local Pastoral Committee of the Australian Workers' Union to federal Employment and Industrial Relations Minister Ralph Willis, two pages, undated, signed by Mr M. Payne, Attunga, NSW 2345.

266. Letter from federal Employment and Industrial Relations Minister Ralph Willis to Mr M. Payne, Secretary, Tamworth Branch of the Australian Workers' Union, 5 January 1984.

267. Correspondence issued by the Minister Assisting the Treasurer, re taxation arrangements applying to New Zealand residents receiving remuneration for services rendered in Australia, issued February 1984, signed by Chris Hurford.

268. Letter from M.J. Ryan, Acting First Assistant Secretary, Department of Employment and Industrial Relations, to the Australian Workers' Union, 14 September 1984.

269. According to the ATO, all four of the following conditions had to be met in order for a New Zealand shearer to avoid paying income tax in Australia: The visit to Australia does not exceed 183 days in the year of income; the employer for whom the work is performed is not an Australian resident; the remuneration received is not deductible in determining the taxable income of a permanent establishment which the employer has in Australia; and the remuneration is subject to tax in New Zealand. The ATO concluded it was extremely unlikely New Zealand shearers would be able to meet all of these requirements.

270. Private and confidential letter from Australian Workers' Union New South Wales branch secretary Ernie Ecob to Commissioner Ian McKenzie and federal Industrial Relations Minister Ralph Willis, 6 March 1984.

271. Commonwealth Reporting Service, Australian Conciliation and Arbitration Commission C No 3105 of 1980, C No 3221 of 1980, Transcript of Proceedings, Melbourne, Tuesday 13 March 1984, p. 2278.

272. 'AWU "will not cop" wide combs', Paul Molloy, *The Weekend Australian*, 2–3 June 1984, p. 5.

273. 'Peace at last in sight in wide combs row', Nigel Austin, *The*

Australian, Tuesday 5 June 1984.
274. 'Combs row spills into bloodshed', Terry Vine, *The Sun*, 9 October 1984, p. 8.
275. 'New tricks, old shearers', Robert Honybun, *The Age*, Wednesday 16 May 1984. This article quotes a Sunbeam representative from Hay in the New South Wales Riverina as saying 90 per cent of Sunbeam's comb production was for wide combs.
276. Australian Workers' Union (New South Wales branch) telex to Commissioner Ian McKenzie, Australian Conciliation and Arbitration Commission, 13 June 1984, signed Ernie Ecob, 12.40 p.m.
277. 'Commissioner: End wide-comb dispute', *Adelaide Advertiser*, 22 June 1984.
278. Ibid.
279. 'It's shear madness: Bullets whistle in wool country', Tom Prior, *The Sun*, Tuesday 9 October 1984, p. 3.
280. Minutes of the meeting of Australian Workers' Union New South Wales branch pastoral industry delegates, Dubbo Golf Club, Saturday 24 November 1984, p. 2.
281. The Parliament of the Commonwealth of Australia, House of Representatives, Hansard, Tuesday 31 March 1992, p. 1525.
282. The Parliament of the Commonwealth of Australia, Employment of Visitors to Australia in the Shearing Industry, Report of the Senate Standing Committee on Rural and Regional Affairs, February 1994.

Index

A

Adam-Smith, Patsy 39, 70
Allan, John 150, 151, 152, 153, 154, 155, 156, 194, 199, 202, 206
Allen, Bill 232
Anderson, Tom 13, 14, 15, 21, 83, 126
Arbitration Commission 11, 39, 45, 49, 56, 78, 80, 81, 85, 89, 90, 94, 96, 98, 99, 101, 104, 108, 110, 126, 130, 132, 134, 135, 139, 141, 152, 154, 156, 157, 158, 164, 167, 171, 175, 176, 178, 179, 180, 181, 192, 195, 196, 197, 200, 205, 212, 213, 215, 225, 230, 238, 239, 241, 242, 243, 252, 253, 254, 255, 257, 268, 273, 275, 279, 285, 299, 300, 301, 305, 312, 313, 314, 319
Arbitration Court 72, 73, 76
Australian Council of Trade Unions (ACTU) 122, 177, 198, 211, 214, 215, 229, 241, 242
Australian Labor Party 34, 71
Australian Wool Corporation (AWC) 50, 51, 54, 81, 162, 217, 329
Australian Wool Harvesting Program (AWHP) 51, 52, 53, 54, 81, 329
Australian Workers' Union (AWU) 9, 10, 11, 12, 13, 14, 15, 16, 19, 20, 22, 24, 26, 27, 28, 30, 31, 33, 34, 35, 36, 39, 40, 41, 42, 44, 45, 47, 49, 61, 63, 68, 69, 73, 75, 76, 77, 78, 79, 80, 81, 82, 83, 84, 85, 86, 87, 88, 89, 90, 91, 94, 96, 98, 99, 100, 102, 103, 104, 108, 109, 116, 125, 126, 128, 134, 136, 140, 144, 149, 150, 152, 154, 155, 156, 158, 159, 162, 164, 167, 170, 175, 176, 177, 178, 179, 183, 185, 186, 192, 193, 195, 196, 197, 198, 199, 204, 207, 209, 211, 215, 218, 221, 222, 223, 224, 225, 226, 228, 229, 231, 234, 235, 238, 241, 242, 243, 244, 245, 246, 247, 251, 252, 254, 255, 256, 262, 263, 265, 267, 268, 272, 274, 276, 277, 281, 284, 288, 289, 291, 293, 294, 297, 298, 299, 302, 303, 304, 305, 306, 307, 308, 309, 312, 313, 315, 316, 317, 319, 320, 321, 323, 325, 327, 328, 329, 330, 331, 332, 333, 334, 337
Australian Workers' Union Annual Convention 125, 129, 130, 149, 151, 175, 332
Australian Workers' Union Executive Council 42, 82, 85, 86, 98, 144,

151, 156, 176, 177, 196, 200,
213, 214, 215, 216, 228, 238,
240, 243, 245, 252, 255, 316
Australian Workers' Union New
South Wales branch 9, 13, 17, 21,
31, 32, 33, 34, 35, 36, 41, 47, 83,
125, 126, 174, 177, 200, 266,
267, 268, 315
Australian Workers' Union
Queensland branch 105, 185,
316
Australian Workers' Union South
Australian branch 84, 159, 164,
204, 213, 237, 264
Australian Workers' Union
Tasmanian branch 84, 284, 287
Australian Workers' Union Victorian
branch 84, 98, 144, 162, 299,
321
Australian Workers' Union Western
Australian branch 84, 170

B

Balcomb, Harold 139, 212, 214
Ballard, Peter 298
Bangate Station, Walgett 289, 291
Bannon, Charles (Joe) 201, 202,
203, 204, 205, 238, 252, 254
Barr, Gil 84, 85, 170, 171, 308, 309
Bathurst 44, 45, 47, 49, 125, 127,
128, 188, 218, 229, 325
Beck, Dennis 46, 47
Begg, Allan 84, 85, 159, 204, 205,
316
Begg, Keith 103
Bendigo 96, 97, 331
black ban 15, 16, 17, 20, 21, 22, 23,
35, 83, 87, 89, 90, 91, 94, 95, 98,
128, 130, 135, 138, 139, 142,
148, 149, 155, 217, 218, 317
Black, Dwayne 115
Blainey, Geoffrey 58
Blayney 14, 188, 189, 190, 244
Bleby, David 195, 198, 199, 201,
204, 205, 313
Bourke 45, 62, 63, 69, 74, 75, 85,
176, 178, 185, 219, 269, 270,
271, 272, 274, 292, 294, 295,
296, 297, 298, 312
Brigadoon, Trangie 269
Brindingabba Station, north-west
NSW 271, 272
Brinkworth, Thomas 236, 237
Broken Hill 61, 159, 219, 220, 223,
229, 231, 232, 233
Bryant, Ross 296
Butler, John 84, 85, 287, 288, 289

C

Cameron, John 276, 277, 278
Canomodine Station, Canowindra
13, 14, 15, 16, 17, 18, 20, 21, 83,
84, 87, 95, 126, 142
Canowindra 13, 14, 15, 16, 47, 83,
89, 90, 126, 142
Capital Hill Camp 321
Cargo 14, 183, 275
Challenor, Peter 169
Charleville 68, 185
Clark, Allan 184
Clarke, Brian (Dubbo) 217, 218,
219, 220, 233, 241, 257, 258,
278, 292, 293
Clarke, Brian (Eaglehawk) 96, 97,
98
Clause 32 (with restriction clause)
78, 80, 81, 85, 90, 91, 98, 99,
125, 126, 127, 130, 131, 134,

136, 168, 170, 193, 198, 208, 240, 241
Closer Economic Relations free trade agreement 302, 303, 321
Cole, Edward 'Ted' 78, 87
Coleraine 317, 318, 319
Collareen Station, Moree 260, 261
Collarenebri 244, 247
Commonwealth Hill Station, South Australia 157, 163, 164, 165, 166, 167
Coolah 176, 276, 277
Coonamble 30, 31, 34, 49, 176, 191, 219, 235, 236, 245, 247, 248, 250, 251, 252, 295, 312
Cowra 13, 15, 293
Cox, Frank 221, 223, 224, 225
Crane, Arthur 167, 168
Crawford, Kevin 245
Cumnock 24, 25, 26, 27, 83, 107
Cuttler, Ian 84, 85, 144, 299

D

Diamond Shears Competition, Longreach 101, 143
Didicoolum Station, South Australia 236, 237
drought 16, 17, 59, 62, 72, 73, 142, 209, 231, 322, 330
Dubbo 18, 20, 23, 24, 26, 27, 29, 30, 40, 41, 45, 47, 48, 49, 83, 84, 87, 90, 91, 94, 95, 107, 139, 151, 156, 175, 176, 179, 180, 186, 192, 196, 197, 198, 200, 212, 213, 214, 217, 218, 219, 220, 222, 225, 229, 233, 240, 241, 244, 246, 247, 253, 255, 256, 257, 258, 274, 277, 278, 292, 319, 329, 330, 331, 332

Duggan, Richard (Dick) 111, 279, 280, 281
Dunedoo 176, 276, 277
Dunlop Station, north-west NSW 74, 328

E

Ecob, Ernie 9, 10, 13, 15, 20, 21, 22, 23, 26, 28, 29, 31, 32, 33, 34, 36, 40, 41, 49, 83, 84, 85, 87, 88, 89, 90, 91, 93, 95, 96, 99, 101, 103, 104, 105, 106, 125, 127, 128, 129, 130, 138, 139, 155, 174, 175, 176, 180, 186, 187, 188, 192, 193, 195, 197, 198, 199, 200, 205, 208, 212, 213, 217, 221, 222, 225, 229, 247, 253, 255, 256, 257, 263, 265, 267, 312, 315, 317, 319, 331, 332, 333
Ecob, Joan 31
Ecob, John 29, 30, 31
Ecob, Russell 28, 29, 30
Ellery, Neil 164, 165, 221, 246, 247, 263, 274, 275, 294, 296, 305
Ennerdale Station, Victoria 157, 162
Eromanga 182, 184, 187, 188, 193, 225
Erudina Station, South Australia 157, 160
Euroka Station, Walgett 73

F

Fermoy 157, 168
field research trials of wide combs 79, 80, 88, 94, 192, 329, 331
Forshaw, Michael 226, 227, 228, 268
Foster, Robert 265, 303

Fraser, Malcolm 209, 210, 211
Frawley, Bernie 266
Frodsley Station, Tasmania 157, 161

G

Galambo Station, Bourke 294, 295, 296, 297
Golden Shears Competition, Euroa 143
Grazcos 189, 217, 218, 219, 220, 233, 236, 247, 257, 265, 276, 278, 292, 293, 297, 298
Griffith 13, 176

H

H.R. Nicholls Society 37, 121
Haddon Rig, Warren 256, 269, 276, 281, 293
handpiece 18, 73, 74, 75, 76, 105, 110, 150, 152, 203, 232, 261, 270, 272, 273, 276, 285, 296, 313, 326
Hawke, Bob 37, 118, 122, 210, 211, 215, 229, 241, 243, 303, 308, 309, 333
Hay 151, 158, 189, 245, 320
Hayden, Bill 209, 210, 211, 213, 242
Healey, Cliff 15, 125, 126, 127
Hebblewhite, Ted 262
Heiniger 151, 152, 155, 300, 301
Hodder, Errol 84, 85, 105, 106, 107, 185, 186, 198, 316
Hollenberg, Peter 165
Hollis, Dave 40, 41, 42
Houlihan, Paul 11, 31, 37, 38, 89, 90, 91, 93, 94, 98, 124, 132, 133, 135, 137, 138, 139, 141, 142, 143, 144, 147, 158, 161, 162, 166, 170, 173, 187, 188, 191, 193, 225, 226, 227, 228, 254, 268, 275, 280, 283, 284, 286, 287, 288, 289, 315, 325, 330, 331
Humphries, Kevin 236, 256, 281, 293
Hunter, Bill 260, 262
Hurford, Chris 305, 306, 308
Hutchinson, John 158, 159

I

implacable hostile opposition to wide combs 24, 100, 116, 213, 238, 239, 253, 285

J

Johnston, Garry 144, 148, 178, 198, 199, 200, 201, 238, 281, 282, 283, 284, 288, 313
Johnston, Mel 101, 102, 276, 278

K

Korean War 32

L

Larsen, Carl 267, 269, 271
Lawson, Henry 67, 85
Lee, Peter John 167
Letchford, Ivan 267, 290, 291
Lightning Ridge 244, 246, 289, 296
Lister, R.A. 151, 152, 153, 155, 199, 301
live sheep export dispute 120, 121, 122, 124
Livestock and Grain Producers' Association (LGPA) 9, 11, 13, 21, 56, 78, 79, 80, 81, 83, 85, 87, 88, 90, 91, 92, 93, 98, 99, 100, 101, 103, 104, 108, 126, 128, 136, 138, 139, 141, 142, 143, 147, 148, 152, 175, 176, 177, 178, 179, 180, 181, 188, 190,

192, 196, 198, 201, 204, 205,
211, 212, 214, 215, 219, 220,
234, 235, 236, 244, 248, 250,
257, 260, 269, 274, 289, 299,
317, 329, 330, 331, 332, 334
Lucindale 164, 233, 240

M

Mack, George 219, 220, 248, 251, 256

MacKenzie, Alistair 130

Manning, Ian 78, 81, 82, 87, 88, 89, 90, 91, 93, 94, 95, 96, 99, 103, 104, 128, 132, 133, 134, 135, 136, 138, 139, 144, 145, 146, 148, 217, 228, 232, 235, 265, 269, 277, 278, 279, 282, 283, 291, 336

Massy, Charles 51, 59

Mawbey, Reg 34, 41, 42

McInerney, Fred 21, 191, 250, 251, 272, 295, 296

McKenzie, Ian (Commissioner) 89, 90, 133, 134, 135, 136, 137, 138, 139, 141, 145, 146, 147, 148, 153, 157, 166, 170, 173, 174, 176, 177, 178, 179, 180, 181, 187, 191, 192, 193, 194, 195, 196, 197, 198, 199, 201, 202, 203, 204, 205, 206, 207, 208, 212, 214, 216, 225, 226, 227, 228, 239, 241, 252, 257, 266, 268, 274, 275, 280, 283, 284, 289, 293, 312, 313, 316, 317, 331, 332, 333, 334

McKenzie, Peter 260

McLachlan, Ian 82, 94, 108, 120, 122, 123, 124, 165, 166, 190, 241, 331

McVeigh, Tom 215, 242

Merenele, Warren 269

Millambri, Canowindra 14, 21, 126, 332

Mirrabooka Station, Molong 274, 275, 276, 278

Mitchell, Frank 12, 41, 42, 84, 85, 86, 89, 154, 155, 175, 196, 213, 308

Moree 260, 261, 262, 310, 317

Mount Margaret Station, Queensland 182, 183, 184, 185, 186, 187

Mudgee 13, 24, 107, 176, 245, 282

Mudginberri abattoir dispute 123, 124

Murdoch, Forbes 256, 293

Murphy, Allen 189, 190

Murphy, Shane 285, 286

Mutooroo Station, South Australia 231, 233, 234, 236

Myers, Frank 125, 126, 127, 128, 324

N

Nankervis, David 152, 153, 199

Naracoorte 20, 84, 159

National Farmers' Federation (NFF) 11, 31, 53, 78, 86, 87, 89, 90, 93, 99, 104, 108, 117, 118, 120, 121, 123, 124, 152, 170, 176, 178, 181, 190, 193, 198, 205, 219, 225, 228, 252, 257, 269, 284, 289, 299, 315, 317, 329, 330

New Zealand Golden Shears Competition 151

O

O'Brien, Max 272

O'Brien, Peter 236, 237, 336

O'Brien, Thomas Dalby 272
O'Connor, Timothy 270
O'Malley, Rory 38, 75
O'Shea, Michael (Mick) 13, 21, 24, 25, 26, 30, 31, 83, 89, 103, 104, 106, 216, 222, 224, 225, 229, 276, 282, 283
Oberon 47, 49, 144, 229, 244
Oliver, Charlie 18, 20, 21, 23, 28, 33, 34, 35, 36, 48, 81, 83, 90, 93, 94, 95, 102, 106, 176
Orange 14, 57, 83, 88, 90, 103, 176, 183, 186, 188, 189, 247, 274, 276, 330

P

Pastoral Industry Award 13, 18, 21, 23, 24, 32, 39, 41, 42, 46, 47, 57, 72, 73, 74, 76, 77, 79, 80, 81, 82, 84, 85, 88, 89, 90, 91, 95, 96, 99, 125, 126, 127, 128, 129, 130, 131, 132, 134, 136, 137, 141, 142, 147, 148, 153, 168, 170, 176, 179, 180, 193, 198, 214, 216, 225, 226, 227, 228, 239, 263, 264, 267, 271, 304, 305, 307, 312, 314, 315, 317, 323, 328, 329, 330, 331, 332, 333
Paterson, A.B. (Banjo) 24, 70
Pittaway, Stephen 159
Polomka, Laurie 164, 165, 192, 336
Pora, Graeme 233, 234
Preece, Bill 195, 310
Prentice, Peter 246

Q

Quilpie 182

R

raddling 62
Rees, Allan 291
Reserve Price Scheme 50, 119
Richardson, Alan McDonald 52, 53, 110
Ridley, Adrian 15, 125, 126, 127
Rockdale, Canowindra 14, 89, 91, 95
Rodman, Jack 89
Rodwell, Laurie 'Buey' 21, 24, 25, 26, 49, 83, 89, 107, 214, 330
Romani Station, Bourke 270, 271, 274
Rothwell, John 14, 15, 16, 17, 18, 142
Rule 123 170, 171, 172
Ryan, David 'Daffy' 161, 162
Ryan, Gerry 266, 269

S

Sams, Peter 133, 135, 136, 137, 138
Sarre, Kevin 45
scabs 63, 66, 69, 89, 212, 216, 229, 239, 265, 298, 306, 327
Schick, John 25, 26, 27, 102, 261, 262
second cuts 22, 54, 55, 101, 102, 105, 106, 143, 158, 159, 161, 165, 167, 173, 269, 270, 271, 272, 275, 290, 327, 328
Senate Standing Committee on Rural and Regional Affairs 12, 320, 322, 334
Shearers' Hall of Fame, Hay 101, 150, 158, 159
Shearing Contractors' Association 236, 244, 245, 255, 256, 266, 267, 269, 290, 291, 317
Sinclair, Bill 261, 262
60 Minutes (Channel 9) 184, 222, 224, 225, 262, 283

skin cuts 23, 54, 56, 101, 106, 168, 195, 288, 290, 327
Small, Allan 248
Smith, Russell 247, 248, 249, 250, 251
Snaigow Station, Western Australia 157, 163, 169, 170, 171
Somerset, Col 247, 296, 336
Still, Geoff 134, 143, 144
Storemen and Packers' Union 23, 89, 91, 214, 311
strike 10, 12, 22, 32, 33, 35, 36, 64, 65, 66, 67, 69, 70, 71, 87, 88, 99, 104, 121, 122, 124, 135, 137, 139, 149, 151, 176, 179, 180, 185, 186, 195, 196, 197, 198, 200, 209, 212, 213, 214, 215, 216, 217, 218, 219, 220, 221, 222, 223, 226, 229, 231, 233, 234, 237, 238, 239, 240, 242, 243, 244, 245, 246, 247, 248, 254, 255, 256, 257, 260, 281, 283, 286, 290, 300, 312, 314, 327, 328, 329, 332, 333, 334
Summerville Station, Bourke 297
Sunbeam 47, 147, 149, 150, 151, 152, 153, 154, 155, 156, 194, 199, 202, 270, 285, 300, 301, 316, 332
Sydney Showground 99, 104, 132, 133, 139, 141, 144, 152, 205, 332

T

Tabratong, Tottenham 269
Talerno Station, Western Australia 157, 173
Tally-hi shearing method 45, 46, 51
Tenanburg, Cumnock 24, 25, 27, 107

Thompson, Jack 329
Thompson, James 'Percy' 107, 108
Thompson, Neville 237
Tottenham, NSW 269
Trangie 219, 244, 245, 248, 269
Trans-Tasman Travel Arrangement 302, 303
Trebeck, David 53, 121
Turton, Bruce 310, 311, 312

W

wage claim 178, 180
Wagga Wagga 62, 221, 222, 223, 224, 225, 229, 265
Waitemata, Western Australia 157, 168
Walgett 73, 176, 191, 244, 245, 258, 259, 260, 289, 334
Wallace, Jim 260, 261
'Waltzing Matilda' 70
Warren 219, 244, 256, 269, 281
Watson, Alistair 60
Watson, Arthur 183, 184, 185
Watt, Allan 24, 25
Watt, Betty 25
weekend work 263, 264, 265, 295
Wellington 229, 236, 281, 293
Western Australian Department of Agriculture 40, 54, 81, 329
White, Gayle 14, 25, 134, 184, 188, 190, 225, 324
White, John 87, 139
White, Peter 44, 45, 47, 49
White, Robert 14, 15, 19, 20, 21, 25, 43, 44, 45, 48, 83, 84, 87, 89, 94, 95, 96, 104, 110, 125, 126, 127, 129, 130, 133, 134, 135, 140, 142, 144, 145, 146, 147, 148, 152, 183, 184, 185, 186, 187,

188, 189, 190, 191, 192, 195, 205, 221, 222, 223, 224, 225, 245, 247, 260, 305, 314, 316, 324, 325, 330, 332, 334
Willis, Ralph 11, 214, 229, 242, 243, 255, 266, 304, 310, 312
Wolseley, Frederick 73, 74
Woodside, Coonamble 247, 248, 251, 252
Wool Council of Australia 79, 80, 82, 94, 98, 143, 165, 190, 207, 241, 331
Woollaston, Paul 12, 15, 125, 126, 127, 224, 225
Woomera rocket range 163
Wyoming, Nevertie 269
Wythes, Phillip 89, 95

Y

Yass 49, 182, 183, 245, 310, 311, 317

www.ingramcontent.com/pod-product-compliance
Lightning Source LLC
Chambersburg PA
CBHW071802080526
44589CB00012B/655